0 Introduction

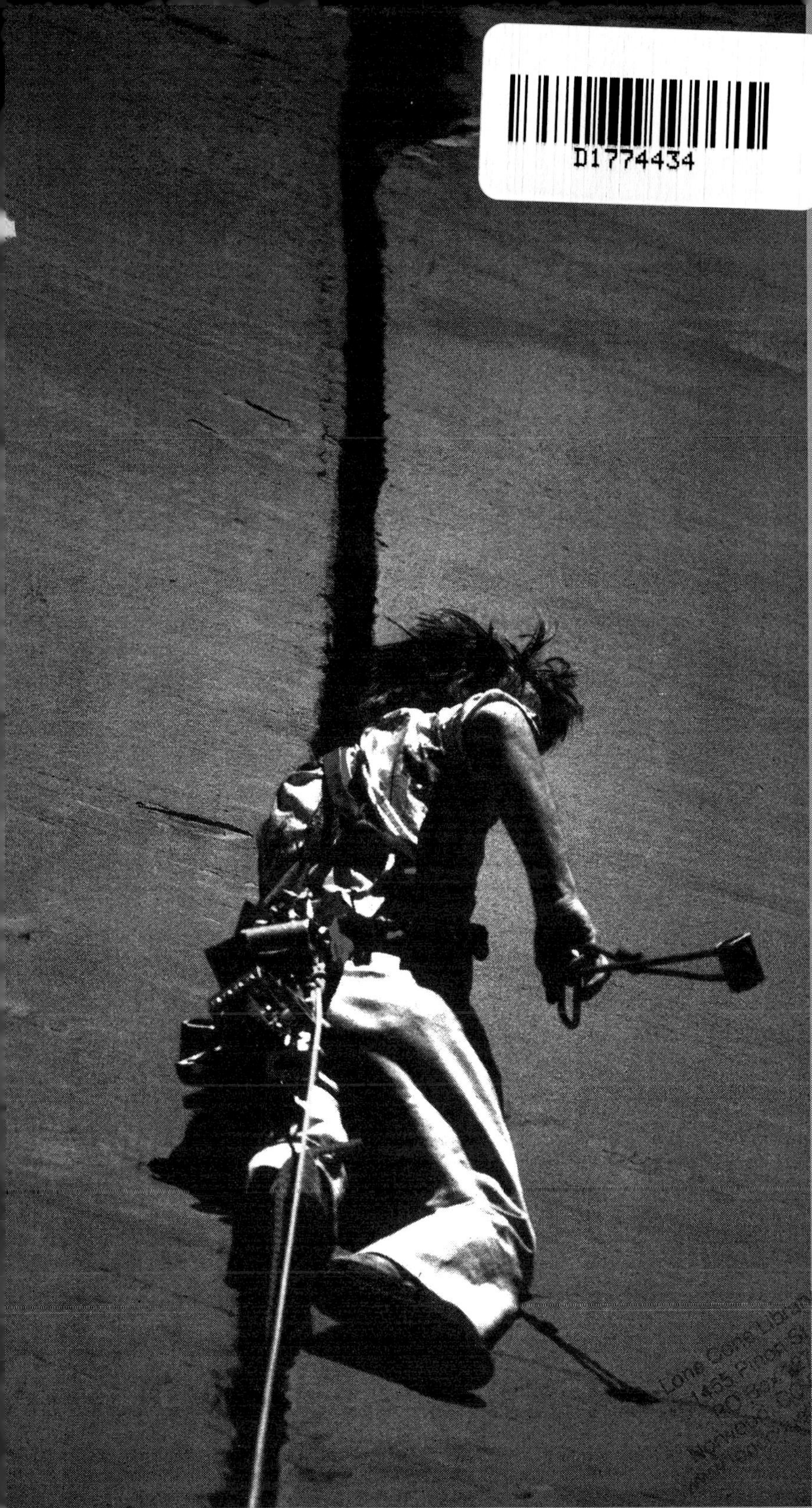

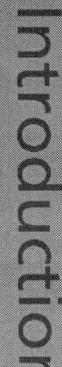

On the climb that started it all, the teenage Earl Wiggins is seen here on the first ascent (pre-cams) of **Luxury Liner**, more commonly known today as **Supercrack**.

Read This

Indian Creek: A Climbing Guide by David Bloom
©2008 Sharp End Publishing. All rights reserved. No part of this book may be used or reproduced in any manner without written permission of the publisher.

Published and distributed by
Sharp End Publishing, LLC
PO Box 1613
Boulder, CO 80306
t. 303.444.2698
www.sharpendbooks.com

ISBN: 1-892540-33-9
Library of Congress Control Number: 2004101640

Cover Photo Credits
On the front: Jimmy Haden on **King Cat** 5.11+, photograph by Eric Draper

Opening page photo credit
Earl Wiggins on **Luxury Liner** (a.k.a **Supercrack**), photograph by Stewart M. Green

READ THIS BEFORE USING THIS BOOK
WARNING:

Climbing is a very dangerous activity. Take all precautions and evaluate your ability carefully. Use judgment rather than the opinions represented in this book. The publishers and authors assume no responsibility for injury or death resulting from the use of this book. This book is based on opinions. Do not rely on information, descriptions, or difficulty ratings as these are entirely subjective. If you are unwilling to assume complete responsibility for your safety, do not use this guide book.

THE AUTHOR AND PUBLISHER EXPRESSLY DISCLAIM ALL REPRESENTATIONS AND WARRANTIES REGARDING THIS GUIDE, THE ACCURACY OF THE INFORMATION HEREIN, AND THE RESULTS OF YOUR USE HEREOF, INCLUDING WITHOUT LIMITATION, IMPLIED WARRANTIES OF MERCHANTABILITY AND FITNESS FOR A PARTICULAR PURPOSE. THE USER ASSUMES ALL RISK ASSOCIATED WITH THE USE OF THIS GUIDE.

It is your responsibility to take care of yourself while climbing. Seek a professional instructor or guide if you are unsure of your ability to handle any circumstances that may arise. This guide is not intended as an instructional manual.

Table of Contents

Introduction 4

Friction Slab to Battle of the Bulge 33

Fringe Wall to Reservoir Wall 69

Cat Wall Area 101

Meat Walls, etc. 137

Six Shooters and Bridger Jack Area 163

Cottonwood West 183

Cottonwood East 199

New Walls 215

Index 222

Introduction

Author's Word

The purpose in writing this book is to make available to the climbing community a comprehensive and accurate guide to the rock climbs of Indian Creek. Prior to this publication, the only attempt to document the huge number of ascents that have been made in this expansive area is the book *200 Select Indian Creek Climbs* by Marco Cornacchione and subsequently updated by the staff at Sharp End Publishing. This guide did an adequate job of directing visiting climbers to the more popular of the 40-plus buttresses that make up Indian Creek. Prior to that the only route information available was found in the classic *Desert Rock* by Eric Bjornstad, which has been out of print for almost fifteen years. A couple of mini-guides were later published in the climbing magazines. Many climbers continually visit the same buttresses they are familiar with, largely due to the inaccuracies, omissions and lack of updated information available in the collective climbing literature. I have tried to fill in the cracks by passing along my knowledge of the climbing routes by spending a significant portion of my adult life climbing as many routes as possible in the Creek, and writing down the relevant beta. I have personally climbed over 300 routes at Indian Creek, but it would be impossible for me to climb them all. Therefore I have occasionally relied on secondhand information supplied to me by friends and acquaintances. I can vouch for their good intentions but not their accuracy.

Lastly when no other information was available I referenced the most recent descriptions listed in the "Other Resources" section of this book (pg 227). Many of the routes referred to as "Unknown" may have less than accurate descriptions, since the only details known about them is that they have a visible anchor. In an area this large, there are going to be routes that I have missed entirely, misnamed, misgraded, under- or overestimated in length, or made mistakes in the sequencing of the routes. Subsequent editions will attempt to clarify these problems.

This book could only have come to fruition with the help of some very special people. Fred and Heidi Knapp and the staff at Sharp End Publishing, for their encouragement and technical expertise; Leslie Hutchinson for the generous use of her space and trusty iMac; Eric Draper, Kris Passie and Nils Davis for their photographs and their time. And to my friends and climbing partners: Heavy Duty, Mini Manson, The Knitter, The Nutter, The Beserker, Lurker #1, Lurker #2, The Host, The Hostess, Lover Boy, Old One Eye, Xtreme Jew, The Tall Jew, The Masseuse, The Camp Director, Rodman, The Southern Belle, The Canucks, The Nurse, Jethro, Jim O, Brent O, VarCo, and all of the dogs.

Publisher's Thanks

The creation of this guidebook was an incredible task, as anyone who has climbed at Indian Creek is aware. With over thirty guidebooks behind us, the Sharp End staff is familiar with the effort a first-time comprehensive guide requires. It took David 3+ years to catalog the routes, label the hundreds of photos, draw countless topos, and personally review the gear lists. As publisher, I also recruited the help of many Indian Creek pioneers to look over the manuscript and they deserve special thanks. Particularly, I'd like to thank Karl Kelley. Karl owns the Desert Bistro in Moab and spends almost every morning climbing in the *Creek*. He helped fill in the blank spots, took me to his recently developed crags, and relentlessly proofed this guide. So, when you're in Moab, treat your rope-gun to the best meal in town. Also, thanks to Scott Carson of IME in Salt Lake City for his help. Scott has been a part of Indian Creek climbing for decades and has contributed routes and enthusiasm to the area. Lisa Gnade and Steve Petro of Excalibur Distribution (Friends, DMM, and Red Chilis) also gave the book a once-over and helped with some errors. Thanks to Bret Ruckman, a modest Indian Creek visionary who along with his brother established many of the venerable classics. Bret's personal experience and decades-old map helped polish this book. A big thanks to the advertisers, support them as they are core companies who care about climbing. Our graphic designers Gary Ludwig and Tara Brouwer deserve a heartfelt thanks for turning our vision into a sleek publication. Lastly, thanks to the photographers who have captured the essence of both this amazing land and the people who love it.

Heavy Duty (a.k.a. Alan Stevenson) on the Roman Candle Hula   Photograph by Steve "Crusher" Bartlett

Publisher's Word

I first climbed in Indian Creek in August 1986—a Wild Country ad guiding my partners and me to Supercrack. We were the only climbers in the canyon, but that, perhaps, was due to the season not the era. I returned the following year and have visited perpetually since then. The area has grown, become discovered, and rediscovered. Much about The Creek has changed and much remains the same. This guidebook will certainly have an effect on the area, as have the nearly endless photographs, articles, and promotions. I've listened to the pros and cons presented by advocacy groups, locals, passionate visitors, and environmentalists. I wanted this book to express more than the location of routes; it needed to express the tradition, personality, and passion that is part of Indian Creek.

I needed this book to be perfect because, unapologetically, climbing and the desert are a big part of who I am. This project became epic and personal. I know many climbers have waited for years and the author was getting antsy. As we struggled to make this book as perfect as we could, I was guided by those Indian Creek climbers I highly respect, most notably my dear friend Bret Ruckman and my new friend Karl Kelley. Both deeply love the desert and Indian Creek, not just as an arena for physical accomplishments, but as a temple, a place of beauty, of spirit, of childlike wonder and discovery.

A rumor of Ernest Hemingway comes to mind. When questioned as to why he rewrote the final paragraph of *For Whom the Bell Tolls* hundreds of times, he replied that it had to be perfect. Indian Creek deserves a guidebook requiring the same dedication. Luckily, many passionate people have joined the effort.

The author and I met nearly two decades ago in Freemont Canyon and have reconnected several times over several book projects. We've roped up in Eldorado, reminisced, and reconnected. Returning to a vagabond lifestyle of sorts, David helped me revisit to those carefree days where jamming for a full rope length was the epitome of joy. David isn't the only writer with whom I've climbed. With 29 titles on the shelves, I've climbed with all but two authors (and I'd like to change that to all).

For years now, Steve "Crusher" Bartlett, a Cutler devotee and veteran of over 100 desert tower ascents, has been a driving force behind Sharp End. He is responsible for more than the maps, edits, and photos that he contributed. Crusher sabbaticaled in Moab with his wife Fran and acted as a liaison between the Moab locals and the Sharp End Headquarters in Boulder. His proximity to The Creek and involvement in the desert climbing community spurred him beyond his usual perfectionism. Much of the inclusiveness and accuracy of this book is due to his efforts on the technical as well as the personal front.

It was a treat for me to set up a satellite office in Crusher's place for week, and a bonus to tick my 47th desert tower (the Gooney Bird) with him. Though we've climbed together on solid rock, joining Crusher in his element was eye-opening. He also introduced me to Karl Kelley, Moab restauranteur and current Indian Creek developer. Karl gave me the tour of new and obscure crags. He and his friends thrashed my hands and ego, but showed me a great time. If I lived in Moab, we'd, no doubt, rope up regularly and have even more rattlesnake encounters together.

Though we didn't make it to Moab together specifically for this book (we have many times in the past), this project was the perfect catalyst for Bret Ruckman and I to reconnect. Our lives are decidedly different from when we became friends almost two decades ago—employees of Boulder's venerable Neptune Mountaineering. Children, mortgages, (somewhat) respectable jobs, and the other confines of adulthood (scheduling similar time off) limit us to occasional outings together, but this project inspired weekly get-togethers that continue to the present (if even for gym climbing or taking our kids to the pool). When Bret and I are in the desert together, words seem trite. We simply joke about the beauty because we know language can't express our feelings.

I pray that the essays, the photographs, and the blood, sweat and tears, that went into this book have an effect on you, the reader. I hope that you, too, are speechless over the beauty of the landscape; that you are humbled by the exposed rock that makes us feel so exposed; that you develop friendships with kindred spirits; and that your actions—both in the desert and back at home—help preserve this fragile beloved environment.

Fred Knapp
Sharp End Publishing

Greater Holding Power

Fat Cam

The world's only cam designed specifically for soft rock!

METOLIUS
metoliusclimbing.com

Travel

From the north:
I-15 south to Provo, southeast on Highway 6 past Price to I-70, east to Highway 191, south to the town of Moab, continue 40 miles south and turn west on Highway 211.

From the northwest:
I-70 east to Highway 191, south to the town of Moab, continue 40 miles south and turn west on Highway 211.

From the northeast:
I-70 west to Highway 128 south at the Cisco exit (River Road), to Moab, then Highway 191 south 40 miles to Highway 211 west.

From the east:
Highway 145 from Telluride to Naturita, then Highway 90 west through Bedrock and the Paradox Valley, which becomes Highway 46 west at the Utah border, to Highway 191 south, and Highway 211 west.

From the southeast:
Highway 160 west from Durango to Cortez, then Highway 666 from Cortez to Monticello Utah, north on Highway 191 for 14 miles to Highway 211 west.

From the south:
Highway 191 north to Monticello Utah, and north 14 miles to Highway 211 west.

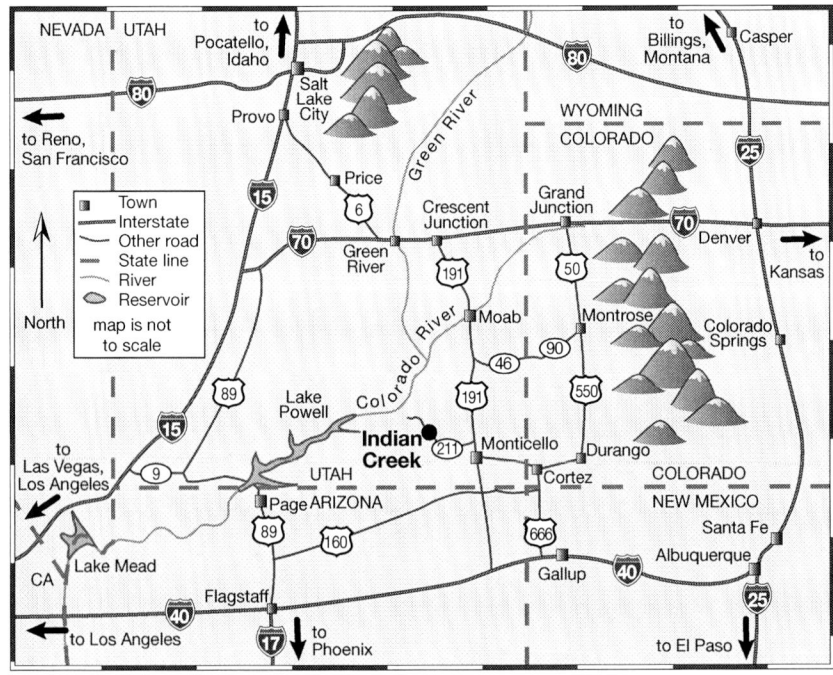

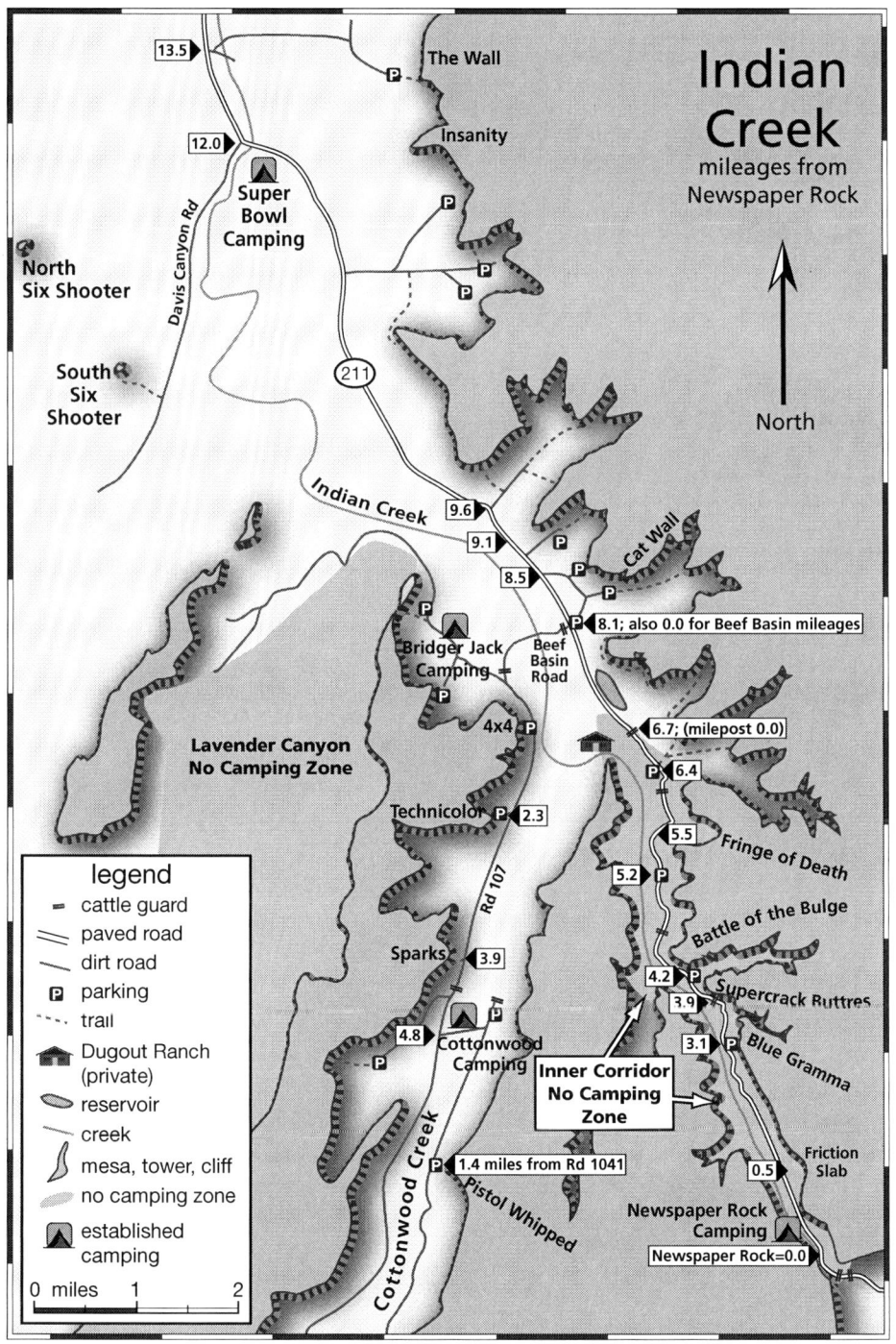

Mileages

From the junction of Highway 191 and Highway 211 to key landmarks:
  Newspaper Rock State Park- 12.2 miles
  Friction Slab- 12.8 miles
  Blue Gramma- 15.4 miles
  Supercrack cattle guard- 16.0 miles
  Supercrack/Donnelly Canyon/Battle of the Bulge- 16.3 miles
  New Wave Wall- 16.8 miles
  New Wall/Scorpion Corner- 17.3 miles
  Fringe of Death- 18.0 miles
  The Fringe Wall- 18.2 miles
  Power Wall/Scarface- 18.5 miles (the large gravel parking area)
  Reservoir Wall/Cat Wall-east/Beef Basin Road- 20.0 miles
  Cat Wall-west- 21.0 miles
  Broken Tooth/The Fin- 21.5 miles
  Six Star Canyon- 22.2 miles

From the junction of Highway 211 and County Road 107 (Beef Basin Road):
  Cross over Indian Creek- 0.5 miles
  Road to Bridger Jack (2nd cattle guard)- 0.8 miles
  4x4 Wall (3rd cattle guard)- 1.2 miles
  Tricks Wall parking- 2.2 miles
  Technicolor Wall- 2.4 miles
  Sparks Wall- 3.8 miles
  Turn for Critic's Choice (barbed wire fence)- 4.2 miles
  Junction County Road 107 and County Road 104I (Way Rambo/Pistol Whipped)- 4.8 miles

Moon over the Bridger Jacks   Photograph by Dan Hare

Crag Map

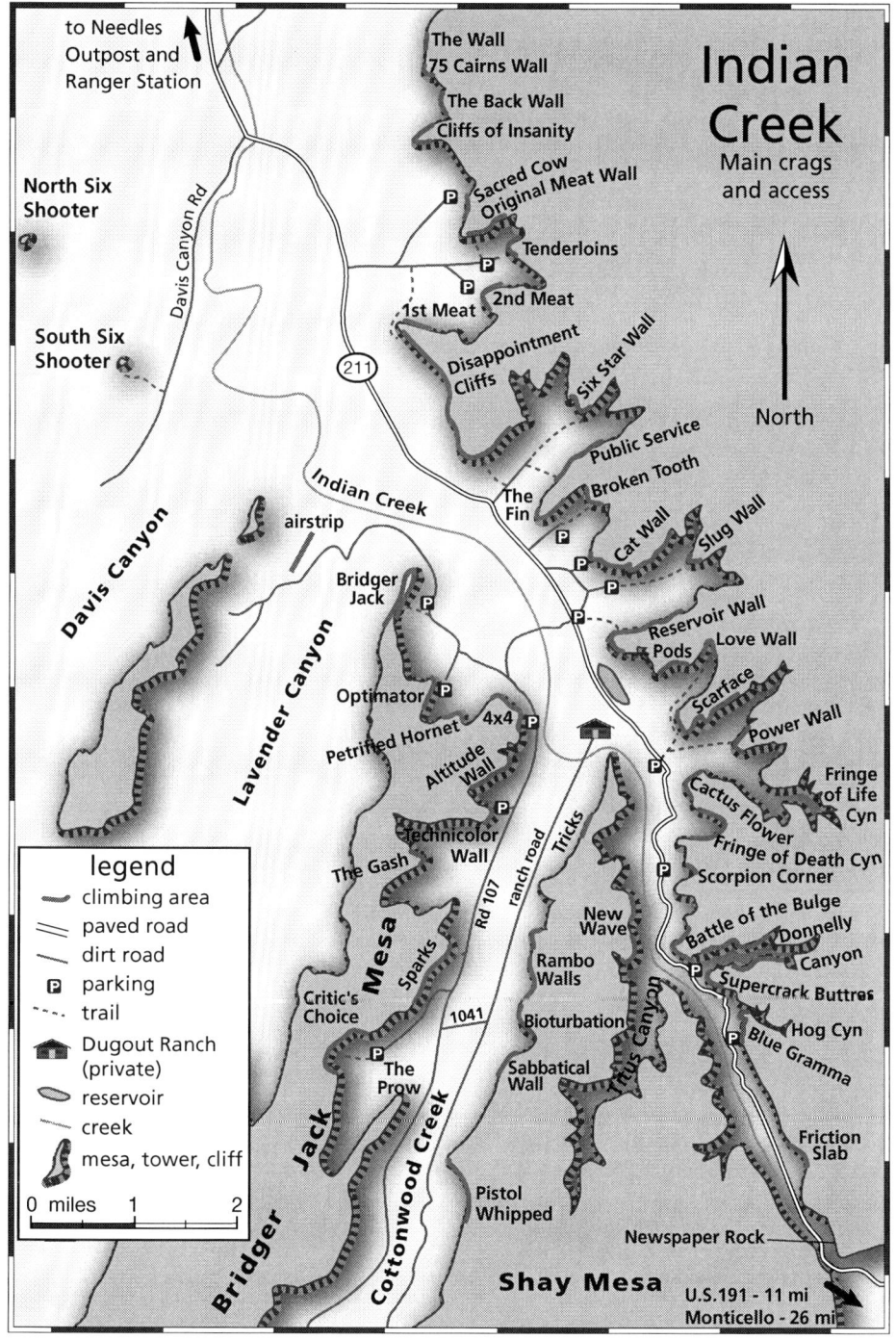

Climate

It is possible to climb comfortably at Indian Creek (weather permitting) during any month of the year, but spring and fall are the most desirable times.

Feb. 15–May 15:
This is a good time to visit; the days are getting longer and the desert is in bloom. However, there can be stretches of stormy weather and the wind is often a factor.
Daytime temperatures range from the low 50s to high 70s.

May 15–September 15:
Summer in the desert is not everyone's cup of tea. You will be climbing exclusively in the shade thus limiting which walls you will visit, as most walls at Indian Creek face south. An early start is advised to avoid heat stroke on the approach, and one gallon of water per person is advised. Daytime temperatures range from the upper 80s to about 100.

September 15–November 15:
The days are getting shorter, but generally high pressure can stay in place for weeks at a time. A primo time to be in the Creek. Daytime temperatures from the 50s to the 70s.

November 15–February 15:
Winter is hit or miss and long cold nights are guaranteed. Storms can last for days at a time, or beautiful sunny days can remain for a while. Daytime temperatures in the 30s to 50s.

Remember that Indian Creek is part of the high desert and extremes of temperature and wind are common. Violent storms can appear out of nowhere, and they don't call the classic on North Six Shooter Peak, Lightning Bolt Cracks for nothing!

The Bridger Jacks under the stars   Photograph by Richard Durnan

Camping

The established areas are Beef Basin, Hamburger Rock, Super Bowl, Cottonwood Creek, and Newspaper Rock (see map). Please try to reuse established camping spots, and do not start new ones. The days of free and unregulated camping at Indian Creek may be drawing to a close. The final plan, to be decided by the various land-managers and landowners involved, and the Access Fund, should be ready by spring 2004. Please check the Monticello BLM website for up-to-date info: <http://www.blm.gov/utah/monticello/> or phone them at 435-587-1500, or check the Access Fund website.

Water and Food

There are no facilities of any kind at Indian Creek. All of your food and water must be brought in from civilization. Small sundries, showers and gasoline can be purchased at The Needles Outpost, but expect to pay more for these items than you would elsewhere. The owners Tracy Napolitano and Gary Knecht have always been very kind to the climbing community, so support them when you can. There is no public water available at the Outpost as they must truck it in themselves. Cell phone reception is pretty non-existent, but seems to exist in one spot: right at the turn-off into Beef Basin.

Photograph of Garrett Kemper by Tommy Chandler

Trash

There is no trash removal here so pack out everything that you bring with you. Please keep your camp area free of loose trash as the first good wind will blow everything into the sagebrush. Two items of particular importance are toilet paper and tape. When you relieve yourself always dig a hole and bury it, and please either burn or pack out your toilet paper. Never defecate near a water source and if you have an emergency at the cliff please walk as far as possible from the base of climbs and hangout areas. Old tape gloves that have been improperly disposed of are a growing problem at the crags. It is not uncommon to see old tape inside the cracks, at the base of climbs or scattered around the hillsides. So please don't discard your tape anywhere but in your own pack, and pick up what others may have left behind.

Erosion

The earth around these parts is very fragile and takes years to regenerate when damaged. Most of the walls have an established trail that follows the path of least resistance up to the base of the wall. Please locate the trail and use it. Do not find a "shortcut" that cuts through untrampled ground. Some of the more obscure buttresses, especially those along Beef Basin Road, have never had a trail or it has faded over time. Take a moment to survey the land and choose a path that will minimize the destruction of vegetation and the erosion of the soil. Usually this means hiking in a drainage or along an adjacent exposed ridge. Of equal importance is the awareness that much of the desert vegetation relies on a fragile component known as cryptobiotic soil. This soil is necessary as an anchor for plants to set their roots in the sandy soil of the region. Once stepped on, the cryptobiotic soil will take generations to repair itself, as it grows very slowly and is not adapted to human interference.

Nature

Geology

The geology of southeastern Utah is among the most magnificent in the world. If you desire to learn about this voluminous topic I suggest you purchase a geology book from one of the fine stores in Moab. For those with less time here is a brief summary. Indian Creek is part of the vast geographic area known as the Colorado Plateau encompassing Southeast Utah, Southwest Colorado, Northeast Arizona and Northwest New Mexico. Most of the rock in this area is sedimentary in nature and is composed primarily of hematite, a form of oxidized iron, with smaller amounts of copper and manganese. Almost all of the rock at Indian Creek is composed of a homogenous layer of Wingate sandstone up to 450 ft. in height. Of the twenty or so named layers of sandstone found on the Colorado Plateau, Wingate is considered by almost all to be the layer of choice for rock climbing. Wingate has a tendency toward eroding very slowly and fracturing cleanly in the vertical plane. This allows for the formation of long, parallel crack systems that the desert climber hungers for. The rock is dense and fine grained in nature, and often covered in a dark desert varnish. The name Wingate comes from the town of Fort Wingate, New Mexico. Chinle sandstone is the layer found under the Wingate and is visible at the base of several Indian Creek Walls, such as The Cat Wall. This layer is softer and does not have the perfect crack systems seen in the Wingate. The layer on top of the Wingate is the Kayenta formation and forms a caprock that preserves the Wingate. This can be seen on the summits of the Bridger Jack group.

Flora and Fauna

The biologic diversity of the high desert surrounding Indian Creek is simply amazing. Much of this is due to the presence of the innumerable canyons found throughout the area, which create small ecosystems catering to plants and animals with specific needs. I am not trained in botany or zoology but I've seen the following during my time in the area. Coyote, fox, mice, deer, falcons, vultures, wild turkey, rattlers and the ever-present equines and bovines of the Dugout Ranch. During a particularly dry September I witnessed a bear foraging for food below the New Wall. He or she probably wandered down from the nearby Abajo Mountains. Common species of plants include sage, cactus, pinyon pine, cottonwood, juniper and the glue that holds it all together, cryptobiotic soil. All of the plants and animals that inhabit this region have to constantly battle extremes of temperature, weather and drought to survive in this harsh land. Let us as humans do what we can to preserve the nature of the land so that the true locals may thrive in the environment they are accustomed. Therefore bury your waste away from water, stay on the trails, don't step on the cryptobiotic soil, and pack out your trash. Although fires are not prohibited at Indian Creek there is not an abundance of downed wood. If you plan on building a fire bring your wood from elsewhere.

Sample of the exceedingly fragile cryptobiotic soil.

NPS Photograph

Unknown climber on **Supercrack** 5.10   Photograph by Michael Clark

Past

The Anasazi Indians had Indian Creek to themselves for hundreds of years, yet they neglected to record their ascents. Unless, of course, their markings on the burnt cliffs are indicative of vertical explorations. Many of the buttresses bear traces of their ghosts in the form of house ruins and petroglyphs.

Modern rock climbing at Indian Creek began when Rick Horn, Huntley Ingalls and Steve Komito established the **Southeast Chimney** route (5.9+, A2) on North Six Shooter Peak in April of 1962. Seven years later, Chuck Pratt and Doug Robinson completed the **West Face Route** (5.10-, A3), and a day later Bill Roos and Paul Sibley added a variation to the first pitch. Various routes on South Six Shooter Peak were climbed between 1969 and 1975. These early pioneers focused their attention on the summits of the area and if they did climb on the buttresses of Indian Creek they did not herald their accomplishments. In fact there has been a noticeable lack of written information documenting first ascents in Indian Creek throughout its history from the 1960s to the present. The first guidebook documentation was a chapter in Eric Bjornstad's 1988 *Desert Rock*, and this only covered Supercrack, Battle of the Bulge, Bridger Jack, and the Six Shooters. Information on the other walls at the Creek were first printed in *Climbing Magazine* #128 (1991) in an article by Steve Petro.

Climbing development in the 1960s and 1970s was limited to a few dedicated and daring individuals who had the mental stamina necessary to climb the parallel sided cracks with a rack consisting of nuts, Hexes, and tube chocks. These individuals include Jimmy Dunn, Earl Wiggins, Bryan Becker, Ed Webster, and Mugs Stump. One tactic that was occasionally employed to give the leader some peace of mind was to hammer a Hexcentric into the crack like a large copperhead. Some early notable ascents include Jimmy Dunn's 1975 ascent of **Y-Crack** in Fringe of Death Canyon and **Generic Crack** in Donnelly Canyon, and the climb that changed Indian Creek forever, **Supercrack**. First climbed by Earl Wiggins, Ed Webster and Bryan Becker in November 1976, this quintessential splitter was originally named **Luxury Liner**. Like other early climbs, this was done without drilling fixed anchors and was taken to the rim of the buttress.

Climbing at Indian Creek began in earnest around 1978 with the introduction of the spring loaded camming device (S.L.C.D.) known as the Wild Country Friend. Once climbers got their paws on these revolutionary crack protectors it became possible to safely climb a crack of unwavering dimensions.

One person in particular deserves attention for the innumerable classic lines he climbed, and that is Steve Hong. Along with Andy Hong and Karin Budding, Steve located and climbed many of Indian Creek's most classic routes. Prior to the opening of State Highway 211, the road into Indian Creek was a private ranch road, and Canyonlands National Park had yet to be established. Hong and his partners are rumored to have flown a plane into the Needles Outpost where they had motorcycles waiting for them. Armed with a high-powered spotting scope Hong scoured the cliffs for five-star cracks, found them and climbed them. During the period from 1977-1988 Hong and partners raised the level of desert climbing with such classics as **Battle of the Bulge, Hydraulic Pump**, the Cat Wall routes and, of course, the climb that symbolizes difficult Indian Creek cracks—**Tricks are for Kids**.

A tradition that began during this area was the placement of plaques at the base of routes to denote the name, grade and date of an ascent. A climber would find a smooth, flat piece of sandstone at the base and etch the relevant information into it for future climbers' reference. This, in effect, became the first guidebook. During the 1980s and 1990s many of these plaques began to disappear and were probably broken by climbers that wanted to keep this information from reaching future visitors. After speaking with many Indian Creek regulars I have found that most climbers enjoy the presence of these plaques and feel that they help preserve the history of the area. Plaque making has made a recent comeback. If you don't like plaques, don't look at them, but please leave them for others to enjoy. Unfortunately, most of the plaques at the popular walls have been lost or destroyed, but at the less frequented cliffs these relics remain.

It is fairly easy to distinguish a Steve Hong plaque as he took great care in crafting these modern petroglyphs. Another tradition that has evolved over time is that of naming a wall after its most classic climb. Examples include; Supercrack, Battle of the Bulge, Scarface, 4x4, Six Star Wall, Critic's Choice, Way Rambo and The Optimator. Many of these are Steve Hong routes, so he may be responsible for this tradition as well.

The next major wave of activity at the Creek centered around Bridger Jack Mesa, where most of Indian Creek's multi-pitch routes and summits are located. Leonard Coyne and Ed Webster started it off with an ascent of **Wild Flower** in June of 1983 and in less than three years all seven summits had been reached. Other developers of this area include Jeff Achey, Chip Chace and Peter Gallagher.

The number of climbers visiting Indian Creek in the 1980s remained relatively small compared to other major rock climbing areas in the United States. This can be attributed to the lack of printed information on the area and to the emergence of sport climbing. In the early- to mid-1990s this changed, perhaps, in part, with the publication of Steve Petro's magazine article and Marco Cornaccione's *200 Select Indian Creek Climbs*. By the late '90s climbers were also beginning to rediscover their traditional roots and Indian Creek was again back in vogue. During the '90s and into the new millennium development of new routes was revitalized by a large and diverse group of individuals. Most of the activity was centered around the more out-of-the-way buttresses such as the Meat Walls, the Beef Basin Walls and by filling in the less obvious lines on the major buttresses. Even today new quality lines are being done on Battle of the Bulge and the Cat Wall, buttresses that were considered climbed out years ago. Since new route information at Indian Creek is spotty I have made a list of the many people who are known to have done first ascents here. My apologies to those who should be on this list, but were left out due to lack of information.

First Ascentionists

Jeff Achey, Jason Ackerman, Jay Anderson, Drew Bedford, Noah Bigwood, Merrill Bitter, Eric Bjornstad, David Bloom, Karin Budding, Steve Carruthers, Tom Carruthers, Scott Carson, Harvey T. Carter, Justin Cassels, Katy Cassidy, Chip Chace, Kevin Chase, Steve Cheyney, Greg Child, Tim Coats, Kyle Copeland, Leonard Coyne, Eric Decaria, Brian Delaney, Gordon Douglas, Jimmy Dunn, Ralph Ferrara, Pete Gallagher, Josh Gross, Lisa Gnade, Chuck Grossman, Stevie Haston, Andy Hong, Steve Hong, Brad Jackson, Jason Keith, Karl Kelley, Ace Kvale, Nathan Martin, Dave Medara, Bob Novellino, Steve Petro, Dean Potter, Steve Quinlan, Chris Ann Quinlan, Tate Rees, Keith Reynolds, Stu Ritchie, Mark Rolofson, Bob Rotert, Bill Roos, John Rosholt, Bret Ruckman, Stuart Ruckman, Pat Savage, Antoine Savelli, Bob Scarpelli, Paul Sibley, Ken Sims, Aron Smith, Jay Smith, Alan Stevenson, John Storn, Mugs Stump, Ken Trout, John Varco, Tim Wagner, Dylan Warren, Robert Warren, Ed Webster, Earl Wiggins, Chip Wilson, Jonny Woodward, Ken Wyrick, The Telluride Crew, The Crested Butte Crew, and the innumerable others that have contributed to new routes at Indian Creek.

Photograph by Tommy Chandler

Ed Webster

Indian Creek Love Affair, circa 1976

On my first climbing trip to Canyonlands I was twenty years old. Jimmy Dunn eased his VW bus onto the creaking wooden timbers of the Dewey Bridge north of Moab one cold November night in 1976, then turned off the headlights and the engine. Hopping out, Dunn, Bryan Becker, and I stood completely still, leaning against the old bridge's railing, listening to the invisible rush of the Colorado River below us, and gazed upwards at a pulsating tapestry of stars. Thus passing across the threshold, we continued down the canyon towards our goal for the night, the Fisher Towers parking lot.

"Look at these cliffs!" I exclaimed, noting the mile-after-mile-after-mile vertical sandstone escarpments glowing ethereally in the silver starlight.

Ed Webster atop Humming Bird Spire after the first free ascen
Photograph by Jeff Achey

"You haven't seen anything yet," said Dunn intently.

Earlier, in exited yet reverential tones, Jim described the crack we were going to attempt, a route he'd first found and sized up several years earlier. It was a line so perfect that his description of it was nearly impossible to believe. Think of a telephone pole 300 feet tall against an otherwise featureless, vertical sandstone wall, he said—and that's what this crack looks like. But because the crack was so utterly parallel, and smooth-sided, there was a good chance that the Hexentrics we planned to use for protection would all rip out if the leader fell. Obviously, on this climb, the leader absolutely could not fall. However, Jim and Earl Wiggins, our other climbing partner, insisted: this was a route worth dying for. It was that superlative of a crack. I'd never heard either of my friends speak like that before, and it made me shudder. As we drove farther south toward Indian Creek Canyon, I tried to visualize the commitment level we'd need to accomplish this climb, and why Jim and Earl spoke so earnestly about a route they considered so calculatedly dangerous.

Late the following afternoon, we descended what would become a familiar set of switchbacks, and halted at Newspaper Rock. Many peoples, including tribes of migrating Native Americans, had lived here and traveled in and out of these canyons for centuries. I was fascinated by the designs of the petroglyphs incised and pecked into the rock's tough black skin of manganese-coated "desert varnish." Here were buffalo, hunters on horseback with arrows drawn, herds of deer, spacemen, dancers, even a wagon wheel. We had entered Indian Creek.

"Well, that crack must be it!" I shouted excitedly, pointing out the windshield as we drove along the meandering road past golden-leafed cottonwood trees, at a yet another perfect hand-width crack coming into view.

"No, it's farther down the canyon," replied Jim.

"OH MY GOD! LOOK AT THAT CRACK!" I blurted out.

"No, that's not it either. It's around the next bend."

Indian Creek Love Affair, circa 1976

When Jim finally stopped the "Youth Challenge" VW bus, Bryan and I leapt out in unison, our eyeballs riveted upwards by the sight of the most perfect, parallel-sided, unbelievable crack—maybe in the entire universe—slicing up the center of the reddish-brown Wingate sandstone wall above the hillside. Then, as Jim pointed out the other sandstone buttresses nearby, each seamed by hundreds of nearly identical crack systems, he said simply: "None of these cracks have ever been climbed."

My mind experienced an altered state; I felt I had passed through Alice's Looking Glass into a magically exotic world where cracks had been sculpted by God into masterpieces of rock climbing perfection. Indian Creek obviously represented the future of hand and finger jamming, and crack climbing. Then, pausing to take a deep breath, I returned through the magic portal to realize I was living in the present, and that tomorrow the true test would come. Could we, mere humans, climb cracks like these? And—how would we protect them?

Earl Wiggins was a principal leader amongst our vision-seeking band from Colorado Springs. Peering through his coke bottle-thick glasses, he racked up to lead the first pitch of his "Luxury Liner" that afternoon. (Much to Earl's disappointment, the climb became forever known as The Super Crack of the Desert—Dunn's original name for the route—after I wrote a story about the climb that was published in Mountain Magazine.) Two other friends, Stewart Green and Michael Gardiner, wanted to film our hoped-for ascent, so we waited around till after the heat of midday when the light was softer. Then, inexplicably, Jim Dunn became disenchanted with the scene. "Too many people," he said, before disappearing in search of new spiritual directions. Fortunately, Dennis Jackson, who'd also tagged along, provided his gentle humor to ease the palpable tension as Earl, Bryan, and I got ready. The fatal consequences of a leader fall were burned into our minds.

With his psyche revved up to the highest possible notch, Earl started up the crack—and instantly became unstoppable. He churned up the first pitch of Super Crack in a blur of synchronized hand and toe jams until he became a perpetual motion machine, halting only momentarily every 20 feet to slot another Hexentric before blazing farther into the unknown. He climbed so quickly that his entire lead took maybe ten minutes. Meanwhile, I ran madcap around the base, frantically taking about a dozen pictures. And when Earl threw himself into the belay niche at the top of the difficulties, a tremendous, spontaneous whoop of congratulations by every one of us reverberated and echoed through the soon-to-be hallowed walls of Indian Creek Canyon.

Earl Wiggins, a climber of understated, yet undeniable brilliance, had accomplished the impossible, mentally preparing himself for, then mastering, with his mind and body a route no one was sure could be climbed. That day in November, 1976, Earl created the new frontier of desert sandstone crack climbing. It was a lead the likes of which none of us present had ever witnessed—and so smoothly did he accomplish it! Like all true visionaries, Earl had made it look effortless. Now Bryan and I had to give it our best. I followed Wiggin's lead of Super Crack's first pitch, removing the Hexes he'd placed for protection—which actually seemed fairly solid. Then, after a rest, I led the second pitch, struggling up a wider, semi-offwidth that narrowed all the way down to fingertips. I also experimented with a new kind of protection device we'd taken along as a last resort: a prototype Lowe, double-prong camming unit that seemed distinctly untrustworthy, yet at least gave me some protection to look at as I gained height. In retrospect, it too represented the wave of the future.

Earl followed pitch two up to my hanging belay, now only 100 feet short of the canyon rim. We were "real climbers" in those halcyon days, so it was absolutely unthinkable for us to consider our climb as the first ascent of Super Crack until we reached the very top of the cliff. Earl swung to the right off my drilled angle piton anchor into a crumbling, shortbread-quality flake, laybacked wildly up it, and disappeared up more 5.10 ground until I heard his loud yell once he reached a juniper tree on top. Poor Bryan had to follow the first two pitches as one, climbing on a single 9mm rope, but soon all three of us were celebrating on the canyon rim—and wondering how we were going to get down. Fortunately, we found several semi-reliable trees to rap off.

19

Indian Creek Love Affair, circa 1976

We never once thought our climb would be repeated, let alone become one of the most famous, sought after, and photographed rock climbs in the world. Protecting smooth-sided, soft sandstone, parallel cracks with only a rack of hexentrics wasn't going to be very appealing to most climbers. But when we reached the ground after our final rappel to enjoy the congratulatory hugs of our friends, I realized our perceptions of what rock climbs were possible had truly changed—and would never be quite the same again.

Indian Creek Canyon probably would have remained a scenic, but isolated climbing backwater except for the invention and popularization of camming protection in the late 1970s and early 80s. To my knowledge, only one team ever repeated Super Crack in traditional, all-hexentric style. The route that Jim Dunn and Earl Wiggins conceived of, and that Earl, Bryan, and I climbed would have remained an obscure footnote but for the invention of Friends and Camalots.

A handful of other new pure crack climbs were pioneered in Indian Creek slightly before, and after, the 1976 first ascent of Super Crack. Wiggins and Dunn barely survived the Fringe of Death, a 5.11 with groundfall-potential in 1975, while Mark Rolofson and I ascended the beautiful three-pitch Cactus Flower Crack (5.10+) in 1978. Standing again on the canyon rim, this time toward sunset, I gazed across the green fields and quiet houses of the Dugout Ranch, listened to the mooing cattle, and admired the most lovely evening silhouette of Bridger Jack Mesa, North and South Sixshooter Peaks, and Island in the Sky.

In the late 1970s, the Redd family, who owned and operated Dugout Ranch, were very kind to us climbers, and curious about these new folks coming to climb on their red rock walls and towers. One day (having not bothered to bring any headlamps), Peter Gallagher and I got completely lost trying to find our car in the dark following our climb of North Sixshooter Peak. After a painful hour of stepping on sharp-spined cactus in our running shoes, we gave up and bivvied on a dirt road we stumbled across. At 5 AM the next morning, a battered old pickup truck sauntered up to us, and stopped. Nervously, we picked ourselves up out of the dust.

"Morn'in," said we, sheepishly.

"What in the heck are you two do'in out here?" asked old Mr. Redd.

"We were climbing the Sixshooters," I said proudly.

"Damn!" exclaimed Mr. Redd. "I always wanted to see someone standing up there on top of one of those! Now next time you're down here to climb them again, I want you to let me know first so I can watch, you hear?"

"Yes, sir," we answered.

Several years later, in the early 1980s, I explored all of Bridger Jack Mesa, making the first ascents of all but one of the mesa's seven summits with a variety of partners. They are each lofty "space stations," and well worth climbing: Bridger Jack, King of Pain, Hummingbird and Sunflower Towers, Easter Island, Sparkling Touch, and Thumbelina. Again, the ranch hands accepted us—as long as we shut the cattle gates after driving through them, which we always did. Once we watched the cowboys assist several calves being born; another time, we witnessed the annual cattle roundup from high on a new route up Bridger Jack (the aptly named Roundup Route), watching the cowboys gather all the stray cattle from our unique aerial vantage point. But always, in the beginning, there was friendship between the Redd family at Dugout Ranch, and the climbers.

Eventually, as it was bound to, word about the extraordinary cracks in Indian Creek "got out." Steve Hong, Karin Budding, Jeff Achey, Peter Williams, Brian Delaney, Leonard Coyne, Steve Cheyney, Steve Petro, Ken Trout, Bob Rotert, Mugs Stump, and many others climbed the first ascents of many of the area's classic cracks. In more recent times, foreign climbers have swelled the ranks of Indian Creek visitors, their imaginations sparked by magazine and movie images of Super Crack, Incredible Hand Crack, and the Lightning Bolt Cracks, amongst others. Put plain and simple, popularity and too many climbers wore out the climbers' welcome on the lands of the Dugout Ranch. Like many love affairs, the original innocence and balance in the relationship was lost. To help show that climbers do care, in the early 1990s the American Mountain Foundation built a trail up the hillside to Super Crack, began revegetating Donnelly Canyon, and opened a dialogue with the Redd family about climbing access, camping issues, and other important environmental concerns.

In 1996 came the news that the Nature Conservancy was raising funds to purchase Dugout Ranch from the Redd family. Money was raised successfully, and Dugout Ranch was deeded to the Nature Conservancy in 1997, thus preserving the lands, and the ranch's traditional way of life, for all time. The pristine beauty and singular rock climbs of Indian Creek Canyon are an irreplaceable treasure whose memories are shared in the hearts of many climbers around the globe. I am happy to know Indian Creek's natural splendor, its red rock vistas, and ancient soul are now safely preserved for future generations of climbers to experience, and become transformed by.

    Ed Webster
    July 12, 2003
    Topsham, Maine

"The Best Ascent of Everest in Terms and Style of Pure Adventure." — Reinhold Messner

HAILED BY READERS AROUND THE WORLD AS ONE OF THE CLASSIC EVEREST BOOKS

SNOW IN THE KINGDOM
MY STORM YEARS ON EVEREST

by Ed Webster

The gripping Everest autobiography of one of Canyonland's most renowned pioneers recounts his historic new route up Everest's Kangshung Face in Tibet, climbed in 1988 without oxygen, radios, or Sherpa support.

Signed copies available. $40 includes postage and handling, from
Mountain Imagery PO Box 35,
South Freeport, Maine 04078 USA
www.mtnimagery.com

"Webster gives us his heart and soul on a platter!" "Brutally Honest" "Magnificent!"

Hardware

Nowhere in the world are one-pitch routes more gear intensive than at Indian Creek. The pitches can continue for a ropelength, and they are often unchanging in size for long stretches. I have given gear suggestions for routes, when the information is known. I have used Wild Country Friend sizes even though many people are more accustomed to Black Diamond and Metolious camming units. The reasons are as follows: When many of these climbs were put up in the 1970s and 1980s, Friends were the only camming device available, and the size of a Wild Country cam, i.e. #2 Friend, most closely approximates the size of the crack, i.e. a two-inch crack. To familiarize yourself with the conversion of cam sizes from product to product please refer to the cam conversion chart on page 24. Loosely translated a #1 Friend is equivalent to a 0.5 (purple) Camalot or orange Metolious, a #1.5 Friend equals a 0.75 (green) Camalot or red Metolious, a #2-#2.5 Friend is a #1 (red) Camalot, a #2.5-#3 Friend is a #2 (yellow) Camalot, and a #3-#3.5 Friend is a #3 (blue) Camalot.

Although a properly placed cam in Wingate sandstone should hold a significant leader fall, due to the soft nature of the rock, (as compared with granite), it is suggested that pieces be placed approximately every 6ft. or one body length. This may often mean that between 6 and 12 units of the same size may be needed to safely lead one pitch. This accounts for the large number of climbers that can be seen congregating around one climb, as all of the groups' cams may be used at once. Sometimes the size of the crack will change slightly and therefore a combination of different cams is preferred. For example, on **Slice and Dice**, a sustained finger-stacking splitter that is 1.5 inches, a combination of 1.5 Friends and 0.75 Camalots, will offer the best protection. It is often possible to leapfrog gear when one is lacking the proper number of the same sized cam. This is usually done on cracks that are hand size or bigger. It is the rare individual that will attempt a tips crack without the recommended number of cams.

The suggestions offered in this guide for specific routes are just that, suggestions. If you feel weak at a particular size crack then bring more cams than are recommended. Similarly one may feel comfortable using fewer cams when climbing an "easier" sized crack. When no suggestions are given take into account the length of the climb, the size of the crack, and how good you are feeling that day. It is always better to have units left over than to run out of gear on the sharp end of the rope. A minimum rack for most climbs would be one set of TCUs, a triple set of cams from 1.0–3.5 inches, a few stoppers and several slings. Two ropes are a good idea unless you know that the climbs you will be doing are under 100 feet in length. Almost all climbs have two-bolt belay anchors but many of the older routes have unsafe bolts and rotten webbing. Many climbs at Supercrack, Battle of the Bulge and the Cat Wall have had their anchors replaced by the dedicated individuals of the American Safe Climbing Association.

When in doubt back up your anchor and/or replace the bolts and the webbing. It is not uncommon for one person to lead a climb and several others to toprope the route. When doing this never thread the rope directly through the rappel rings or chains. Put a couple of quickdraws directly into the bolt hangers and help lengthen the life of the rings.

Many climbers find their cam triggers stiffening after climbing in the desert, due to the ever-present sand. Simply applying a lubricant such as WD 40 will temporarily relieve the problem, but will ultimately make the cams even stiffer as more dirt adheres to the lubricant. A better method is to boil the cams in water, pick out any remaining grime with a tooth pick or small toothbrush and then apply a non-greasy lubricant such as Metolius Cam Cleaner or Elmer's Slide-All. This will lengthen the life of your cams and make them easier to use.

Super Rack of the Desert: If you've got it flaunt it.... Photograph of Mary Buchmayer by Richard Durnan

Hardware

GEAR CONVERSION CHART

Body Part	Inches	Black Diamond	Wild Country	Wired Bliss	Metolius	Aliens	BIG BRO
<tips	< 0.5		"zeros"	0.40	.00	0.33	
		0.20				0.38	
Tips	.5/.65	0.30	0.00	0.50	.0	0.50	
		0.40	0.5		1.0		
Fingers	.65/1.0		1.0	0.75	2.0	0.75	
				1.0	3.0	1.0	
Off Fingers Thin Hands	1.0/1.3	0.75	1.5	1.5	4.0	1.5	
Hands	1.3/1.7		2.0	2.0	5.0	2.0	
					6.0		
Big Hands Fist	1.5/2.5	2.0	2.5	2.5	7.0	2.5	
			3.0	3.0			
Off Fist	2.0/3.0		3.5	3.5	8.0		
Small OW	2.5/4.0	3.5	4.0	4.0	9.0		
Big OW	3.0/4.5				10.0		Big Bro #1
> Big OW	3.5/5.5	4.5	5.0				Big Bro #2
	5.0/7.0		6.0				Big Bro #3
	> 7.0						Big Bro #4

Difficulty Grades

The difficulty of any climb at Indian Creek is a combination of the length of the route, the size of the crack, steepness, the availability of rests and—most importantly—the size of one's fingers and hands. In general perfect hand cracks are about 5.10, cupped hands will be 5.10+ to 5.11, thin hands usually weigh in at 5.11 to 5.12-, finger cracks check in between 5.11+ and 5.12+, tips cracks range from 5.12- to 5.13- and finger stacks top the charts at 5.12–5.13. Because the routes are so size-dependent the standard Yosemite Decimal System utilizing + and - grades will be used here. 5.10- is usually 5.10a, 5.10 is 5.10b or 5.10c and 5.10+ equals 5.10d. The amount of gear that gets placed will also affect the grade slightly. The grades given here are for leading routes while placing protection. Toproping reduces the grade about two or three letter grades.

Plan for Hand

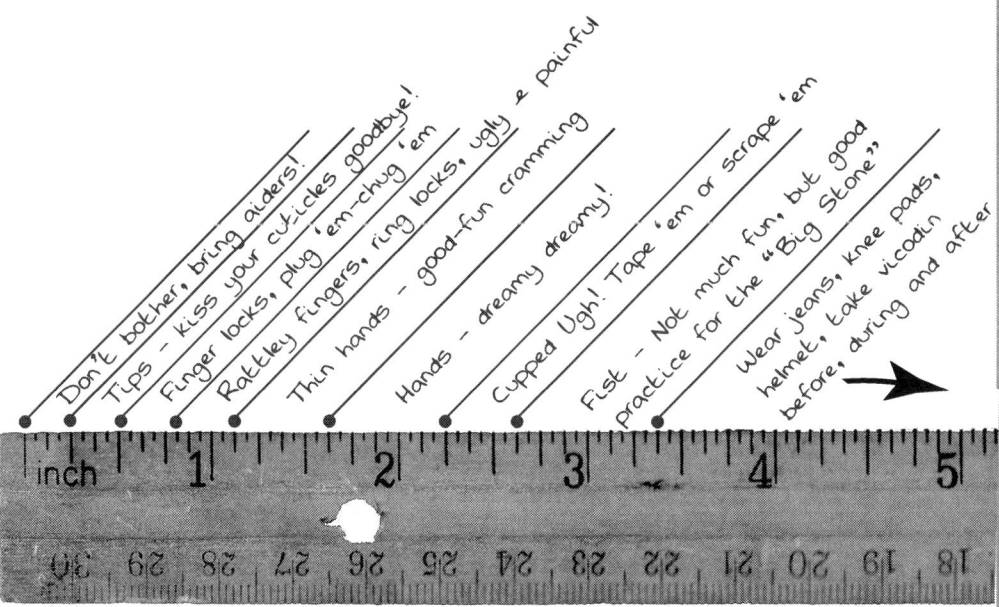

*slide boundaries to fit your preferences

Alan Lester's

Plan for the "Average" Hand

Photograph by John Dickey

Hardware

Anchors

Most of the bolts in use at Indian Creek were placed as rappel anchors. Over the years the types of bolts used include: buttonheads, Star Drives, studs, machine bolts, drilled baby angles and expansion bolts. Many of these have been found to be inadequate for the purpose they were intended. Rawl five-piece expansion bolts, 3/8"-1/2" in diameter are considered the safest choice. Until the 1990s webbing was used on the anchors, but due to the dry and sunny weather this webbing needs to be replaced frequently. It is therefore recommended that chains be used instead of nylon webbing. There are some routes that have protection bolts in place where natural gear is absent. Many of these bolts have become unnecessary with the introduction of the micro-camming units. On the buttresses adjacent the Dugout Ranch bolts are only permitted as rappel anchors. These include, but are not limited to, Supercrack, Battle of the Bulge, and the Reservoir Wall. When putting up a new route try and use only natural gear, but if the climb is worthy and only a bolt will work, place as few as possible, use only Rawl five-piece expansion bolts, and camouflage the hangers with reddish-brown paint.

Ari Menitove replacing a Cat Wall anchor.   Photograph by Andrew Burr

Pagan Mountaineering

59 South Main #2   Moab UT 84532

435. 259. 1117

www.paganmountaineering.com

Alternative Lifestyle

Bouldering
If scaling the small stones is your bag then go to Bishop or Hueco. However if your hands hurt or you need a change of pace then decent bouldering can be found near the road by Fringe of Death Canyon, at the base of Bridger Jack, at the 4x4 Wall trailhead, and on the large boulder on the trail to Way Rambo. If you're really jonesing check out the Big Bend Boulders along River Road, 15 minutes northeast of Moab.

Rest
If you are spending more than a few days at Indian Creek then your body will eventually wear down and you'll be forced to rest. There are a multitude of enjoyable rest-day activities to choose from:
1) Go for a hike in one of the local canyons, i.e. Donnelly or Titus Canyon
2) Explore in Canyonlands National Park
3) Hang around aimlessly at The Needles Outpost
4) Take your mountain bike out for a spin
5) Clean your cams
6) Stay in camp and rest
7) Search for ruins and petroglyphs
8) Heckle your friends who are climbing
9) Party in Moab

Urbanism
If you need water, food or gas the nearest town to Indian Creek is Monticello, located 14 miles south of the junction of Highway 211 and Highway 191. Friday and Saturday nights you could hang around the gas stations with the local youth, but otherwise, not much happens here. Most people will opt for the one-hour drive to Moab. One can find motels, supermarkets (City Market and Boomers, both on Main St), a laundromat, a movie theatre, and gear shops. A great place for climbing gear and beta is Pagan Mountaineering next to Eddie McStiff's on the corner of Center and Main. Climbers can get showers for $3 at the Center Motel. Gearheads (Main St., often a big tent sits out front) is a source for free filtered water as well as cheap energy bars and a well stocked climbing section. Matrimony Spring, a pipe on the right side of the River Road just outside of town, can also fill up your Nalgene.

Craig Luebben and Tommy Caldwell making friends.   Photograph by Topher Donahue

Book Learning

Book Format

The buttresses are listed from east to west (right to left) along the north side of Highway 211 from The Friction Slab to the crags northwest of The Cliffs of Insanity, ending at Suburbia. These are the north side walls.

The south side walls begin with Bridger Jack Mesa and are laid out from north to south (right to left) along the west side of Beef Basin Road as far south as Critic's Choice. The loop is completed with the walls along the east side of Beef Basin Road from Pistol Whipped to Tricks Wall, and around Paragon Prow to the south side walls (The New Walls) of Highway 211.

Routes at all buttresses are described from left to right.

Excuses for failure

- [ ] 1) The crack is too big (or small).
- [ ] 2) My tape is too tight (or loose).
- [ ] 3) I don't have enough gear.
- [ ] 4) I placed way too much gear.
- [ ] 5) This guidebook sucks.
- [ ] 6) It's too hot (or cold).
- [ ] 7) My hands hurt.
- [ ] 8) I suck at crack climbing.
- [ ] 9) I have no endurance.
- [ ] 10) It's not granite.
- [ ] 11) _____
- [ ] 12) _____

Corrections and Additions

Since this is the first major update on Indian Creek climbing in several years there are bound to be errors and omissions. Subsequent editions can only improve with the input of other climbers. Please send any corrections or additions to Sharp End Publishing, P.O. Box 1613, Boulder CO 80306 or sharpend@comcast.net.

Jason Lakey on the first send of the Bridger Jack highline. Photograph by Josh Cross

Jason Keith

Access, Climbers, and Cows

Many climbers are drawn to Indian Creek not only for its unique hard-core crack climbing, but also its primitive, wide-open feeling. If the "Creek" doesn't exemplify the Wild West and freedom then no place does. Still, what climbers may perceive as public land might actually be private Dugout Ranch property; what now seems like unmanaged use could in the future be closed or restricted.

Photo of Jason Keith on Way Rambo by Celin Serbo
Jason serves as Policy Director for the Access Fund.

Private Land. Climbers cross private property at least a little every time they approach Supercrack Buttress, Battle of the Bulge, Donnelly Canyon, New Wall, New Wave Wall, Paragon Prow (AKA the Sundial), Tricks Wall, Scarface, and Love Wall. We drive across Dugout property (on a county right-of-way) every time we camp or climb at Bridger Jack. For many years, crossing Dugout land was tolerated because of the positive relationship forged between a few climbers and longtime owner of the Ranch, Heidi Redd. Even when a few careless climbers let their campfire burn down a few of Heidi's cottonwood trees, she continued to allow access. When campers began to trash the side canyons near Supercrack and Battle of the Bulge, Heidi graciously made an arrangement with climbers: she'd allow continued access across her land to Supercrack and Battle of the Bulge if these side canyons were blocked off from auto access and allowed to restore.

For nearly forty years, Heidi Redd has run the Indian Creek Cattle Company and held the Bureau of Land Management grazing leases adjacent to the Ranch. These grazing "allotments" cover significant Indian Creek locations including the popular campsites along the Bridger Jack Road and Superbowl Site, and the fields below Cat Wall. On most days you can see Heidi's cows or horses grazing on these public land allotments.

In 1997, The Nature Conservancy bought Dugout Ranch and currently manages it to fulfill three major stewardship goals: the preservation of the property's ecological and open space features, the use of the property as a resource for ecological research and natural history interpretation, and the continuance of a historic ranching operation, with the least environmental impact. Under the terms of the Dugout Ranch sale Heidi retained a life lease of 25 acres and her home (she can live there until she dies) and a 10-year lease of the Ranch to continue her cattle operation. Heidi owns the cattle and the Indian Creek Cattle Company and currently holds the grazing permits associated with Dugout Ranch.

Public Land. There are real impacts associated with grazing on public lands, and some would rather not see cows grazing at all along the Bridger Jack Road and other public land allotments. However, Heidi's Indian Creek Cattle Company pays for that right, and has for several decades now. Climbers, on the other hand, have only been climbing at Indian Creek in *significant* numbers for the last ten or so years. Although some folks would rather see the BLM terminate these grazing leases, under the current system if Heidi ends her grazing lease then another rancher could step in and install their ranching operation. Since she began ranching the land in the mid-1960s, Heidi has been conservation minded. Indian Creek Cattle Company has always run fewer cattle than its predecessors and often fewer than current permits allow. Heidi and her cattle company have worked to maintain native grasses and restore/maintain the critical riparian corridor of Indian Creek. There's no assurance that another rancher would do the same.

Access, Climbers, and Cows

Climbers and cowboys. In a number of areas at Indian Creek, conflicts have sprouted between climbers and Heidi's cattle operation. The most common is the dog/cow issue. Even if you feel you have an absolute right to camp and climb at the Creek, following these few basic guidelines may help keep you climbing on some of Indian Creek's best crags.

- **Control your pets.** Whether or not you hate cows, Heidi has a right to graze them at Indian Creek. If you see cattle or horses approaching your camp, or as you drive to your parking area, TIE UP YOUR DOG! Don't assume that your mellow beast won't cause any problems, because even distant barking can aggravate cows and horses. Granted, some cowboy/climber interactions have gone over the top (there's no excuse for threatening to shoot someone's dog), but remember, whether or not *your* dog has tried to round up some cattle, someone else's dog has probably done so recently. Heidi and her cowboys are at the end of their rope in terms of giving campers the benefit of the doubt with their pets, so be proactive and keep the hounds under control.

- **Courtesy.** Be respectful of Heidi and her cowboys if you see them. Remember, Heidi and The Nature Conservancy own the private property of Dugout Ranch and control access to some of the best crack climbing in the world and in some cases they may actually own the climbing routes too! Mouthing off does everyone a disservice and may result in the loss of these access privileges. More importantly, being friendly to local landowners that endure a transient and often large climbing population is the right thing to do.

- **Climb elsewhere.** Consider not climbing at a few key locations that require walking across Dugout property, especially Paragon Prow, Fist Fight Wall and New Wall. There are literally a thousand other climbs, and these routes in particular infringe on the privacy of the Ranch.

- **Leave No Trace.** The better we care for the place, the more Heidi will think us responsible stewards, and the more likely we can continue to approach our chosen climbs across Dugout land. Leaving the land in as good or better shape than we found it reflects respect for the land, local landowners, and other visitors.

Finally, ask yourself how long you've been climbing at Indian Creek and how often you visit. Ten years? Twenty-five years? Four years? Heidi has called Indian Creek *home* for nearly four decades. She's seen the national park come in, a nuclear dump proposed for Lavender Canyon, uranium miners dynamiting their claims, massive OHV use, and now hordes of climbers descending on the area, many of whom trespass across her land at their whim. Still, Heidi continues to try to work with climbers, allowing them to cross private property and often helping people in need. Let's try hard to continue a positive relationship with the Dugout Ranch and hopefully maintain access to some of our favorite climbs.

Jason Keith

The Petroglyphs
One more consideration from David Bloom and Sharp End Publishing

There are numerous sites throughout Indian Creek where the Native people indigenous to this area have left their mark. Many impressive panels of petroglyphs and pictographs can be found with a little exploring. As luring as they are, merely touching these ancient panels can cause them harm as oils from one's skin affect the pigments. Protection of these resources could likely become another major access issue. Please don't ruin our prividges, only put up or repeat a route if it is possible to do so without harming these treasures.

Fred Knapp on the venerable classic, **Incredible Hand Crack** 5.10   Photograph by Stewart M. Green

Friction Slab to Battle of the Bulge

Area Overview
Friction Slab to Battle of the Bulge

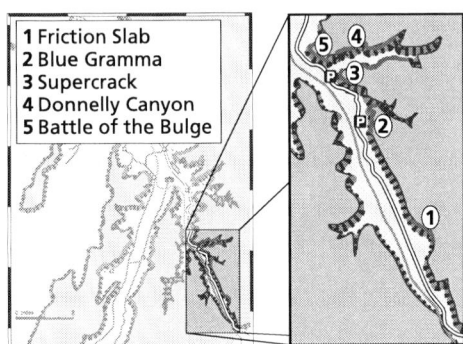

1 Friction Slab
2 Blue Gramma
3 Supercrack
4 Donnelly Canyon
5 Battle of the Bulge

Friction Slab

Let's face it folks, you don't come to Indian Creek to climb slabs, but if your hands are all chewed up these climbs are a nice diversion. These routes are on a light-colored slab 0.5 miles down the road from Newspaper Rock.

Friction Slab

1 **Laurel 5.11**
Two pitches
The first pitch is 5.10R and has three bolts and a 1-bolt anchor. The second pitch is the crux and has about six bolts. Rappel the route or walk off to the east.

2 **White Waltz 5.10 90'**
Three bolts to a 2-bolt anchor.

3 **Unnamed 5.9 90'**
Start left of a juniper tree and climb past four drilled pitons to a 2-bolt anchor.

4 **Sundance 5.7 70'**
Located about 50' left of a forming arch on the right side of the slab. Two bolts to a 1-bolt anchor.

5 **Split Pinnacle 5.9 25'**
Past the Friction Slab on the right side of the road is this short tight-hands to fist splitter on a pillar tucked in the trees. Mostly hands.

6 **Y-Crack Simulator 5.9 30'**
Located on the right side of the road two miles past Newspaper Rock is this short but quality wide-hands crack. 3.0–3.5

Patrick Griffin on the first ascent of **Orion's Bow** 5.10   Photograph by Ed Webster

Blue Gramma Cliff

Blue Gramma Cliff

This is the first wall with cracks that a visiting climber will see upon arriving at Indian Creek. There is an excellent selection of moderate (5.10-5.11) climbs close to the road.

The single most important issue facing climbers at The Creek relates to climbing near petroglyphs. Some of the best-preserved petroglyphs are adjacent to climbs at Blue Gramma. In the future, the anchors atop some of the Blue Gramma climbs may be removed. Please respect the rock art and the BLM in their efforts to preserve these irreplaceable resources—and watch for missing anchors!

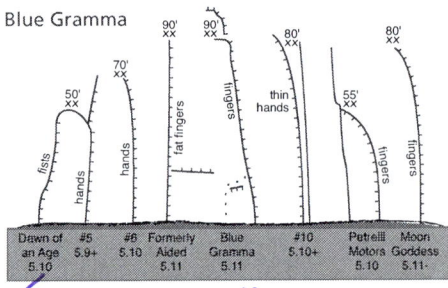

Blue Gramma

1 **Unnamed 5.10- 60'**
This straight-in hands to fist crack is 500' left of **Dawn of an Age**. *(2)3.0, (2)3.5, (1)4.0*

2 **Unnamed 5.10 50'**
Left-facing flake.

3 **Unnamed 5.10 50'**
Hands to offwidth in a left-leaning corner. One-bolt anchor. *2.5–4.0*

4 **Dawn of an Age 5.10 50'**
Fists in a left-facing corner. *3.5–6.0*

5 **Unnamed 5.9+ 50'**
Hands to wide hands in a left-facing corner. Offwidth second pitch. *2.5–4.0*

6 **Unnamed 5.10 70'**
Fingers to wide hands in a left-facing corner. *(1)0.75, (1)1.0, (2)1.5, (2)2.0, (3)2.5, (2)3.0, (1)3.5*

7 **Formerly Aided 5.11 90'**
Off-fingers in a left-facing corner.

8 **Unnamed 5.11 90'**
Begin below an obvious flake at the left side of a white slab. There is a fixed piton on the route.

9 **Blue Gramma 5.11 90'**
Slabby start to fingers in a beautiful varnished left-facing corner. You can practically smell the aroma of this sweet grass as you layback effortlessly up this gem of a climb. *0.5–2.5*

10 **Unnamed 5.10+ 80'**
Climb twin cracks in a thin-hands right-facing corner. *1.0–2.5*

11 **Petrelli Motors 5.10 55'**
Climb the varied splitter, mostly fingers, left of a right-facing corner, and left of some petroglyphs. *0.5–2.5, heavy in the smaller sizes*

12 **Moon Goddess Revenge 5.11- 80'**
Follow thin cracks past a bolt and a ledge, and up a left-facing dihedral. *(3)1.0, (5)1.5, (2)2.0, (1)2.5, (1)3.0*

13 **Orion's Bow 5.10 50'/130'/170'**
This three-pitch face climb ascends the slab between Blue Gramma and Supercrack Buttress. Start at the toe of the buttress.

Pitch 1: Follow a left-facing flake (5.6).

Pitch 2: Climb steepening rock past some bolts and a thin crack (5.10).

Pitch 3: Angle up and left past a few more bolts to a bolted belay (5.9).

Rap the route with two double-rope rappels. *(7) quickdraws, nuts*

Wendy Davis on **Blue Gramma** 5.11 Photograph by Ben Moon/MoonFoto

Karin Budding

The Desert

For those of us who frequented Indian Creek in the 70s and 80s, "the desert" was a relatively short stretch of road that offered one beckoning side canyon after another. Much of the day was spent exploring—hiking up endless loose talus slopes with unpleasant packs only to be disappointed in the size of the crack—the perfect finger or hand crack was wide enough for a fist upon closer inspection.

On the well established Indian Creek star rating scale, however, there were many "five stars" to be had. Some required lassoing loose blocks at the base that obstructed the bottom portion of a faultless crack. Others required parking automobiles on climbing shoes for extended periods of time in order to enhance the shoe's toe-jamming capability. They all required massive tape jobs (another highly technical operation that evolved in complexity, but not necessarily effectiveness over the years) and, of course, the giant rack. And they all got ONE bomber bolt at the top—but it was bomber.

Karin Budding   Photograph by Dan Hare

The classics required a name plate—the name and rating were meticulously carved into a loose stone with the drill bit and hammer, and ceremoniously placed at the base of the route. Friends, hot on the trail of a new route, have told me they were disappointed to discover a name plate at the base of some obscure crack they were going to claim as their own. The naming of the route was yet another feat—particularly if you had to adhere to the theme name of the cliff. The theme could be in honor of a new pet cat or the cut of meat to be grilled on the campfire that night.

The plentiful wood supply fueled the fire and the endless stream of climbing spew long into the night. Plans had to be made, though, for the next day's adventure—there were more canyons to explore and countless more "five stars" to be discovered. Each time the cycle was repeated, the climbing was truly incredible.

Karin Budding
July 7, 2003

Neptune Mountaineering

Weekdays 10am - 8pm   Weekends 8am - 6pm
633 South Broadway, Boulder, CO 80210, 303-499-8866

gear to get you vertical

photo Peter Holcombe
www.holcombephotography.com

www.neptunemountaineering.com

Supercrack Buttress

Prior to 1976 this was just another unnamed buttress of Wingate sandstone. This all changed when Earl Wiggins, Ed Webster and Bryan Becker had the vision to climb a staggeringly beautiful wide hands splitter armed with only nuts and Hexcentrics; the rest is history. Jimmy Dunn first discovered Supercrack but did not climb on the first ascent as he was in charge of metaphysical support that day.

The Supercrack Buttress/Battle of the Bulge area sees more climbing traffic than all the other crags at Indian Creek combined. The reasons are many. Supercrack Buttress is one of the first cliffs one comes to at the Creek, it's a short approach from the road, there are a high concentration of 5.10s, and its name recognition is unparalleled. Having heaped so much praise on this pioneer cliff, there are a couple of drawbacks. Spring and fall weekends can make one feel like they are waiting in a bread line to do any of the popular routes. Compared with some less traveled buttresses some of the climbs here can be a little generic.
Park 0.3 miles past Supercrack cattle guard, on the right.

Heidi Redd has been very accommodating of climbers over the years, even after some careless climber campfires burnt down some of her trees. Please return the favor and be respectful of private property rights and ranching practices of the Dugout Ranch (i.e. keep dogs from harassing cows).

John Adams on **3 AM Crack** 5.10   Photograph by Dan Hare

Supercrack Buttress

1 Unnamed 5.11- 60'
Tight hands in a shallow left-facing corner. Stays shady.

2 Unnamed 5.11+ ?
A wavy tips splitter through a bulge. Anchors not visible.

3 Bad-Rad Duality Crack 5.10+ 110'
Everything from thin hands to offwidth in a long left-facing corner. Mostly hands. 2.0–4.0

4 The Onslaught 5.11 70'
Fingers in a tight straight-in corner.

5 No Name Crack 5.10 120'
Hands to wide hands in a right-facing corner. 2.5–4.0

6 Triple Jeopardy 5.7 70'
Climb the left side of a broken pillar. One of the few climbs at this grade.

7 Twin Cracks 5.9 60'
Climb twin hand/finger cracks in a right-facing corner. 1.0–3.0

8 3 AM Crack 5.10 110'
Hands to wide hands in a right-facing corner. (2)2.0, (3)2.5, (4)3.0, (2)3.5

9 Wild Works of Fire 5.11R 100'
Start over stacked blocks and climb a hand to finger crack, to face climbing along a seam. A new anchor was placed below the dicey section. It is 50' of 5.10b to the new anchors. *Nuts, 2 sets of TCUs, 2 sets of cams*

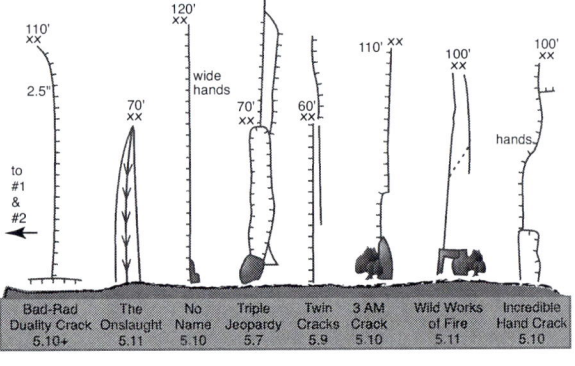

44

10 The Incredible Hand Crack 5.10 100'
Originally climbed as a four-pitch route to the top, way back in 1978. This may be the most climbed route in all of Indian Creek. Over the years the crack has gone from a tight 2.5" to big 2.5" from all the traffic, and the feet have gotten a lot smoother. Climb the right side of a pillar to slammer hand jams in a right-facing corner through a roof. The original name of the route was **Sedimentary Journey**, then renamed **The Ultimate Hand Crack** on the second ascent. The route is now referred to by all by its present name. *(6)2.5, (1)3.0*

11 Binge and Purge 5.11 70'
Thin hands to offwidth on the left side of a pillar. It may be advisable to do your binging and purging prior to getting on this route. *0.75–#5 Camalot*

12 Pringles (a.k.a. Into the Abyss Route) 5.12- or 5.11 110'
A little contrived, as it comes very close to **Gorilla Crack**, but a fine fingers lieback nonetheless. Climb sustained fingers in a shallow right-facing corner without using the crack to the right (5.12-). Most people toprope the route from the Gorilla anchors and stem over to the right (5.11). *0.5–3.0, heavy on the 0.5, 0.75*

13 Gorilla 5.10 110'
Mostly wide hands and fists up a poddy splitter. This climb has acquired many different names over time including: **Intruder in the Dust, Gorilla Crack, Cave Man, and Manhattan Faggot**. *(1)1.5, (2)2.0, (3)2.5, (5)3.0, (3)3.5*

14 Three Pigs in a Slot (a.k.a. Buffalo Slots) 5.10 90'
Climb a left-facing corner to a chimney/slot through a roof.

15 Unnamed 5.10 60'
Climb the black corner to a fixed nut anchor.

15.5 International Affair 5.12 50'

16 The Wave 5.10+ 100'
An enduring classic that climbs a left-facing corner on the left side of the Key Flake formation. *Nuts, 2 sets of Friends from 1.0–3.0*

Supercrack Buttress

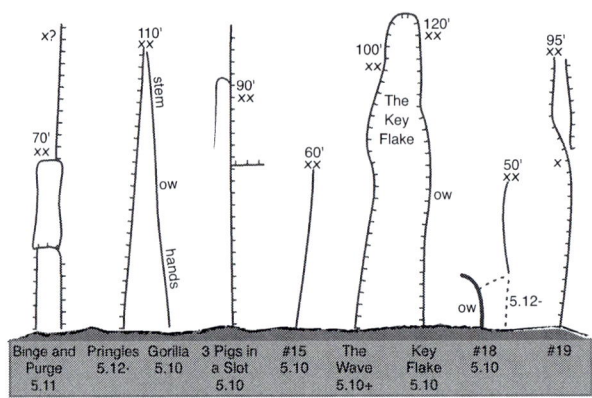

17 Key Flake 5.10 110'
Climb the offwidth crack on the right side of the key-shaped flake. *Lots of 6" gear*

18 Unnamed 5.10 50'
Immediately right of **Key Flake**, climb an offwidth flake and step across right to a finger crack. The direct boulder problem start is 5.12-. *0.5–2.0*

19 Unknown ? 95'
Start in a right-facing corner, pass a bolt, and up a corner that switches aspects.

20 Keyhole Flakes 5.10 80'
Fingers to hands on the varnished right wall of a dihedral. *1.0–4.0*

21 Unknown ? 70'
Climb a flared splitter to tips in a left-facing corner.

22 Coyne Crack (a.k.a. One Eyed Poker, The Left Side of Darkness) 5.11+ 70' or 120'
An amazing thin-hands splitter. Harder for those with big hands. Named after Leonard Coyne, one of the original Indian Creek pioneers. First led yo-yo style by Coyne in 1978 with #7 and #8 Hexes hammered into the crack. Coyne later returned for an all-Friends ascent before the introduction of the half-sized units. Using tipped out #1 Friends Coyne took a whipper blowing a couple of pieces and sustaining a painful eye injury when his glasses shattered. Before he could fully recover Coyne's climbing partner Ken Sims sent the route in good style. There is a seldom-done second pitch (hands). The first ascent party went all the way to the rim. *(3)1.5, (7)2.0 —and (4)3.0 for pitch 2*

23 Fingers in a Lightsocket (a.k.a. Super Dooper, Super Corner) 5.11+ 60'
Beautiful fingers in a right-facing corner, awesome crux sequence at the end. *(1)0.4, (2)0.5, (3)0.75, (2)1.0*

24 Unnamed 5.9 20'
Pretty darn short, but good. Hands on the left side of a block.

Supercrack Buttress

Supercrack (a.k.a. Super Crack of the Desert, Luxury Liner) 5.10 100'
The climb that started it all. The classic wide-hands splitter. Harder for those with small hands. Originally went another pitch (5.11) to the rim. *(1)1.5, (1)2.0, (1)2.5, (2)3.0, (5)3.5*

26 **The Little Face Climb 5.11 60'**
This route climbs the first 15–20 feet of Amaretto, then traverses left onto a pillar, passes one bolt and finishes at the anchor on top of pitch one of Amaretto.

27 **Amaretto (a.k.a. Amaretto Corner, Alma Redd Corner) 5.9/5.11+ 60'/100'**
Start on the right side of a pillar and climb hands to offwidth.
Pitch 1: Worthy in its own right.
Pitch 2: Ascend the sustained, varnished thin-hands right-facing corner above a ledge.
Pitch 1: 2.0–5.0; pitch 2: heavy on the 1.5, 2.0

28 **Painted Pony (a.k.a. Ride the Pink Pony, Pink Polypropylene Fantasy) 5.11 130'**
A long pitch that climbs over some big blocks (nuts useful) turns a roof and finishes with sustained thin hands. *1.0–3.0, nuts, extra slings, heavy on the 2.0*

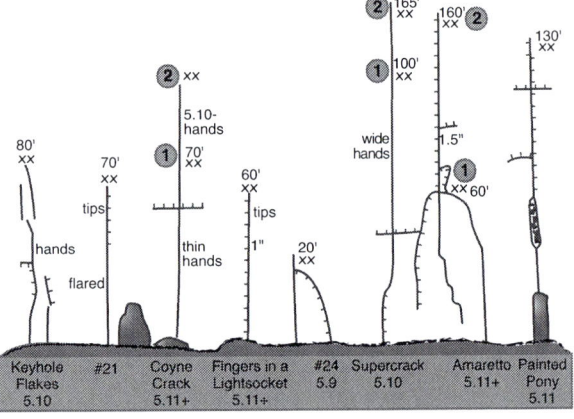

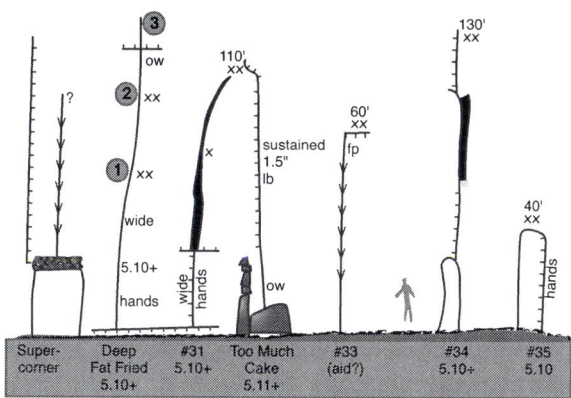

29 **Supercorner**
   (a.k.a. Finger in a Corner) ? 130'
   Climb the right-facing corner that begins on a ledge with some ruins. Mainly larger Friends. Nothing else is known.

30 **Deep Fat Fried 5.10+ ?'**
   A three-pitch line right of the Anasazi ruin. Start with hands in a straight-in corner. Then climb the ever-widening corner for three pitches. The first pitch is 5.10+ and may be called Honest Ozzie.

31 **Unnamed 5.10+ 110'**
   Wide hands in a shallow right-facing corner to flare with a bolt to bulge. Shares anchor with **Too Much Cake**.

32 **Too Much Cake 5.11+ 110'**
   Offwidth start (#5 Camalot) to sustained 1.5" laybacking in a right-facing corner. .75 Camalots will work better than the suggested 2.0 Friends. Finishes with a roof. *(1)0.75, (1)1.0, (10)1.5, (1)2.0, (1) #5 Camalot*

33 **Unknown ? 60'**
   Very thin stemming corner. There are petroglyphs to the right of the route.

34 **Unamed 5.10+ 130'**
   Climb over stacked blocks to a right-facing corner that turns into a chimney.

35 **Unnamed 5.10 40'**
   Climb hands in a right-facing corner on the right side of a pillar, just left of a big block.

36 **Anasazi 5.11- 120'**
   Start in a double corner right of the big block and climb fingers to big fingers in a long right-facing corner. Gets a little soft near the top, but still a classic. *(1)0.75, (7)1.0, (5)1.5, (1)2.5, (1)3.0, (1)3.5*

Note: The corner to the right (chimney flare) has been toproped

49

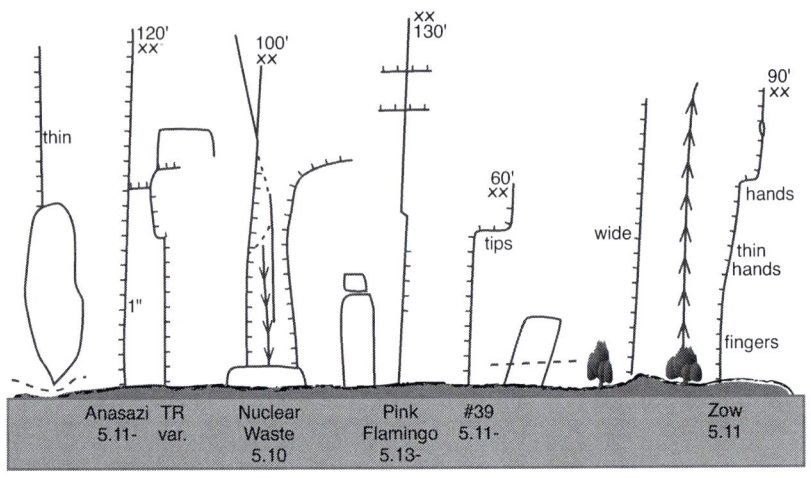

Nuclear Waste 5.10 100'
Start on a small ledge and climb a left-facing thin-hands crack, switch right to a fingers splitter and back left to the left-facing crack. Finish with a short hands splitter. A very interesting route. *(1)0.75, (1)1.0, (2)1.5, (3)2.0, (2)2.5, (2)3.0, (1)3.5*

There are several unknown cracks to the right of this climb and to the left of **Pink Flamingo**.

38 Pink Flamingo 5.13- 130'
An incredible one-inch splitter through a small roof that favors those with bigger fingers. *(3)0.5, (4)0.75, (10)1.0, (4)1.5*

39 Unnamed 5.11- 60'
Right of **Pink Flamingo** is a finger crack to some face climbing through a roof. *(4)0.5, (2)0.75, nuts*

40 Zow 5.11 90'
A steep right-facing corner. Fingers to thin hands in a clean right-facing corner, to a hands roof. Located to the right of a long wide left-facing corner.

Bill Morse on **Coyne Crack** 5.11+   Photograph by Lisa Hensel

Donnelly Canyon

Donnelly Canyon Overview

Donnelly Canyon
A good wall to begin your tour of Indian Creek. This popular wall is home to a high concentration of quality moderate routes. Park in the first large pullout on the right after passing the Supercrack cattle guard.

_1_ **Unknown 5.10 ?'**
On the leftmost side of Donnelly Canyon is this left-facing corner that goes from hands to offwidth. Anchor not visible.

_2_ **Unnamed 5.10+ 60'**
To the right of a prominent pillar, climb over a large wedged chockstone and into this ever thinning corner. Very cool climbing. 0.4–2.5, mostly 0.5, 0.75

_3_ **Fuel Injected Hard Body 5.12- 60'**
Thin technical stemming past an unnecessary bolt to perfect fingers in a left-facing corner. (2)0.4, (4)0.5, (6)0.75

_4_ **The Naked and the Dead 5.8/5.10/? 40'/80'/?**
Pitch 1: Climb hands on the left side of a pillar.

Pitch 2: Follow twin cracks in a left-facing corner.

Pitch 3: An offwidth of good quality, which climbs past two bolts. *Two sets of Friends, extra 2.0 and 3.5*

Var. Pitch 1: The right side of the pillar is a 5.11 tips crack. Nuts are useful.

_5_ **Generic Crack 5.10- 120'**
It may be generic, but it sure is fun! Climb the obvious flared hands splitter. There is a seldom-done offwidth second pitch that goes at 5.10. (2)2.5, (8)3.0, optional 3.5, and optional #4.5 Camalot (other combinations of 2.5s and 3.0s will work)

Robert Lemley on **Generic Crack** 5.10-   Photograph by Michael Clark

Donnelly Canyon

6 Unnamed 5.11 60'/100'
This two-pitch left-facing corner is just right of a small pillar. Pitch one is thin.

7 Unknown ? 80'
Flared offwidth splitter.

8 Binou's Crack 5.9 50'
Begin in a right-facing corner, then climb any combination of three cracks. One of the better climbs at the grade. *(1)0.4, (1)0.5 and a few thin-hands/hand pieces*

9 Let 'er Buck 5.12 100'
The only pure sport climb at the Creek, and an excellent one at that. A boulder problem start to technical arete climbing. *11 bolts*

10 Unnamed 5.10 80'
Climb a wide right-facing corner and angle right just before a squeeze section.

Var. Continue up the corner through the squeeze. No anchors are visible.

11 Unnamed 5.10 100'
Flared fingers to hands splitter. *1.0–3.0*

12 Mr. Peanut 5.11+ 60'
The left-facing offset crack on the left side of the Elephant's trunk feature.

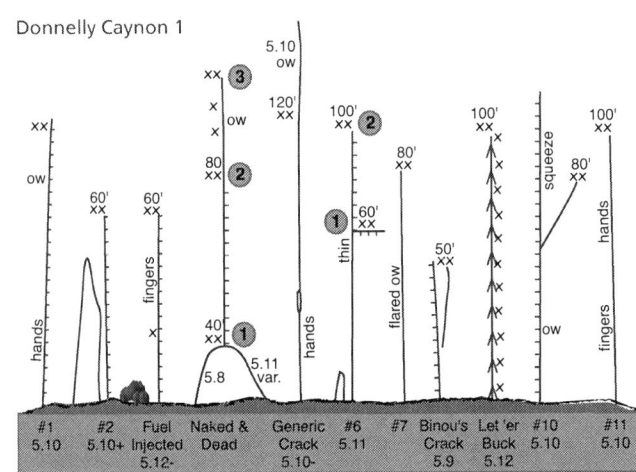

GearHeads

Moab's most complete

Outdoor Store

- BLACK DIAMOND
- WILD COUNTRY
- METOLIUS
- ALIEN
- PETZL
- PRANA
- 5.10
- MSR
- STERLING
- MAMMUT
- LA SPORTIVA
- YATES
- CHACO
- TEVA

- Mountain Hardwear
- Cascade Designs
- Therm-a-rest
- Smart Wool
- Camelbak
- Lowe Alpine
- Dana Design
- Osprey
- Bibler
- Merrell
- Salomon

Mail Order
888-740-4327
FREE SHIPPING
USA Only

Climbing Shoe Rental $5.00/day
FREE FILTERED WATER
471 S. Main St. #1 Moab, Utah 84532
888-740-4327   www.gearheadsoutdoorstore.com
8:30AM -10:00PM March - Oct.   9:00AM - 6:00PM Nov. - Feb

Donnelly Canyon

Donnelly Caynon 2

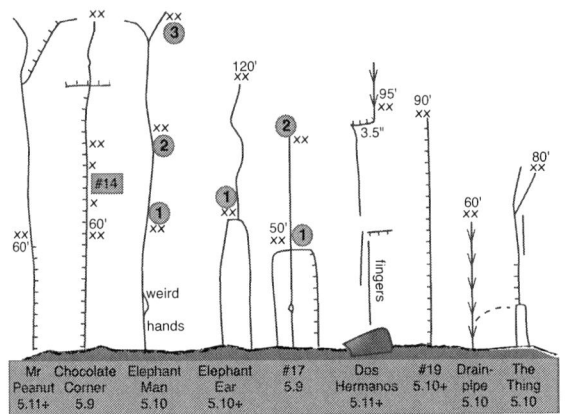

Chocolate Corner 5.9 60'
The clean, dark right-facing corner in the center of the Elephant's trunk. Superb at the grade. *(2)2.0, (3)2.5, (1)3.0*

Ocean Negro 5.9/5.12/5.12+
Climb **Chocolate Corner**, then continue up two more pitches to the top of the Elephant. Pitch two has been led without clipping the fixed gear. *0.4–3.5 with (6)2.0 for pitch 3, small nuts for pitch 2*

Elephant Man 5.10/5.11/5.11
Three pitches of funky cracks and slots on the right side of the Elephant. *Pitch 1: (1)0.75, (1)1.5, (1)2.0, (1)2.5, (2)3.0, (1)4.0 Pitches 2&3: 0.75-3.5, with (5)2.0 and extra 2.5–3.0, two ropes*

Elephant Ear 5.10+ 120'
Another funky crack that is climbed in two short pitches. *1.0–5.5, heavy on the 3.0–4.0*

Unnamed 5.9 50'
A hands splitter up the center of a block. There are anchors above for an unknown second pitch.

Var. Climb the thin-hands to offwidth crack on the right side of the block.

Dos Hermanos 5.11+ 95'
Start above a boulder and climb twin cracks to a hands splitter, finish with a wide hands roof. Many of the early climbs were put up by the *Dos Hermanos* (The Hong Brothers), but this is the only one named after them. *(1)0.5, (2)0.75, (5)1.0, (2)1.5, (1)2.0, (2)2.5, (1)3.0, (2)3.5*

__19__ **Unnamed 5.10+ 90'**
Flared hands and fingers with pods in a steep right-facing corner, just left of **The Drainpipe**. (2)1.0, (4)1.5, (1)2.0, (3)2.5, (1)3.0, (1)3.5, (1)4.0

__20__ **The Drainpipe 5.10 80'**
Start on top of a large boulder pile and climb thin hands and fingers in a water-polished crack. 0.75–2.0, (4)1.0

__21__ **The Thing 5.10- 80'**
Start on top of a small pillar that is located up a gully to the right of **The Drainpipe**. Climb a small left-facing corner to twin diverging splitters. 0.5–3.0

__22__ **Unknown ? 180'**
A long flared splitter of many sizes.

__23__ **Ansaid Tower 5.7 ?'**
A small Lost Arrow-like spire up canyon. One rope, small rack. Not shown on topo.

Battle of the Bulge

Battle of the Bulge
The sister buttress to Supercrack. If varnished 5.11s are your bag then this is the cliff for you. Home to three of Indian Creek's testpiece cracks, the beautiful **Ruby's Café**, the devious **Disco Machine Gun**, and the currently unrepeated hair-raising **Air Swedin**. Parking is 0.3 miles past the Supercrack cattle guard on the right. (Same as Donnelly Canyon and Supercrack Buttress.) On busy days or if you are planning on climbing mainly on the left side of the Bulge, there is a small parking area 0.1 miles down on the left side of the road. Do not camp anywhere in this area.

Battle of the Bulge-left

1 **Unnamed 5.11 150'**
A long and wide left-facing offwidth corner.

2 **Think Pink 5.11- 100'**
Steep hands and fists in a right-facing corner. Pitch 2 is called **Think Again**. (1) 1.0, (3) each 2.5–3.5

3 **Grits Grunt 5.8 2 pitches**
A long unprotected chimney, a la Earl Wiggins.

David Bloom on **Disco Machine Gun** 5.12   Photograph by Nils Davis

Battle of the Bulge

4 Unknown ? 130'
Climb the offset offwidth in a right-facing corner past two bolts.

5 Elbow Vices 5.10 90'
A left-facing corner that is mostly hands. 2.0–3.0

6 Pigs in Space 5.10+ 120'
This west-facing climb ascends a slabby wall with features for the feet. 0.75–3.0

7 Unknown ?' 90'
Climb a right-facing corner past two bolts and out left through a small roof flake.

8 Crack Attack 5.11- 90'
There is a little bit of everything on this stellar route, but the business is thin hands. (4)1.5, (5)2.0, (2)3.0

9 Fat Boy Slim 5.11 90'
You can practically feel the Techno pumping in your veins as you ascend this fists-to-fingers stembox.

10 Dogs in Space 5.10 90'
Broken straight-in corner to big-hands roof. There is even a head jam on this burly route.

11 Drive-by Nailing A1+ 130'
Ugly, pinned-out aid seam. Pitch 1 is 130'. Goes to top in three pitches.

Battle of the Bulge 1

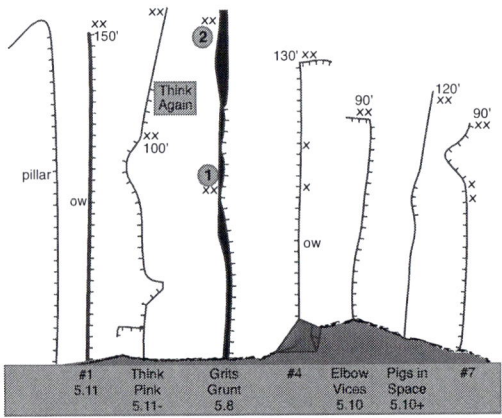

12 Christmas Tree 5.12+ 160'
Lieback and stem up this never-ending right-facing tips corner. *(2)0.4, (15)0.5, (3)0.75, (4)1.0, (2)1.5*
-

13 Unnamed 5.11+ 120'
A neglected classic. Varied right-facing corner, all sizes from hands to tips. *(1)0.4, (1)0.5, (1)0.75, (3)1.0, (5)1.5, (5)2.0, (2)2.5,(1)3.5*
-

14 Disco Machine Gun 5.12 70'
Almost flashed onsight on the first ascent by Keith Reynolds. First redpointed by Beth Rodden. Tips locks, stemming and laybacking in a shallow left-facing corner. *(2)0.33, (3)0.4, (4)0.5, (1) each 0.75, 2.0, 2.5, #3 Rock*

15 Let's Dance 5.12 110'
Climb up a grassy ramp to a pillar to a shallow right-facing corner that narrows to tips. This is the last climb before the trail goes downhill on some broken rock. *(2)0.4, (5)0.5, (4)0.75, (2)1.5, (2)2.5, (1) #5 Camalot*

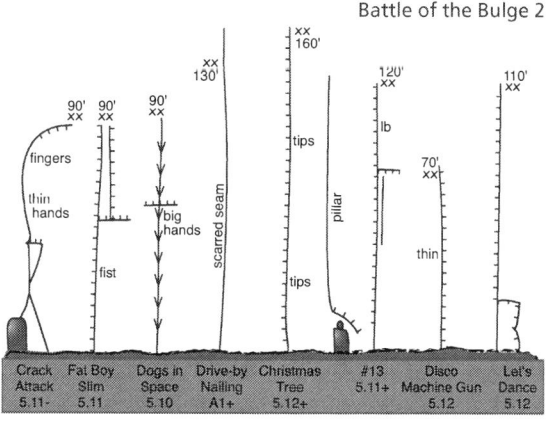

Battle of the Bulge 2

Battle of the Bulge

Battle of the Bulge 3

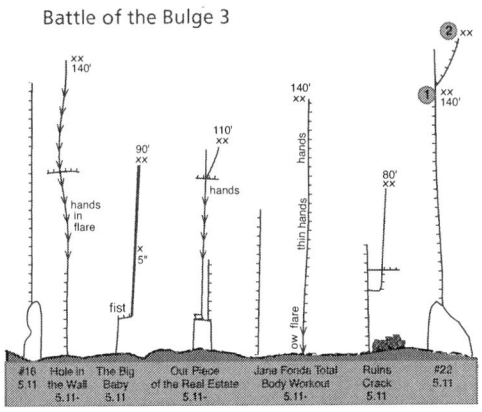

16 Unknown 5.11 ?
This prominent right-facing corner probably has an anchor but it is not visible.

17 Hole in the Wall 5.11- 140'
Start in a small right-facing corner that leads to straight-in flared hands and big hands. Pretty stout! *(2)2.5, (9)3.0, (7)3.5, (1) #4 Camalot*

18 The Big Baby 5.11 90'
A dream climb for some, but a nightmare for most. The quintessential Indian Creek wide crack. Climb steep fists, turn a roof and struggle up this sustained 5.0"–7.0" crack. *(1)3.5, (2) #4 Camalots, (2) #4.5 Camalots, (1) #5 Camalot, 1 pussy bolt*

19 Our Piece of the Real Estate 5.11- 110'
Most of this route is an excellent 5.10 hand crack. The start gives some people fits. *(1)1.0, (2)1.5, (2 or 3) 2.0, (2)2.5, (1)3.0, (2) #3 Camalots*

20 The Jane Fonda Total Body Workout (a.k.a. Sheila Longstar) 5.11- 140'
A difficult bombay start yields to all sizes of hands in a left-facing corner that seems to go on forever. *(7)2.0, (6)2.5, (1)3.0, (3)3.5, (1) #4 Camalot optional for start*

Jamie Blythe spelunking on **The Cave Route** 5.10+   Photograph by Richard Durnan

Battle of the Bulge

Battle of the Bulge 4

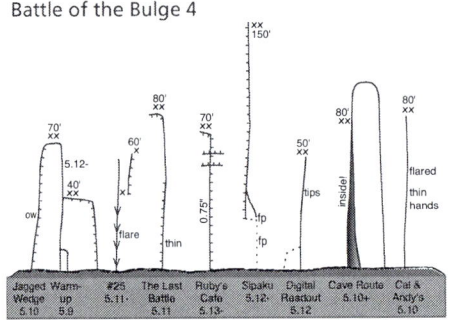

27 Ruby's Cafe 5.13- 70'
A Lisa Gnade masterpiece. Fingers in a changing corner through an amazing roof, then a layback sprint to the anchors. *(3)0.5, (9)0.75*

28 Sipaku 5.12- 150'
This new-wave crack route went up in 2001. Delicate face climbing past two fixed pins and a hanging flake leads to a shallow right-facing corner with fingers and thin hands. *(2)0.5, (2)0.75, (4) each 1.0–2.0, (3)2.5, (1)3.0, (1)3.5, a small nut, double ropes*

29 Digital Readout 5.12 50'
It's short, thin, and hard. Tight fingers and tips in beautiful black varnish. *(1)0.4, (4)0.5, (4)0.75*

30 Wiggins Chimney 5.9X 90'
Climb the chimney that forms the entrance to the **Cave Route**. Protection is difficult. *(1) long sling...*

31 The Cave Route 5.10+ 80'
A one-of-a-kind route. Save it for hot or inclement weather. Sustained thin hands or laybacking. *(1)1.5, (6)2.0, (1)2.5*

32 Cal and Andy's Route 5.10 80'
Flared jamming, mostly thin hands. *1.0–2.5, (1) #4 Camalot, heavy on the 2.0*

33 Quarter of a Man 5.11++ 120'
How much of a man or woman are YOU? Long and sustained thin hands in a left-facing corner on beautiful crimson stone. *(3)1.5, (8)2.0, (2)2.5*

21 Ruins Crack 5.11 80'
Located just to the left of some "ruins." Makes for an excellent warm-up to **Ruby's Cafe**. Climb fingers in a small right-facing corner, make a funky crack switch to the right, and finish up a flared thin-hands splitter. *(1)0.5, (3)0.75, (3)1.0, (1) each 1.5, 2.0, 3.0*

22 Unnamed 5.11 140'/?'
This two-pitch route starts on top of a pedestal and ascends a prominent right-facing corner with light-colored rock. Begin in a hands splitter to a pod. The anchors may be poor—beware!

23 The Jagged Wedge 5.10 70'
Climb a left-facing offwidth flake.

24 The Warm-Up 5.9 40'
A little harder than it looks, but still a good warm-up. *1.5–3.0* sucks

Var. If you keep climbing past the anchors to the **Jagged Wedge** anchors, this is an unnamed Skip—where are you?—Guerin route. This is 5.12-, with thin gear.

25 Unnamed 5.11- 60'
Flare to left-facing flake with a bolt. Starts 1.5".

26 The Last Battle 5.11 80'
Tricky thin start to right-facing corner to flared hand splitter. *(2)0.4, (2)0.5, (3)0.75, (3)1.0, (3)1.5, (1)3.5, (1) #4 Camalot*

62

Jamie Blythe on **Quarter of a Man** 5.11+   Photograph by Richard Durnan

Battle of the Bulge

Battle of the Bulge-right

✓ **The Black Corner 5.11 80'**
Battle of the Bulge's twin brother. A short big-fingers roof to thin hands in a right-facing corner. (2)1.0, (3)1.5, (5)2.0, (1)2.5

✓ **Battle of the Bulge 5.11 70'**
Stellar laybacking or thin-hands jamming. A Hong classic. Most people stop at the first anchor, but you can keep going another 40' to a second set of anchors. (2)1.5, (6)2.0, (1)2.5; for continuation: 0.75–3.5

36 **Unnamed 5.10+ 50'**
Start above some flakes leaning against the base and climb thin hands to a flare in a small left-facing corner. (1) each 1.5–4.0

37 **Unnamed 5.11 80'**
Immediately right of the previous route is this zigzagging crack that goes from tips to hands, passing one bolt. Difficult-to-clip anchors. (1) each 0.5–1.0, (3)1.5, (5)2.0, (3)2.5

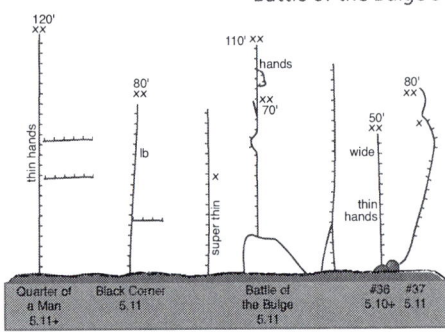

64

Battle of the Bulge 6

38 Slim Chance ? 160'
Start on the right side of a block and climb fingers in a right-facing corner to a straight-in corner that goes from fists to chimney.

39 Railroad Tracks 5.10- 50'
Climb twin cracks to a ledge inside a chimney. *0.75–3.0.* There is a second pitch in the back of the corridor on the right.

40 The Mystery Machine 5.10 100'
Start atop **Railroad Tracks**, in the back of the corridor.

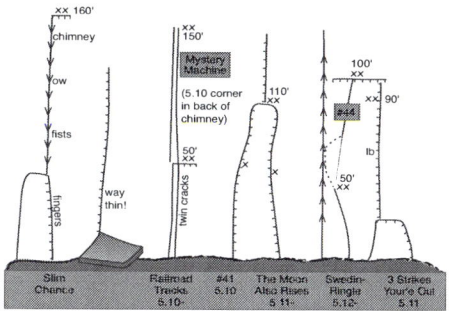

41 Unnamed 5.10 50'
Climb the left side of a prominent pillar to a one-bolt anchor.

42 The Moon Also Rises 5.11- 110'
Climb the right side of the prominent pillar, passing a bolt. *Many 2.0, and offwidth gear*

43 Swedin-Ringle 5.12- 50'
A short, difficult offset splitter, fingers to thin hands, and back to fingers. Do it in good style; don't grab the chains! *(3)0.75, (2)1.0, (3)1.5, (2)2.0*

44 Air Swedin 5.13R 100'
Possibly the most difficult tick at Indian Creek and unrepeated to date. Created by the young Pat Savage—he will be missed. Climb **Swedin-Ringle**, but don't clip the chains. Instead, bust left to an arete for a crazy technical sequence until it is possible to rejoin the crack. Protection is next to impossible, and if you blow it you'll catch more air than Michael Jordan! *Same gear as Swedin-Ringle, plus (1)0.33, (2)1.0, (2)1.5, (1)2.0*

45 Three Strikes You're Out 5.11 90'
Begin on top of a large block, then layback like mad up this immaculate corner. *(2)1.5, (6)2.0, (2)2.5*

46 Unknown 5.10 ?'
Climb the next large dihedral to the right of **Three Strikes You're Out**. No topo.

Steph Davis

Photograph by Eric Perlman

Fragile Host

A place as compelling as Indian Creek can sometimes be too loved. More than any place I've known, the Creek inspires passionate debates about what's "right."

When I first started climbing at Indian Creek, I was charmed to come across stone plaques. The first ascentionists scraped names and dates onto a flat piece of sandstone, then tucked it below the crack. Such plaques are less visible, and even less permanent, than white chalk on the orange-brown rock, or metal and nylon anchors hanging all over the cliffs. But one year a climber appointed himself to patrol the buttresses and smash the plaques to bits, hurling them down the talus slopes. Ironically, the ease with which he destroyed the soft carved rocks demonstrated how impermanent and fragile they actually were. It made me sad. I miss the plaques, and the sense of history and respect I felt when I discovered one. Only a few are still intact.

As far as I can see, the desert is a delicate place. However, part of its beauty lies in its contradictions, and the desert is also a tough place. Visiting does not have to be a crime, if we can remember what it means to be a visitor. We do not own Indian Creek. In the great scheme of things, no one owns it. None of us has been elected "ethics police." All of us are guests in the desert.

Perhaps the best thing we can do at Indian Creek is to treat this sacred place with the utmost respect, and to treat our fellow visitors with respect as well. Above all, let us remember our manners when we come calling. Be polite, helpful and unobtrusive. Do not disturb the other guests. Bring a small gift. Clean up after yourself. Use common sense. Make sure you leave the place better than you found it.

I find that being a good guest is a lot of work. It is, however, the surest way to get invited back.

TECH TIPS: RING LOCKS, SLACKLINING, TAPE JOBS, THE RIGHT BEER

Climbing

INDIAN CREEK
THE BEST CRAG ON EARTH?

OFF ROUTE IN CANYONLANDS
GREAT CLIMBS YOU'LL NEVER FIND

SANDSTONE DELIGHTS
CRUMBLING BEFORE YOUR EYES

"The Original Climber's Magazine"
Subscribe at Climbing.com

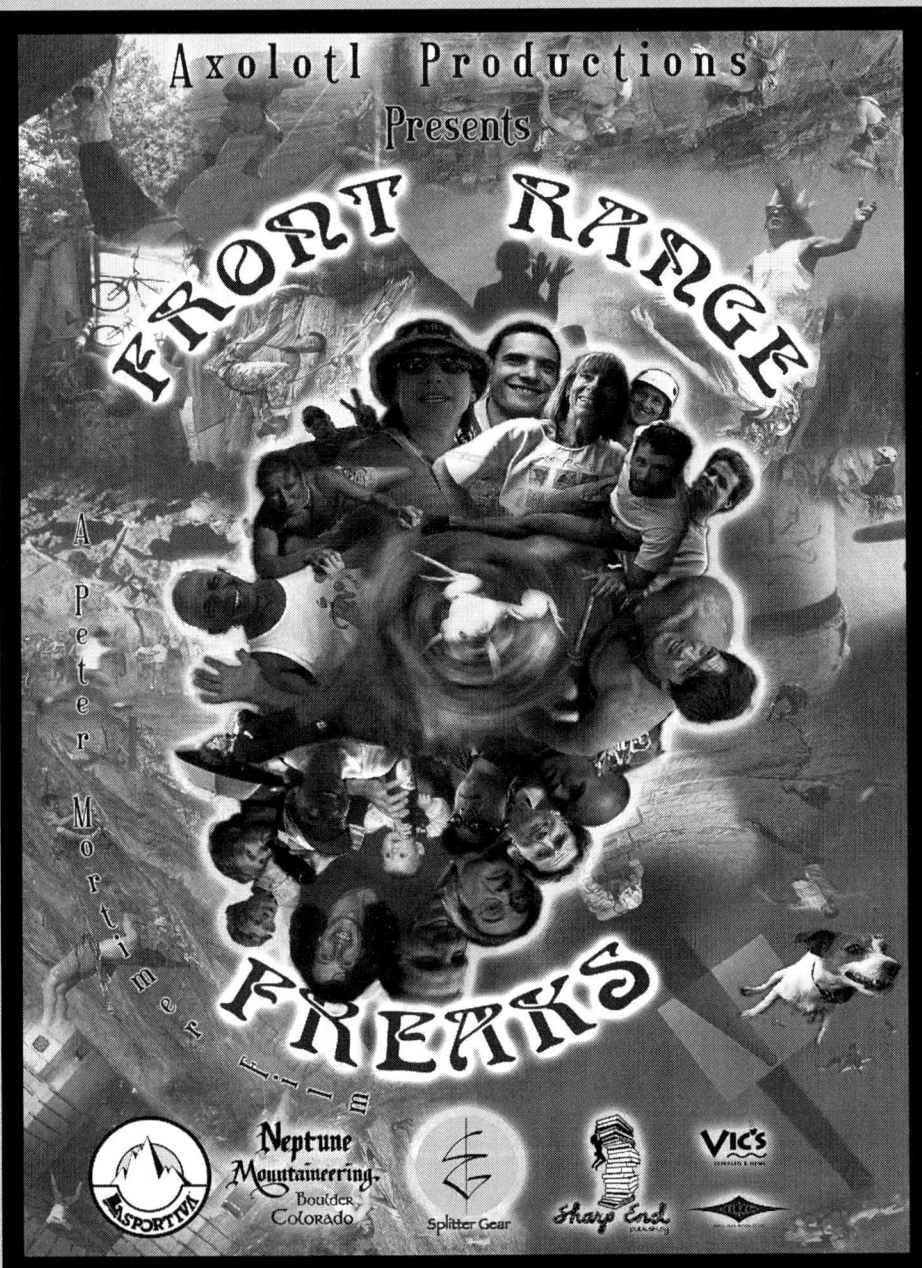

2 Fringe Wall to Reservoir Wall

Stevie Haston on **Death of a Cowboy** 5.13- Photograph by Laurence Gouault

Area Overview
Fringe Wall to Reservoir Wall

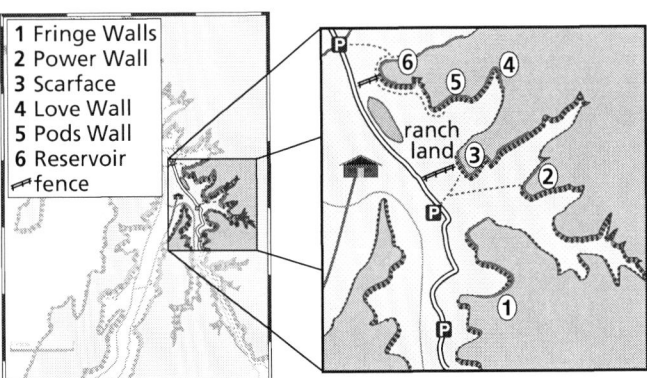

1 Fringe Walls
2 Power Wall
3 Scarface
4 Love Wall
5 Pods Wall
6 Reservoir
fence

Cactus Flower Buttress

The Fringe Walls

These are the walls close to the road just past Battle of the Bulge. From left to right they are Fringe of Life Canyon, Cactus Flower Buttress, Fringe of Death Canyon, and Scorpion Corner. Cactus Flower Wall is also known as Fringe Wall. Many of the earliest routes climbed at Indian Creek were done on these walls, and some of the routes were climbed all the way to the rim and have no fixed anchors. There are more routes than the ones listed here but information is hard to find. Scorpion Corner parking is 1.3 miles past the Supercrack cattle guard, Fringe of Death parking is 2.0 miles, Cactus Flower is 2.2 miles and Fringe of Life is best accessed from the Scarface/Power Wall parking in the large gravel lot at 2.5 miles.

Fringe of Life Canyon

1 Fringe of Life 5.11 3 pitches
This route faces west and begins on the left side of a pillar in a dihedral.

Pitch 1: Climb the left side of the pillar, fingers to offwidth.

Pitch 2: Climb a difficult flaring 5.11 offwidth above the pillar.

Pitch 3: Climb a 5.10 offwidth up into a corner, then finish with a 5.8 groove to the top.

2 The Stupid Crack of the Desert 5.11+ 3 pitches
To the right of #1 is this wide crack in a dark corner that has a slash in its left face.

Pitch 1: A long sustained offwidth.

Pitch 2: Climb a chimney filled with blocks and flakes. At the end of the pitch, tunnel through the crack to a secret belay room.

Pitch 3: A groove that climbs over large gashes.

3 Heir Apparent 5.10+ 3 pitches
Located 200 yards to the left of **Cactus Flower**.

Cactus Flower Buttress

4 Unknown ? 100'
Hands to a flare then hands in a left-facing corner.

5 The Sting 5.11 80'
Steep splitter hands. *0.75–3.0*

6 Bar Exam 5.10+ 80'
Start on top of a block then climb hands to offwidth in a left-facing corner. Shares an anchor with **The Sting**.

7 Cactus Flower 5.10+ 3 pitches
A beautiful three-pitch splitter that is mainly fists and offwidth. *(2) each 1.0–2.0, (3) each 2.5–4.0, (1) each #4, #4.5, #5 Camalot*

8 Unnamed 5.12- 150'
There are several pillars to the right of **Cactus Flower**. This route climbs the thin left-facing corner that is up and to the right of these pillars.

9 Neutron Dance 5.10+ 140'
A short 5.7 approach pitch angles up and right to this steep hands splitter. *Mainly 2.5–3.5*

10 Unknown ? 120'
Big hands to offwidth in a right-facing corner.

11 White Patti 5.10 110'
Off-fingers to offwidth, and through a roof in a right-facing corner.

12 Worm Hole 5.10+ 2 pitches
Pitch 1: Climb a wide crack on the left side of a pillar to an anchor on a ledge.

Pitch 2: Climbs a splitter with several large pods.

Cactus Flower Buttress 1

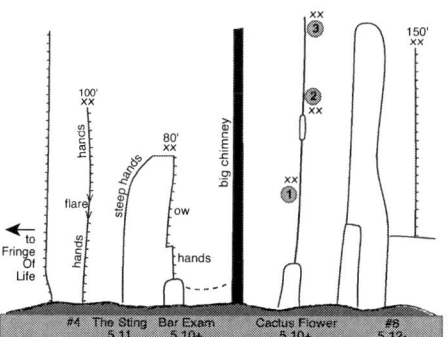

Cactus Flower Buttress 2

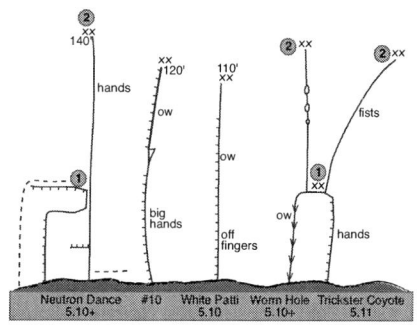

Fringe Walls

13 **Trickster Coyote 5.11 2 pitches**
Pitch 1: Climb the right-facing corner on the right side of the pillar, 5.11 hands.

Pitch 2: A right-angling 5.11 fists splitter.

Fringe of Death Canyon

14 **Unnamed 5.9+ 90'**
Starts on the left side of a pillar in a left-facing thin-hands corner and finishes in a right-facing corner. *1.0–3.5*

15 **Warren's Left-leaning Crack 5.11+ 120'**
Fingers in a small flare to tight hands in a left-facing corner. Clip an intermediate belay and negotiate the off-fingers changing offset. It's 5.10+ to the first set of anchors. *(1)0.33, (2)1.0, (5)1.5, (4)2.0, (3)2.5*

16 **Dunn's 5.10+ 100'**
Climb fingers to thin hands to fingers to hands in a shallow left-facing corner left of an offwidth corner on the left side of a prominent pillar. This climb may continue for another pitch or two.

17 **Unknown ? ?**
Hands to offwidth to chimney past two fixed pitons in a right-facing corner on the right side of the prominent pillar.

Fringe of Death Canyon 1

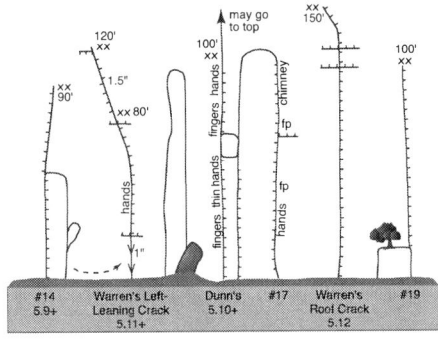

18 **Warren's Roof Crack 5.12 150'**
Sustained overhanging fingers in a left-facing corner to hands through double roofs. *(2)0.5, (3)0.75, (4)1.0, (4)1.5, (3)2.0, (2)2.5, (3)3.0, (1)3.5, (1) #4 Camalot*

19 **Unknown ? 100'**
Hands in a left-facing corner. Starts on a ledge right of a large juniper.

20 **Unknown ? 160'**
A long wavy splitter with a couple of fixed pitons.

21 **Unknown ? 60'**
Fingers in a straight-in corner to an offset offwidth.

Fringe of Death Canyon 2

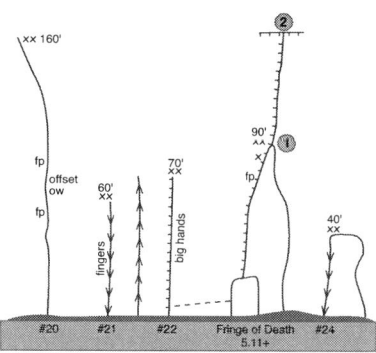

Fringe of Death Canyon 3

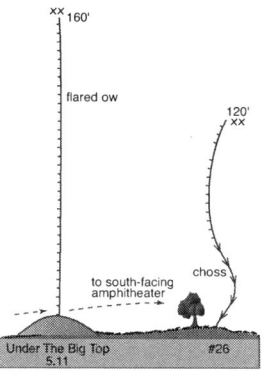

22 Unknown ? 70'
Big hands in a right-facing corner.

23 Fringe of Death 5.11+ 2 pitches
This route is located 30 feet left of a large chimney, and ascends a thin right-facing corner with a small pillar at its base.

Pitch 1: Stem and layback up the right-facing corner (5.11+, 90').

Pitch 2: Continue up the corner (5.9) to the rim. Rappel the chimney to the right. *Nuts, TCUs, (3) each 1.0 and 1.5, (2) each 2.0–4.0, fixed piton and bolt of questionable quality*

24 Unknown ? 40'
Hands in a straight-in corner on the left side of a pillar.

25 Under the Big Top 5.11 2 pitches
Flared offwidth in a left-facing corner just inside the left corner of Fringe of Death Canyon.

26 Unknown ? 120'
A chossy left-angling crack leads to a better-looking right-facing corner. This route is located above a juniper in the south-facing amphitheater of Fringe of Death Canyon. There are a few unknown routes between here and **Y-Crack**.

27 Y-Crack 5.10 150'
First climbed by Jimmy Dunn in 1975, before the ascent of **Supercrack**. A long wide-hands splitter. Most people finish on the left side of the Y. The right side is a little harder. *3.0–4.0*

Fringe Walls

This next route is located a few hundred feet inside the right wall of Fringe of Death Canyon.

28 Immaculate Deception 5.10

3 pitches

Pitch 1: Climb 5.8 hands in a shallow varnished corner.

Pitch 2: Climb past a fixed pin on the left wall and then traverse right below a loose offwidth to the top of a semi-detached spire.

Pitch 3: Go right and up past a fixed pin to the summit.

29 Every Grapefruit For Himself 5.10 100'

This route is right of **Immaculate Deception** and left of a detached pillar. There is a fixed piton high on the route below a vegetated area.

The last two routes are located in the center of the small buttress to the right of Fringe of Death Canyon.

30 Scorpion Corner 5.12 100'

A gorgeous thin-hands left-facing corner to an undercling roof.

31 Prospector 5.11 100'

An excellent corner pitch, just right of **Scorpion Corner**.

Power Wall

A small cliff, with many quality lines, set back from the road. Park 2.5 miles past the Supercrack cattle guard in the large gravel parking area on the left. Hike north on a trail that turns into an old road in between Scarface and The Fringe Wall (Fringe of Life Canyon).

Power Wall Overview

1 Unknown 90'
Start on a small ledge above a juniper. Climb a shallow right-facing corner from thin hands to offwidth. *2.0–7.0, heavy on the OW gear*

2 Power Line 5.12 55'
The BEST pure 1" splitter in the world! *(4)0.75, (5)1.0*

3 Tip Layback 5.11+ 55'
Very popular as it conveniently shares an anchor with **Power Line**. *(1)0.4, (1)0.5, (2)0.75, (4)1.0, (1)1.5*

4 Unnamed 5.12 60'
Technical stemming and face climbing along twin thin cracks. *(1)0.33, (4)0.4, (4)0.5, (1)0.75, (1)1.5*

Power Wall

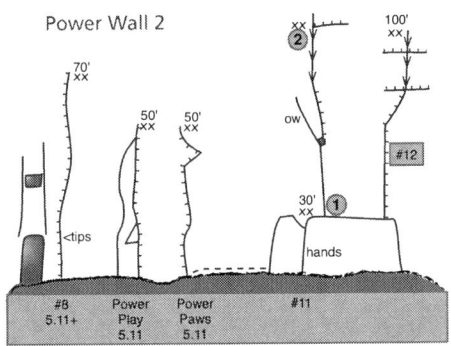

5 Batteries Not Included 5.9+ 60'
Splitter hands to big hands in a left-facing corner. Excellent rock. *(3)3.0, (4)3.5*

6 Unnamed 5.8 35'
One of the better moderate offerings around. Climb twin cracks, mostly thin hands.

7 Flower Power 5.10 160'
Varied and fun corner through a small roof. *(2) each 0.5–3.5, extra 0.75, 3.0, long runners*

8 Unnamed 5.11+ 70'
Appealing right-facing corner with a boulder problem start. Harder for the vertically challenged. *(1) each 0.33–4.0, and (2) each 1.5, 2.0*

9 Power Play 5.11 50'
Twin cracks that pack a punch. *(2) each 0.75–2.0 and (3)1.5*

10 Power Paws 5.11 50'
Another excellent short route. Layback or jam the right-facing flake. *(1)0.75, (2) each 1.0–2.0, (3)2.5*

11 Unknown ? 2 pitches
Pitch 1: Climb a 30' hands splitter in the middle of a large block.

Pitch 2: Splitter offwidth with anchors underneath a roof.

12 Unnamed 5.12 130'
Same short first pitch as the previous route. Pitch two climbs a left-facing corner through two roofs. *(2)0.5, (5)0.75, (5)1.0, (1)1.5, (4)2.0, (1) each 2.5, 3.0*

David Bloom on **Power Line** 5.12   Photograph by Eric Draper

Power Wall

Power Wall 3

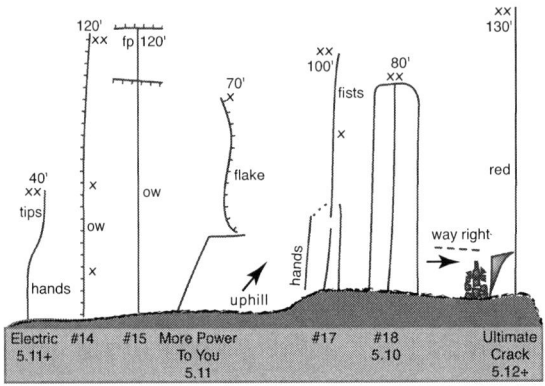

13 Electric 5.11+ 40'
Hands to tips splitter. *(1)0.75, (1)1.5, (1)2.0, (1)2.5, (1)3.0, (1)3.5*

14 Unknown ? 120'
Right-facing offwidth with two bolts.

15 Unknown ? 120'
Splitter offwidth, fixed piece under small roof.

16 More Power To You 5.11 70'
Layback up an obtuse corner. One bolt and one fixed nut anchor. *1.0–1.5*

17 Unknown ? 100'
This route is quite a ways to the right, but still on the main south face. Wavy splitter hands to offwidth with one bolt. *3.0–7.0*

18 Unnamed 5.10 80'
Hands to offwidth on a pillar. *(1)2.5, (1)3.0, (3)3.5, (1)4.0, (2) #4 Camalots, (1) #4.5 Camalot*

19 Ultimate Crack 5.12+ 130'
A stunning line. This crimson fissure is located on the far right side of the cliff at the top of a boulder-filled gully. There is a sharp flake leaning across the bottom of the crack. *(2)0.5, (5)0.75, (3)1.0, (8)1.5*

There are some unknown routes past **Ultimate Crack** to the right.

Scarface Wall

Scarface Overview

Scarface Wall

This wall was first made famous by a nice photo of Derek Hersey on **Scarface**, gracing the cover of an old *Climbing* magazine.

Park on the left side of the road in a large gravel parking lot; 2.5 miles from the Supercrack cattle guard.

1 **Unknown ? 100'**
A splitter offwidth on the southwest prow of the buttress.

2 **Unknown ? 60'**
Thin hands to hands in a changing corner.

✓*3* **Lieutenant Uhuru 5.11- 100'**
Varnished left-facing corner through a small roof. Mainly 1.0–2.0

4 **Black Uhuru 5.10+ 100'**
Praise Jah! The ebony-colored right-facing corner.
(*1*)0.75, (6)1.0, (3)1.5, (1)2.5, (2)3.0

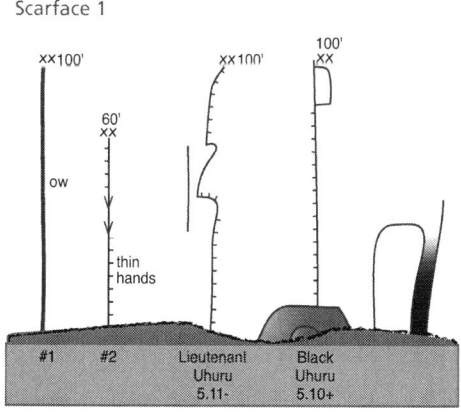

Scarface 1

Scarface Wall

Scarface 2

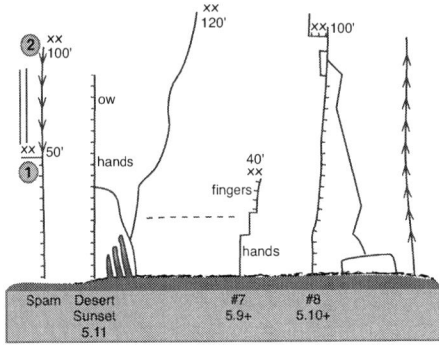

5 Spam ? 50'/100'
Pitch 1: Climb a right-facing crack to a ledge.

Pitch 2: A straight-in corner with a couple of splitters to its left.

6 Desert Sunset 5.11 120'
Climb broken rock above some pillars to a zigzagging hand crack. *0.75–4.0 with (5)2.5, double ropes recommended*

7 Unnamed 5.9+ 40'
Thin hands to fingers in a right-facing flake. *(1) each 1.0–2.0, (3)2.5*

8 Unnamed 5.10+ 100'
A shady left-facing corner with a twin crack start. *(2)1.5, (4)2.0, (3)2.5, (1)3.5*

9 Where's Carruthers? 5.10+ 60'
Hands to wide hands in a clean right-facing corner. Anchor underneath roof. *(2)2.0, (2)2.5, (2)3.0, (3)3.5*

10 Scarface 5.11- 70'
An elegant line. Splitter thin hands to hands. Harder for big-handed folks. *(1)0.75, (1)1.0, (2)1.5, (3)2.0, (5)2.5*

Var. The stemming corner immediately right of Scarface has been led, but is usually toproped.

11 Nubian Slave 5.11 120'
A straight-in corner that jags steeply to the right. Left of a small group of pillars leaning against the wall. *(2)1.0, (2)1.5, (3)2.0, (3)3.0, (5)3.5, (1) #4 Camalot*

Scarface 3

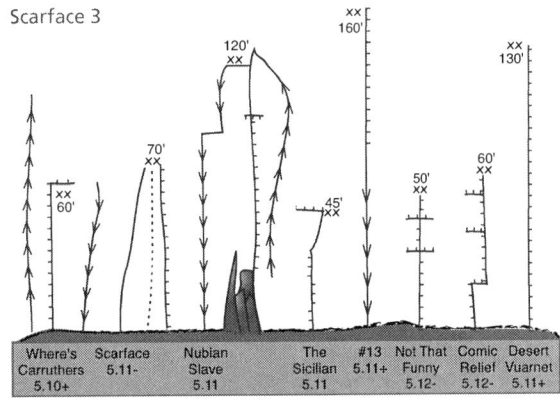

Julia Warwick on **Scarface** 5.11- Photograph by Michael Clark

Scarface Wall

12 The Sicilian 5.11 45'
Off-fingers in a changing corner to thin-hands splitter. A short but quality line that is harder than it looks. *(1)0.75, (3)1.0, (2)1.5, (1)2.0, (1)2.5*

13 Unnamed 5.11+ 160'
Bombay to flare to left-facing corner. *(1)0.75, (2)1.0, (3)1.5, (1)2.0, (2)2.5, (5)3.0, (5)3.5, (1)4.0, (2) #4 Camalots*

14 Not That Funny 5.12- 50'
Big fingers in a changing corner to off-fingers and thin hands over two small roofs. *(1)0.5, (2)0.75, (3)1.0, (2)1.5, (2)2.0*

15 Comic Relief 5.12- 60'
Hands in a right-facing corner to fingers and stemming over three roofs. *(5)0.75, (1)2.0, (2)2.5, (1)3.0*

16 Desert Vuarnet 5.11+ 130'
You'll look pretty cool if you flash this sustained left-facing corner to thin-hands splitter. *(2)0.75, (3)1.0, (6)1.5, (6)2.0, (1)2.5*

17 Unnamed 5.11 2 pitches 60'/130'
Pitch 1: Climb a chimney on the right side of a pillar.

Pitch 2: A nicely varnished fingers-to-offwidth corner.

18 Unknown ? 100'
Hands to offwidth in a right-facing corner.

19 Desert Shield (a.k.a. Desert Storm) 5.12 130'
Another gem! Start on a slab, then climb a shallow left-facing corner, with hard moves past a bolt, to a rest. Gather your guns and charge up sustained fingers in a steep open book. A Steve Carruthers FA. *0.5–2.0 with (6)0.75, (4)1.0*

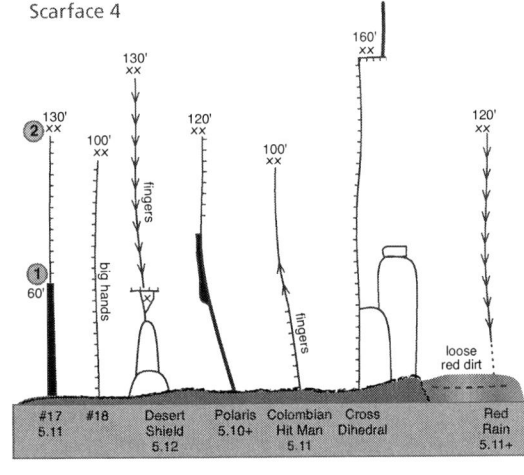

_20_ **Polaris 5.10+ 120'**
A left-leaning offwidth crack that narrows and then widens to a chimney. Finishes in a small left-facing corner.

_21_ **Columbian Hit Man 5.11 100'**
A right-facing offset finger crack to an exposed arete splitter. *(1)0.4, (2)0.75, (3)1.0, (4)1.5, (4)2.0, (2)2.5*

_22_ **Cross Dihedral ? 160'**
A broken right-angling crack system left of some pillars. The anchor is visible at the base of a splitter offwidth.

_23_ **Red Rain 5.11+ 120'**
A loose red start to steep thin hands through a bulge and a tight slot. *1.0–3.0*

_24_ **Steel Pulse 5.11+ 80'**
Difficult ring-locks over a small roof. *(1)0.75, (2)1.0, (5)1.5, (5)2.0, (3)2.5, (1)3.5*

_25_ **Dirt Cheap 5.10+ 70'**
A cruxy start to all sizes of crack in twin corners. *(2)0.75, (1)1.0, (1)1.5, (1)2.0, (4)2.5*

_26_ **Sudden Impact 5.11 160'**
Very sustained thin hands in a right-facing corner with occasional rests. Starts with some loose face moves to gain the ledge. *(1)0.75, (8)2.0, (4)2.5, (1)3.0*

_27_ **Torque Wrench 5.11 150'**
Thin hands and hands to a strenuous roof slot. *(1)1.0, (3)1.5, (5)2.0, (5)2.5, (2)3.0, (1)3.5*

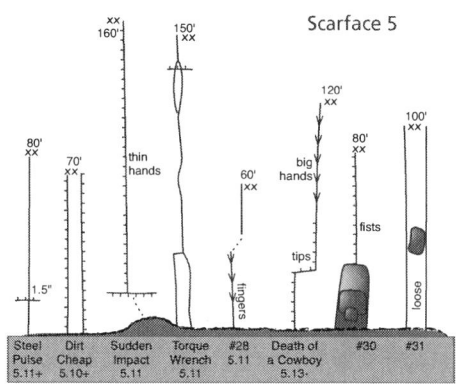

Scarface 5

_28_ **Unnamed 5.11 60'**
Fingers.

_29_ **Death of a Cowboy 5.13- 120'**
Many are called but few are chosen to climb this Petro/Gnade tips crack through a roof. Finishes with a sustained big-hands corner. *(1)0.4, (4)0.5, (1)0.75, (1)1.0, (1)2.0, (2)2.5, (4)3.0, (3)3.5*

_30_ **Unknown ? 80'**
Start on top of loose blocks then climb fists in a right-facing corner.

_31_ **Unknown ? 100'**
Climb the loose chimney past a large chockstone.

Scarface Wall

32 Unnamed 5.9 80'
Big hands in a right-facing corner through two small roofs.

33 Unnamed 5.11- 60'
Off-fingers to thin-hands splitter on a right-facing wall. *(1)1.0, (4)1.5, (1)2.0*

34 Big Guy 5.11- 160'
Splitter offwidth climbing. A good warm-up for **The Big Baby**. There is a lower anchor at 120'. *(1) each 1.5–3.0, (2) each 3.5, 4.0, #4 Camalots, #4.5 Camalots*

34.5 For Dewey 5.12+ 120'
A high quality route with a bit of finger crack, tips crack, and face climbing. Not shown on photo or topo. *Rack from wires to 2" cams*

35 Unknown ? 120'
Twin cracks to a right-facing corner. Starts left of a large juniper.

36 Unknown 5.9 40'
Hands in a small left-facing corner, left of a large boulder. Bad anchor. A continuation (rating unknown) goes up a groove to higher anchor at 80'

37 Wavy Gravy 5.10- 70'
Really fun hands in a wavy left-facing corner. Twin cracks start. *(1)2.0, (3)2.5, (2)3.0*

38 Mantel Illness 5.11 80'
Thin hands in a straight-in corner to twin splitters; thin and wide. *0.5–2.0*

39 Rte. 666 ? 130'
Start in a left-facing corner then switch left to another left-facing corner.

40 Route of all Evil ? 130'
Same start as **Rte. 666** but continue up the first left-facing corner.

41 Twitch! 5.11 60'
Strenuous moves through a flared-hands roof to a thin-hands and hands left-facing corner. *(3)1.5, (1)2.0, (3)2.5, (2)3.0, (2)3.5*

Scarface 4

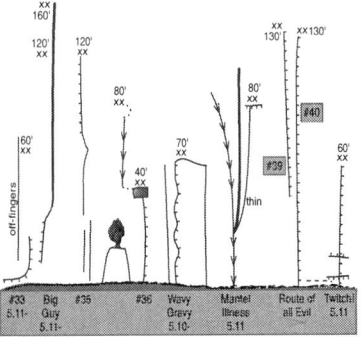

Ari Menitove on **Big Guy** 5.11- Photograph by Andrew Burr

Lisa Hensel

Learning Curve

The first time I climbed there was probably much like everyone's first time: a memorable disaster. I thought I'd try one of the "easy" classics aptly named *Generic Crack*. I managed to get maybe 20 feet up before my flailing caused total exhaustion. I grunted, panted, and cursed the crack for being too tight, too big, too weird, too painful and too damn hard. It was hell, and I swore I hated crack climbing. But, I came back.

What was the draw? Most of my friends couldn't get enough and would drive the two and a half hours from Durango each weekend, or even for the day, just to sink their mitts into the perfect cracks. They were the ones who made it look easy. The cracks fit their hands perfectly and they floated their way up the varnished sandstone walls. They were actually enjoying it.

Slowly, but surely, I began to succeed at The Creek. Toproping my way to victory, and finally leading and sending some of the climbs that previously tortured me. Soon enough I was craving more. That's the thing about The Creek; once you truly succeed on a climb the whole place changes from awful to amazing. Next thing I knew, I was completely hooked.

There is always a challenge in Indian Creek. Each size is new and hard to learn. Hand cracks came first, then wide hands, finger locks, thin hands and what I still believe to be the hardest, rattly fingers. It's not quite a thumb stack and it's not quite a finger lock—it's the size that my climbing partners and I took to a new level.

We had theories about everything: thick tape on the thumbs, thin tape on the thumbs, knuckle tape, combo finger/thumb taping; we did it all. We researched the mags and tried new techniques. Stacking, bridging, twisting, and torquing we eventually figured it out—and no tape was deemed necessary.

It's more than just climbing idyllic cracks. It's about the growth my partners and I have experienced. For me, the process of learning how to use my body so that it fits perfectly into each and every size crack is what fuels my addiction. Climbing here feels limitless and probable. Every new struggle, flail, grunt and pant is now somehow absurdly rewarding and fun.

What brings me back again and again? Perhaps it's the extraordinary splitter cracks or that alluring new challenge. Or maybe it's the smell in the air, the creek below, the high desert wind, the color of the rock, the sea of purple flowers in the spring, the leaves of the cottonwoods, the stars at night, or even the gobies that grace my tired, swollen hands. You tell me.

Lisa Hensel

Lisa Hensel with Kenai   Photograph by Ben Moon/MoonFoto

The Love Wall

The Love Wall

The Love Wall

This east-facing wall is the rightmost side of Reservoir Wall. It is recognized by two large horizontal calcite streaks. Many of the routes were put up by Telluride locals and not all routes are included in the text below. Love Wall is a great place to get away from the crowds and have an adventure. All information on this wall is secondhand, so take it with a grain of sand, and have fun exploring.

Currently, the few climbers who come here park in the large gravel parking area (same as for Scarface), and hike up a faint trail in the canyon between Scarface and the southeast face of Reservoir Wall. Be aware that this involves crossing Dugout Ranch property. Please consider parking and approaching via Reservoir Wall and Pods Wall.

_1 **The Torte ? ?'**
A short 5.11.

_2 **Incredible Hand Job ? ?'**
3.0s and 3.5s

_3 **Unnamed 5.11 ?'**
Fingers to tight hands in a corner and through a roof.

_4 **Strumpet 5.11- ?'**

_5 **Unnamed 5.9. ?'**
Shares its anchor with the **The Power of Love**.

_6 **The Power of Love 5.13- 2 pitches**
Tiny fingers and stemming.

_7 **1-900 5.10 ?'**
Fingers.

Reservoir Wall Overview

Reservoir Wall

A stellar wall with something for everyone. The west face is very popular on warm days. The climbs farthest right require a long approach—at least by Indian Creek standards.

All climbs on the Reservoir should be approached from the parking area opposite the Beef Basin turnoff. The trail leads up to the area around **Slot Machine**. This will keep you off land owned by the Dugout Ranch. (All land in the vicinity of the reservoir itself.)

___1 **Excuse Station 5.11 120'**
This climb and the following route are located on the far left side of the west face. A long walk, but well worth it. Excellent splitter thin hands. *(2)1.5, (3)2.0, (8)2.5*

___2 **No Excuse 5.10+ 120'**
Climb the left-facing corner right of **Excuse Station**. There may be no excuse, but everybody's got one. Hard for the grade. *0.75–2.0, bolt*

___3 **Mega Bucks 5.11 150'**
A wide left-facing corner. Mostly 4–5 inches.

___4 **Gurkha 5.12- 65'**
Named after a group of ethnic Nepalese, known for being short and fierce. Fingers in a tight changing corner to rattly flared fingers through a roof. Starts on a small ledge. *(1)0.75, (6)1.0, (3)1.5, (1)2.0*

___5 **Raja 5.11+ 100'**
The difficult corner in between **Gurkha** and **Ninja**.

___6 **Ninja 5.11+ 100'**
A left-facing fingers lieback. *0.75–2.0, heavy on the 0.75, 1.0*

Reservoir Wall

7 Sharka Zulu 5.10+ 130'
Not the most aesthetic climb on the block. Thin start to hands and strenuous wide moves in a left-facing corner. *0.75–4.5*

8 Pente 5.11- 160'
Exquisite! Slightly tight hands splitter to left-facing corner. Just left of a large pillar. Stays shady. *(2)1.0, (3)1.5, (4)2.0, (6)2.5, (1)3.5, a few extra runners for the start*

9 Slot Machine 5.12- 160'
Incredibly sustained thin hands in a tight corner. A punishing route, put up by Steve Hong. Harder for bigger hands. *(1)0.4, (2)0.5, (3)0.75, (1)1.0, (3)1.5, (9)2.0 (1)2.5, bolt (#1 Camalots work better than #2 Friends)*

9.5 Less Than Zero 5.13 ?'
A very thin crack just right of **Slot Machine**, led in November 2003 by Nathan Martin.

10 Dr. Carl 5.10 60'
Excellent warm-up. Twin cracks. *0.5–3.0*

11 Wigglin' Worm 5.11 150'
A loose start gives way to strenuous hands through a roof and big hands in a corner. A harder variation (likely 5.12) follows **Wigglin'** for about fifty feet, then traverses left to a steep fingers splitter. *(1)1.0, (2)2.0, (6)2.5, (4)3.0, (3)3.5, (1)4.0*

12 Unnamed 5.10 60'
Left-facing corner. Big hands. *3.0–3.5*

13 Unknown ? 150'
Splitter to hands in a right-facing corner to offwidth.

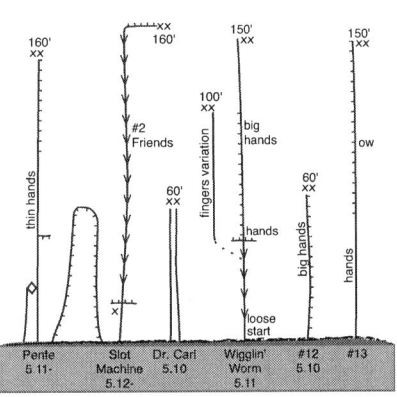

90

Wendy Davis on **Pente** 5.11-   Photograph by Ben Moon/MoonFoto

Reservoir Wall

14 Three Fools 5.10 60'
Fists in a left-facing corner on a pillar. 3.0–4.0

15 Ernie Used to Box 5.11 100'
A striking diagonaling offwidth splitter. 3.5–7.0, heavy on the big stuff

16 Unknown ? 80'
Stembox to a roof.

17 Overlook 5.10/5.11 110'/80'
The first pitch is fun and varied, even though it looks wide. Don't let it scare you from getting to the second pitch, a classic looking splitter.

Pitch 1: (2)1.0, (1)3.0, (3)3.5, (1)4.0, (1) #4 Camalot, (1) #4.5 Camalot

Pitch 2: (2)0.75, (3)1.0, (3)1.5, (2) each 2.0–3.0

18 Speedy Gonzalez 5.10/5.11 60'/60'
One of the first routes put up on Reservoir Wall.

Pitch 1: Hands in a straight-in corner, left of a pillar.

Pitch 2: A good-looking offset splitter, fingers to thin hands.

19 Unnamed 5.11 80'
Excellent splitter fingers. Harder for small knuckles. (4)0.75, (4)1.0, (2)1.5, (1)2.0

20 Unknown ? 120'
Offwidth in a flare.

21 Flesh and Bone 5.11 90'
Small roof at the start to fingers and thin hands.

22 Unnamed 5.10 40'
Hands in a left-facing corner on the left side of a rectangular pillar. Not recommended.

23 Unknown ? 120'
Right-facing corner to offwidth roof, one-bolt anchor.

24 Dreadasaurus 5.10+ 90'
Blocky start. Thin hands in a left-facing corner. (1)0.75, (1)1.0, (2)1.5, (4)2.0, (2)2.5, (2)3.0, (1)3.5

Reservoir Wall 3

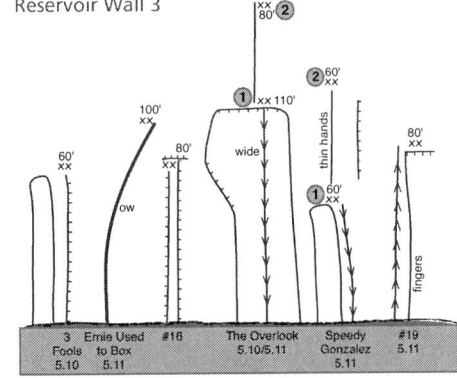

Mandy Hosford on **Slot Machine** 5.12- Photograph by Tommy Chandler

Reservoir Wall

Reservoir Wall 4

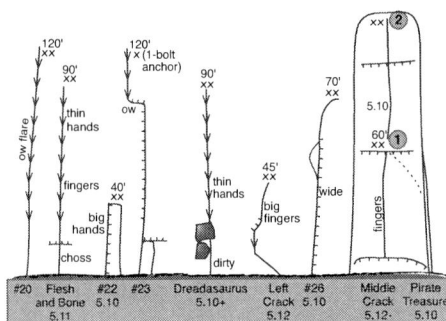

Reservoir Wall 5

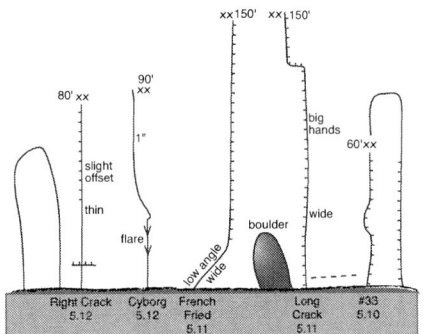

25 **Left Crack 5.12 45'**
Climb an easy ramp up and left and pull over into a small, thin corner, and up the right-angling off-fingers crack. Stout! *(1) each 0.4–0.75, (2) each 1.0, 1.25, 1.5*

26 **Unnamed 5.10 70'**
A left-facing flake with a pod up high. *(4)2.5, (5)3.0, (1)3.5, (1)4.0, (1) #5 Camalot*

27 **Middle Crack 5.12- 60'**
One of Indian Creek's best short splitter finger cracks. *(3)0.75, (4)1.0*

28 **Pirate Treasure 5.10 2 pitches**
Pitch 1: Climb broken rock to the right of **Middle Crack** and into a chimney behind the large pillar. Belay on ledge on the front face of the pillar.

Pitch 2: A striking big-hands splitter. *Heavy on the 3.5 and 4.0*

29 **Right Crack (a.k.a. Marvelous, a.k.a. Fantastic) 5.12 80'**
Thin hands to a technical crux, off-fingers finish. *0.4–2.5*

30 **Cyborg 5.12 90'**
Be afraid! A burly Petro route, up a flare to torturous big-fingers splitter. *(4)0.75, (8)1.0, (3)1.5, (1)2.0, (1) #4.5 Camalot*

31 **French Fried 5.11 150'**
A right-angling, low-angle start leads to a long left-facing corner.

32 **Long Crack 5.11 150'**
Offwidth to hands in a long right-facing corner.

33 **Unnamed 5.10 60'**
Hands in a left-facing flake.

34 **Unknown ? 50'**
Offwidth to fist splitter, left of a 100'-tall pillar.

35 **Unknown ? 140'**
Start up a chossy left-angling ramp to a long crack, immediately right of the previous route.

From here, pass the 100' pillar and some talus to gain the next route to the right.

David Bloom on **Left Crack** 5.12   Photograph by Kris Passie

Reservoir Wall

Reservoir Wall 6

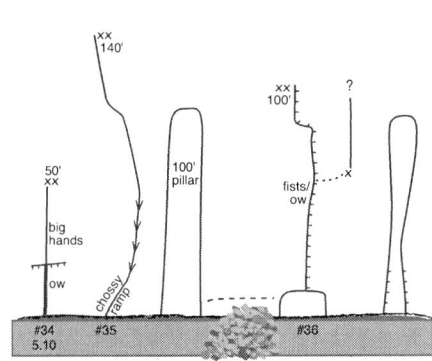

Reservoir Wall 7

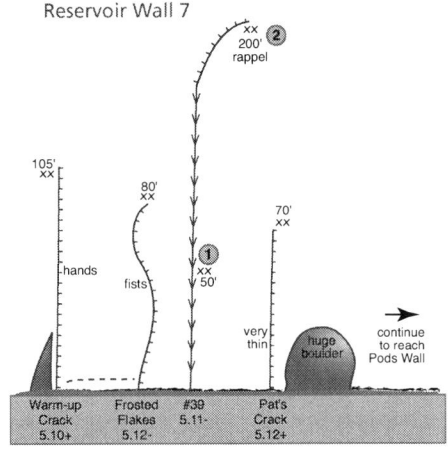

36 Unknown 100'
Left-facing corner that starts on top of a large block.

37 Warm-up Handcrack 5.10+ 105'
Hands in a left-facing corner, with a pillar at the start. If it weren't such a long walk this route would be as popular as **The Incredible Handcrack**. *(1) each 1.0–2.5, (6)3.0, (2)3.5*

38 Frosted Flakes 5.12- 80'
Classic, wavy fist crack. *(1) each 1.5–3.5, (3)4.0, (2) #4 Camalots*

39 Unnamed 5.11- 50'/150'
Two pitches up a straight-in corner. Mostly thin hands. *(1)0.75, (1)1.0, (1)2.0, (7)2.5, (3)3.0, (2) 60m ropes*

40 Pat's Crack 5.12+ 70'
Less-than-tips in a shallow left-facing corner. Left of a huge boulder. Named for Pat Savage of **Air Swedin** fame. *0.33–0.75*

Beyond here are several more routes: **Rosholt's Disease** and **The Cure** are both wide cracks and they share an anchor. **Snakeskin** is a 5.10 big-hands corner.

Pods Wall

Pods Wall-left

The Pods Wall

Continue walking along the base of Reservoir Wall until you reach these fine routes on the southeast prow. A little extra effort is required to get here. **You will be directly across from the Dugout Ranch. Please keep a low profile.**

1 **Ham on Rye 5.12   130'**
Off-fingers splitter to wide-hands flare.

2 **Pecking Order 5.11   150'**
Pitch 1: Climb the left side of a pillar, with big hands.
Pitch 2: Gain a slot.

3 **The Supervisor 5.12   120'**
Starts as tips, then takes a 1.25" overhanging layback.

4 **Unknown ?   80'**
A stembox.

5 **Unknown ?   90'**
A left-facing dihedral up to a huge roof, freed by Steve Hong.

6 **Unknown ?   150'**
Left-facing corner, starts thin hands, goes to fingers.

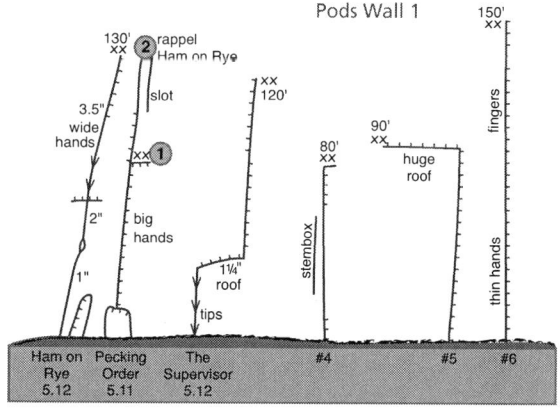

Pods Wall 2

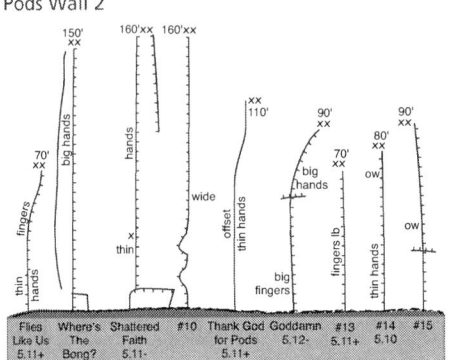

__7__ **Flies Like Us 5.11+ 70'**
Begin in a thin-hands right-facing corner that switches to fingers in a left-facing corner.

__8__ **Where's the Bong? ? 150'**
Climb hands in a right-facing corner with a pillar at the start, that switches to big hands in a left-facing corner.

__9__ **Shattered Faith 5.11- 160'**
A long left-facing corner that starts out thin, passes a bolt and widens to hands.

__10__ **Unknown ? 160'**
A long, wide right-facing corner.

__11__ **Thank God for Pods 5.11+ 110'**
Classic, offset thin-hands splitter with pods. A real beauty. *(3)1.5, (8)2.0, (3)2.5*

__12__ **Goddamn 5.12- 90'**
Big fingers in a right-facing corner to a big-hands arcing splitter. *0.75–3.0*

__13__ **Unnamed 5.11+ 70'**
A right-facing fingers lieback. *(1)0.4, (1)0.5, (2)0.75, (4)1.0, (3)1.5*

__14__ **Unnamed 5.10 80'**
Right-facing corner, thin hands to offwidth. Funky anchor. *2.0–6.0*

Pods Wall-right   Love Wall

__15__ **Unknown 90'**
A wide left-facing corner through a small roof.

Route #15 is the last route on the south face before turning onto the southeast face.

__16__ **Unknown ? 70'**
Start off a ledge, head up a pillar.

__17__ **Unnamed 5.11 100'**
Hands in a left-facing corner. Watch your rope.

Hike a few hundred feet right again to the last two routes. Both look good.

__18__ **Unknown ? 120'**
Flake to short left-facing corner to splitter.

__19__ **Unknown ? 80'**
Sustained fingers in a crisp right-facing corner.

Pods Wall 3

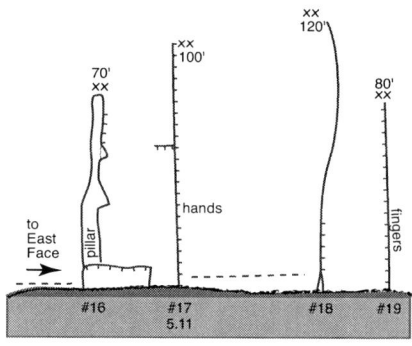

Stewart Green

Indian Creek Sojourn

Indian Creek. To me there has always been magic in that name. That sinuous canyon, lined with soaring walls of ruddy Wingate sandstone, is a special place. A place not just for climbing adventures, but a place to connect with the elemental earth and with the ancient ones who once hid in aeries tucked into the cliffs and scribed their art on desert varnished panels.

The first time I saw Indian Creek was in late November, 1971. Jim Dunn, Billy Westbay, and I drove down the remote canyon in my white VW bug, en route to an early ascent of North Six Shooter Peak. That sunny first afternoon we stopped and scrambled up to the base of several buttresses. The most prominent one towered above the road and cattle guard. We walked along the cliff-base until we reached the most perfect crack we had ever seen. We dubbed it "The Supercrack" and longed to sink our hands into its perfection. But neither bong pitons nor our largest Colorado nuts, a new passive technology that lessened rock damage, could safely protect the parallel-sided slit.

In October, five years and many trips later to Indian Creek and our favorite campsite at Fringe of Death Canyon, I returned to Supercrack. Earl Wiggins, his wife Cheryl, and dog O'Thing, and I had caravanned over from Colorado, while Jim had driven west from New Hampshire towing Ed Webster and Bryan Becker. The following day Earl and Jim had a date with Supercrack. I was to photograph and film the ascent. But Jim elected not to climb, "the vibes weren't right," so Earl, belayed by Webster, jammed his way up the perfect crack toward a vault of azure sky. I recorded it all for posterity on Kodachrome, Super 8 film, and audio tapes. In my mind, that day was the start of modern crack climbing at Indian Creek—the best crack area in the world.

Over the years I've continued to sojourn to Indian Creek, but somewhere along the way I found there were just too many folks there. The cracks were getting worn on the edges and all chalked up. Trails criss-crossed the talus slopes. Toilet tissue flowers sprouted on clumps of sagebrush. Dogs ran everywhere with abandon. People came to climb, but many didn't care enough about the place, its beauty, and its uniqueness.

That seems to be changing, for the better. So now I come to Indian Creek in the off-season, when few other climbers are about. The resolute cliffs still wall the canyon's sides. The fractured cracks still cleave the sculptured sandstone. The ravens still fly on errands through the cottonwoods. The rock and sandy soil still smells dry and dusty under the hot sun. Times change, yes. But time also stands still. At Indian Creek.

Stewart Green

3 Cat Wall Area

Tom Englebach on **Johnny Cat** 5.11+ Photograph by Mark Soot

Area Overview
Slug Wall to Disappointment Cliffs

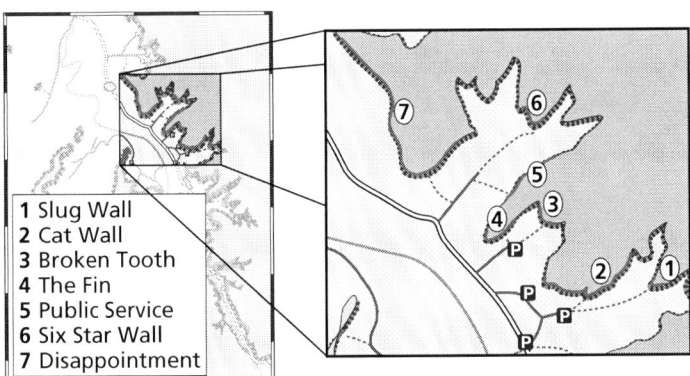

1 Slug Wall
2 Cat Wall
3 Broken Tooth
4 The Fin
5 Public Service
6 Six Star Wall
7 Disappointment

Slug Wall

The Slug Wall
This is a small rounded buttress, resembling a slug, in the canyon behind and to the right of Cat Wall. There are about twenty routes here, most of them on the right side (southeast face) of the buttress. The routes were mainly put up by a group of reticent Crested Butte climbers. The following climbs are close together on the right side. No further beta is available at this time.

1 **Unknown ?'**
   Hands and fists. Short.

2 **Unknown 5.11 ?'**
   A very long route.

3 **Unknown 5.11 ?'**
   Another long route.

4 **Unknown 5.10 ?'**
   Hands; arcs left to right.

5 **Wahinis 5.12+ ?'**
   Short and hard, tips and fingers in a left-facing corner. Starts on a ledge.

Cat Wall

The Cat Wall

Named after the catlike formation that sits on top of Reservoir Wall and faces Cat Wall (this formation has been climbed at 5.10). There are more climbs per square foot here than at any other buttress in Indian Creek. The cliff is so wide there are two distinct trailheads. Most people park at the east end of the cliff (**Johnny Cat** area.) There is also parking and a trail to the west that comes up around **Puma**. Many of the classics are pictured in the classic, but out of print, *Canyon Country Climbs* by Wiggins and Cassidy. All kinds of climbing are found at The Cat from splitter tips cracks, to chiseled corners, evil flares, roofs, and endurance testpieces. The only things lacking at The Cat are an abundance of warm-ups and shade. No matter what time of year, The Cat receives a maximum amount of sunshine. If it seems really cold everywhere the **Johnny Cat** area can still provide excellent cragging conditions.

Cat Wall Overview

1 **Pussy Whipped 5.11+ 100'**
Starts in a stembox, pulls over a small roof, then launches into 1.5s in a left-facing corner. This is the first route to the left of **9 Lives**. *(1)0.5, (2)0.75, (3)1.0, (5)1.5, (2)2.0, (2)2.5, (1)3.0*

2 **9 Lives 5.11+ 120'**
A beautiful splitter that necks down from hands to tight hands and a short stretch of stacks. Cop a rest, then climb fingers in a left-facing corner, make a cool traverse left, and finish steep big hands through a bulge. Yeah! *(1)0.75, (2)1.0, (2)1.5, (4)2.0, (6)2.5, (1)3.5*

3 **Maceo 5.12- 130'**
Climb a light-colored offset flake crack past a bolt, and into a long stemming chimney. *(1)0.4, (1)0.5, (3)1.0, (3)1.5, (1)2.0, (2)2.5, (2)3.0, (1)3.5, extra slings*

4 **Unnamed 5.11+ 120'**
Immediately right of **Maceo**, scramble on top of a pillar, and climb the straight-in corner above. *(2)0.4, (2)0.5, (3)0.75, (3)1.0, (5)1.5, (3)2.0, (1)2.5, (1)3.0, (1)4.0*

Cat Wall

_5_ Acme Plaque Me 5.11 100'
Starts on a small ledge. Climb a short straight-in corner, with a funky stemming crux, to a right-facing corner, fingers to wide hands. (2)0.33, (1)0.5, (2)1.0, (5)1.5, (3)2.0, (2)2.5, (1)3.0, (1)3.5

_6_ The Mousetrap 5.12- 110'
An aesthetic but grueling wide crack. #6 *Friends*

_7_ Unnamed 5.10 70'
Tips in a straight-in corner, through a small flare, finish with splitter hands.

_8_ Cat Walk 5.10+ 120'
Climb a straight-in crack that arcs left to a right-facing corner.

_9_ Cattle Call 5.12- 110'
This route and **Catnap** start on the same small broken ledge. Climb a left-facing corner through three roofs. Second anchor at 160'. A route that keeps coming at ya!

_10_ Catnap 5.11- 70'
Interesting moves in a funky corner. (1)0.5, (2)0.75, (1)1.5, (4)2.0, (2)2.5, (1)3.0, (1)3.5

_11_ Wild Cat 5.11+ 80'
Fun face climbing past an unnecessary bolt gains a ledge. Stellar finger stacking and thin hands up a steep exposed poddy splitter. Wild! (1)0.75, (5)1.0, (6)1.5, (1)2.0

Cat Wall 1

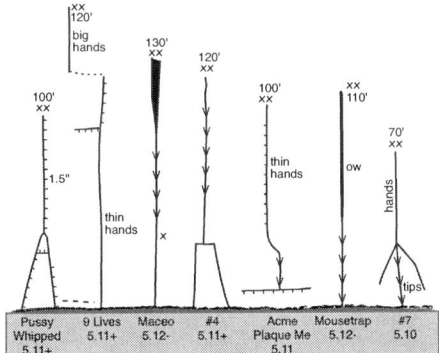

Cat Wall 2

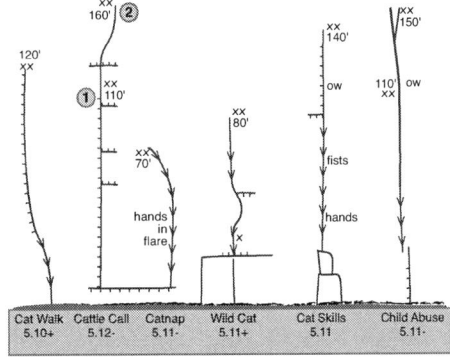

__12__ **Cat Skills 5.11 140'**
Scamper up onto a couple of big blocks then climb a straight-in corner to a right-facing offwidth. *3.0–6.0*

__13__ **Child Abuse 5.11- 150'**
Starts in a small right-facing corner. Mostly splitter offwidth. There is an intermediate anchor at 110'. *2.5–7.0, heavy on the big stuff*

__14__ **Deseret Moon 5.11+ 130'**
A steep technical stemming start past a hard flaring crack move. (There used to be a bolt here, it has since been removed.) It's a little spicy here but not runout. A well-deserved rest then one of Indian Creek's best long hands splitters.

Var. 5.11- Many people avoid the more classic start by climbing broken cracks to the left to gain the hands splitter. *(1)0.4, (3)0.5, (1)each 0.75–2.0, (4)2.5, (1)3.0*

__15__ **Tom Cat 5.10+ 90'**
A well-traveled classic and a great warm-up. Hands to wide hands in a right-facing corner. *(4)2.5, (4)3.0, (1)3.5*

__16__ **Gato Negro 5.12- 195' 2 pitches**
Pitch 1: Climb a long left-facing corner, with wavy flakes at the bottom, to a gear-protected belay below a roof.

Pitch 2: Pull the roof into a left-facing thin-hands corner. *0.33–7.0 with extra 2.0, double ropes, extra slings*

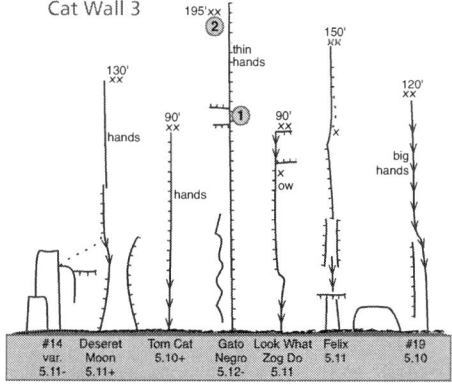

Cat Wall

Cat Wall 4

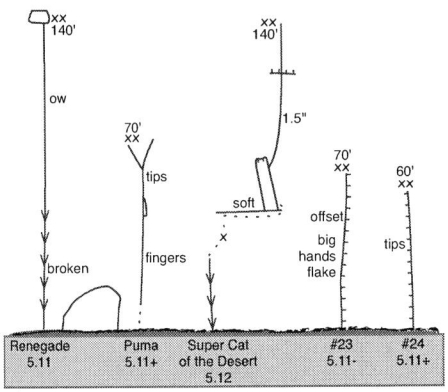

Cat Wall 5

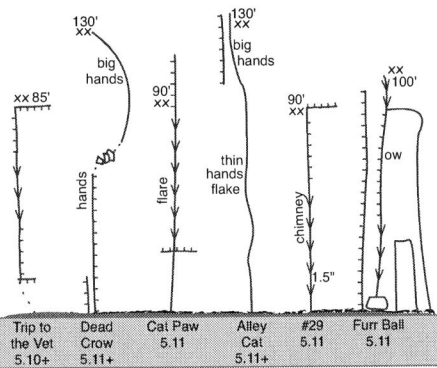

17 Look What Zog Do 5.11 90′
Starting left of a small pillar, climb a straight-in corner, to wide hands in a left-facing corner and through an offwidth roof (fixed piton under roof). One of the first routes done on Cat Wall.

18 Felix 5.11 150′
Consistently interesting stemming and face climbing. *(1)0.33, (3)0.4, (3)0.5, (4)0.75, (2)1.0, (1)1.5, (2)2.0, (2)2.5, (2)3.0, nuts, extra slings*

19 Unnamed 5.10 120′
Hands to wide hands in a right-facing corner. Harder for small hands. *(1)2.0, (3)2.5, (4)3.0, (4)3.5*

20 Renegade 5.11 140′
Climb a broken corner to a splitter offwidth.

21 Puma 5.11+ 70′
Splitter fingers with feet, in black varnished rock, to a tips/face climbing crux. Harder for big fingers. *(3)0.4, (2)0.5, (3)0.75, (2)1.0, (1)1.5*

22 Super Cat of the Desert 5.12 140′
The climb that has it all! It's not called Super Cat for nothing. First climb past a poorly-placed bolt (exciting), then traverse right for 20 feet with no reliable gear. Next, pull up into a knife-edged flake and attack the big-fingers to thin-hands splitter up to the roof. Crank over the roof and sprint up the long hands to fingers splitter. Whew! *(1)0.33, (2)0.75, (3)1.0, (5)1.5, (7)2.0, (2)2.5, (1)3.0, (2)3.5, (1)#4 Camalot, extra runners, double ropes*

23 Unnamed 5.11- 70′
Big hands up a left-facing flake.

24 Unnamed 5.11+ 60′
A right-facing tips corner.

25 Trip to the Vet 5.10+ 85′
A bouldery start (#00 Alien), goes thin hands to hands in a shallow changing corner. More fun than flossing your dog's teeth. *(1)0.33, (1)0.75, (1)1.5, (2)2.0, (4)2.5, (2)3.0, (2)3.5, (1)4.0*

David Bloom on **Super Cat of the Desert** 5.12   Photograph by Eric Draper

Cat Wall

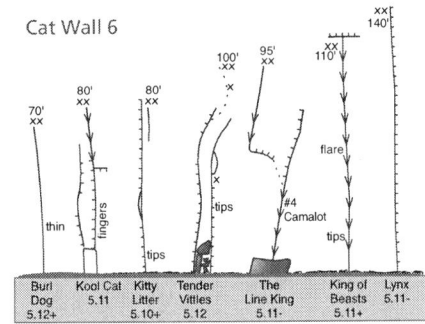

Cat Wall 6

26 Dead Crow 5.11+ 130'
Good hands in a shallow left-facing corner to loose face climbing and a nearly horizontal big hands splitter. Highly recommended. *Heavy on the 3.0 and 3.5*

27 Cat Paw 5.11 90'
Climb the flaring corner that begins with a roof. A Keith Reynolds special.

28 Alley Cat 5.11+ 130'
Sustained thin hands up a left-facing flake to a big-hands finish. *0.75–3.5 with (7)2.0*

29 Unnamed 5.11 90'
Climb a straight-in corner to a chimney slot and finish in a left-facing corner. *(2)0.75, (1)1.0, (3)1.5, (3)2.0, (3)2.5, (2)3.0*

30 Furr Ball 5.11 100'
Another quality Steve Quinlan route. Starts left of a pillar and tackles a straight-in corner to a flake, then heads up an offwidth in a right-facing corner.

31 Burl Dog 5.12+ 70'
Climb the very thin crack in the left-facing corner left of **Kool Cat**. *(7)0.4*

32 Kool Cat 5.11 80'
Fingers in a beautifully varnished corner. Hard, thin finish. *(2)0.5, (5)0.75, (4)1.0, (1)2.0, (1)3.0*

33 Kitty Litter 5.10+ 80'
A right-facing corner that goes through all the sizes. Better than it sounds. *(2) each 0.5–3.5*

34 Tender Vittles 5.12 100'
Not your usual Indian Creek fare. Scramble over some stacked rocks and climb a very thin left-facing corner, then negotiate thought-provoking face moves up and right passing two bolts. *Double ropes, extra runners, small nuts, Lowe balls, (2)0.33, (5)0.4, (2)0.5, (5)0.75, (3)1.0, (1)1.5, (1)2.0, (1)3.0, (1) #4 Camalot*

35 The Line King 5.11- 95'
Start on top of a small block, then head up twin corners to a pod, face climb up and left and finish out the left side of a small roof. *(3)1.5, (1)2.5, (4)3.0, (4)3.5, (2) #4 Camalots*

36 King of Beasts 5.11+ 110'
Thin crack in a flare. Lives up to its name. *(5)0.4, (1)0.5, (1)0.75, (1)1.0, (4)1.5, (2)2.0, (2)3.0*

37 Lynx 5.11- 140'
A long and varied left-facing corner. Some loose blocks but still a good route. *(1)0.5, (3)0.75, (2)1.0, (2)1.5, (3)2.0, (1) each 2.5–3.5*

Wendy Davis on **Kool Cat 5.11**   Photograph by Ben Moon/Moonfoto

Rebecca Roseberry

Scarred Hands Tell A Long Story

Desert rats, cranking hard, living in the dirt or out of beat up pickups…Pink skin and a riddled mess of gobies sparks conversation of the day's climbs. The cringing pain associated with raw skin is often unavoidable. Here, you are classified by your gobies: a beginner trying hard, or a plain stupid climber with not enough tape for his project. Rest days are spent licking battle wounds, being reassured by friends, and compiling a too-long tick list. Eventually your skin will toughen over the miles of corners, slots and, of course, classic splitters.

The red color spectrum across this wild country appears as the subject of a master painter. Those of us who seek less crowded crags and the wild formations of the Fisher Towers make the commitment to climb softer rock. I found myself, two years ago, coated with dirt, sand and silt, scared shitless in Arches National Park with radiant sun striking out through a blue sky contrasting boldly against the La Sal Mountains. Living through the obscure Entrada adventure I extended my stay in Moab a little longer.

Indian Creek is raw beauty, stripped naked, bearing all that is a rock climber's dream. Wishing the night away to countless falling stars, the psyche and obsession of flawless cracks creeps into your dreams. This region uprooted my Pacific Northwest heritage and lured my wandering spirit. A passion for adventure will forever push me further into the sphere of sandbaggers. I accept that only the damned survive such challenges.

We've all had our asses handed to us in defeat. Indian Creek is unique: size is well-nigh everything. My proposal for the next guidebook, in the year 2020, is one that scans extremity dimensions and computes the grades accordingly. The well-rounded grade seeker tests all techniques or strives for boldness on the daring or deadly lines. Stitching up an "off" size crack can improve endurance, as well as social skills—begging to borrow camming units.

Indian Creek has been referred to as a 'sport-trad' area, suggesting that however hard you climb you're not rad. I disagree. Honing in rattley finger jams or levitating up a five-inch crack takes perseverance and advanced technique. Scarred hands tell a story of our best accomplishments and untold defeats. The essence of Indian Creek is reflected in us—rough as the rock we bleed a brilliant red.

To a seasoned Indian Creek enthusiast, style and a varied crack diet matters. I, myself, am guilty of seeking out the long thin hand cracks. Hopefully, before I know it, I'll successfully embrace the wide and gain a tighter grasp of desert climbing fulfillment. For one moment forget about numbers, sizes, who uses tape or chalk, and realize the aesthetic movement of ascending perfect cracks. The miles of Wingate towering above the canyon floor and friends not seen enough is what brings us back for future seasons of stellar rock climbing.

Rebecca Roseberry

Rebecca Roseberry on **Way Rambo** 5.12-
Photograph by Glen Hartman

Cat Wall

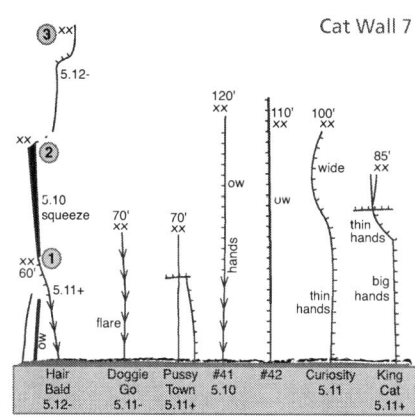

38 **Hair Bald 5.11+/5.10/5.12- 3 pitches**
Pitch 1: (a.k.a. Hairball) Stem in a dark, leaning, left-facing 60' corner. *Bring about four #2 Friends.*

Pitch 2: Up a squeeze chimney to anchor.

Pitch 3: Traverse right and climb the steep S-crack and pull a roof.

39 **Doggie Go 5.11- 70'**
Flare right of Hair Bald.

40 **Pussy Town 5.11+R 70'**
Off-fingers splitter to face moves to fingers with stemming.

41 **Unnamed 5.10 120'**
A long shallow left-facing offwidth corner. The start is fingers, but it's mostly wide.

42 **Unknown ? 110'**
Offwidth in a right-facing corner.

43 **Curiosity 5.11 100'**
Hands in a left-facing corner to flared jamming through a bulge. Highly recommended. Are you curious? *(2)1.5, (2)2.0, (2)2.5, (4)3.0, (4)3.5, (2)4.0*

44 **King Cat 5.11+ 85'**
Big hands in a clean left-facing corner to a tight-hands flake. Blast through the big-hands roof and punch it to the chains. An eye-catching line! *(2)0.75, (2)1.5, (3)2.0, (1)2.5, (1)3.0, (4)3.5*

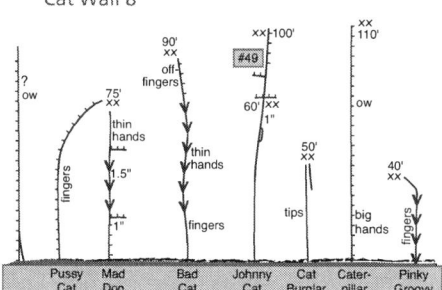

45 **Pussy Cat 5.11 75'**
Mostly fingers in a right-facing corner to a roof that arcs to the right. Clip the Mad Dog anchors. *(2)0.4, (3)0.5, (3)0.75, (3)1.0, (2)1.5, (2)2.0, (1)3.0*

46 **Mad Dog 5.11+ 75'**
Start up finger stacks and thin hands in a tight corner, pull a roof and finish with a thin-hands splitter. This one gives a lot of people fits! *(2)1.0, (5)1.5, (4)2.0, (2)2.5*

111

Cat Wall

47 Bad Cat 5.12 90'
Three hard parts on this killer line. Splitter fingers, thin hands in a corner and an exhausting ring-lock finish. *(1)0.5, (3)0.75, (6)1.5, (6)2.0*

48 Johnny Cat 5.11+ 60'
A cherry of a line. Gorgeous rattly fingers up a blank wall. Harder for small fingers. *(2)0.75, (7)1.0, (1)1.5, (1)2.5*

49 Tasmania 5.12+ 40' (100' to ground)
Finally climbed in the fall of 2000 by Tate Rees. This is the roof overhead from the **Johnny Cat** anchor. *(4)0.5, (6)0.75, (7)1.0, (1)1.5, (1)2.0*

50 Cat Burglar 5.12 50'
Tight fingers up a varnished face, hard crack switch at the end. *(3)0.5, (4)0.75*

51 Caterpillar 5.11 110'
This is the prominent left-facing corner right of the **Johnny Cat** alcove. Hands to mostly wide. *2.5–#4.5 Camalot, heavy on the big stuff*

52 Pinky Groovy (a.k.a. Tweety) 5.11- 40'
Fingers in a tight left-facing corner. Kinda tricky. *(3)0.75, (2)1.0, (1)2.5*

112

53 **Pussy Galore 5.11- 95'**
Wide hands in the back of a flare. *(1) each 1.5–2.5, (2)3.0, (4)3.5, (2)4.0, (1) #4 Camalot*

54 **Free Berlin 5.11 50'/150'/100'**
Pitch 1: Climb broken rock above a pillar.

Pitch 2: Hands to big hands in an offset splitter (5.11-).

Pitch 3: Finish up a left-facing corner to the rim. *Heavy on the 3.0, 3.5, (2) 60-meter ropes (they just reach the ground from the top of pitch 2)*

55 **Cathedral of the Mad Feline 5.12+ 60'**
Steep tips in a right-facing corner. A Lisa Gnade testpiece. *(1)0.4, (10)0.5*

56 **Pit Bull Terror 5.11 120'**
Demanding liebacking and jamming in a clean right-facing corner, fingers to big hands. *(1) each 1.0–2.5, (4)3.0, (3)3.5*

57 **Catastroph 5.11 100'**
A funky soft start gives way to thin-hands and hands in shallow changing corners. There is a second pitch which gains the rim. *(1)0.4, (1)0.75, (4)1.5, (4)2.0, (3)2.5, (2)3.0, (1)3.5*

58 **Unnamed 5.11 160'**
A Jay Smith route. There is a second pitch for this route, rating unknown. *(1)1.0, (3)1.5, (5)2.0, (3)2.5, (3)3.0, (3)3.5, (1)4.0*

59 **Fat Cat 5.11- 85'**
Mostly a big-hands splitter, a tricky start is thrown in for good measure. *(1)1.5, (1)2.0, (3)2.5, (3)3.0, (3)3.5*

60 **Unnamed 5.10 80'**
Hands in a left-facing corner. Hard start. Excellent warm-up. *(1) each 0.75, 1.5, 3.0, 3.5, (2) each 2.0, 2.5*

61 **Crewcut 5.11 100'**
Left-facing corner to flake, big hands through double roofs and a hard finish. *Extra 3.5s*

62 **Cat Man Do 5.10 90'**
Interesting offset splitter. Also a good warm-up. *(1)0.75, (4)2.0, (2)2.5, (2)3.0, (1)3.5*

63 **Bachelor Party 5.11+ 80'**
A hard face move to splitter off-fingers with feet. Named for Bret Ruckman's pre-marital desert voyage. *(2)0.4, (1)0.5, (3)0.75, (3)1.0, (3)1.5, (1) each 2.0, 2.5, 3.5*

Cat Wall 9

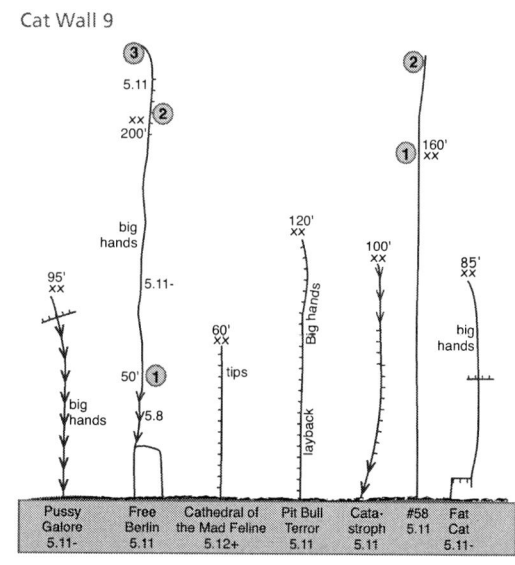

Cat Wall

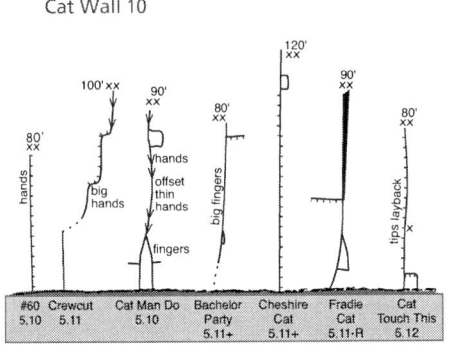

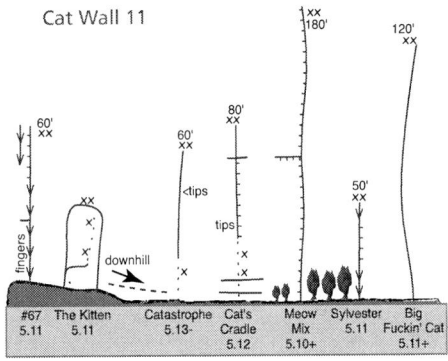

64 Cheshire Cat 5.11+ 120'
Fingers in a left-facing flake to a right-facing corner.

65 Fradie Cat 5.11-R 90'
Right-facing corner to a flare. (1)1.5, (1)2.0, (2)2.5, (2)3.0, (1) #4.5 Camalot

66 Cat Touch This 5.12 80'
A punishing Woodward pun. Right-facing tips dihedral with a bolt. Mostly 0.4s, with some 0.25s halfway

67 Unnamed 5.11 60'
Fingers in a shallow corner, just before the prominent pillar. (3)0.4, (5)0.5, (2)0.75, (1)1.5

68 The Kitten 5.11 ?'
Climbs the pillar, past a couple of bolts, just left of **Catastrophe**. Start in the gap between the tower and the cliff, and follow a horizontal out to the west face. A "Heavy Duty" special.

The following routes are downhill and to the right of the prominent pillar and offer some afternoon shade.

69 Catastrophe 5.13- 60'
Even if you're blessed with small fingers and you smash your tips down with a hammer, they still won't fit into the top of this elegant splitter. (2)0.4, (8)0.5, bolt

70 Cat's Cradle 5.12 80'
Climb face past two unnecessary bolts and layback up this tips crack in a steep left-facing corner. 0.33–0.75, heavy on the 0.5

71 Meow Mix 5.10+ 180'
A classic, long right-facing corner with some wide sections. (2)1.0, (2)1.5, (4)2.5, (7)3.0, (2)3.5, (2) #4 Camalots, extra runners, use double ropes or break up into two pitches

72 Sylvester 5.11 50'
Fingers and bigger in a tight corner. This is to the right of three junipers. 0.1–0.4

73 Big Fuckin' Cat 5.11+ 120'
This goes from fists to fingers.

BECAUSE IT'S A LONG WAY DOWN

ELI LYNN ON "INCREDIBLE HANDCRACK", A LONG WAY UP

DRY CORE
MARATHON
PHOTO: RALPH LINSENFELD

STERLING ROPE
THERE IS A DIFFERENCE
WWW.STERLINGROPE.COM

Broken Tooth

Broken Tooth Overview

Broken Tooth

Broken Tooth is the small-but-stellar buttress between Cat Wall and The Fin and set back from the road. The center of the wall is host to several excellent splitters. The left side has some shade and excellent moderate lines. The right side is home to many difficult offwidths and the classics **Broken Tooth** and **Unbelievable**. Turn right on a gated dirt road, 1.5 miles past Beef Basin Road (5.5 miles past the Supercrack cattle guard) and park at the end of this road.

1 **Mondo 5.12- 140'**
Maybe the best long fist crack at The Creek. A hard fingers start, then an unrelenting fists splitter. Shady. *(1) each 0.75–3.0, (2)3.5, (9)4.0, (1) #4 Camalot*

2 **Unknown ? 60'**
Fingers.

3 **Chemotherapy 5.12 100'**
Pretty right-facing corner.

4 **Unnamed 5.11+ 70'**
Difficult fingers in a flare. *(2)0.5, (6)0.75, (2)1.0, (1) each 1.5, 2.0, 3.5*

5 **Unnamed 5.11- 50'**
Climb a short splitter and traverse left to a right-facing corner.

6 **Blue Sky Mining 5.10+ 50'**
A right-facing corner. *(1) each 0.4, 0.5, 0.75, 1.0, 2.0, 3.0, 3.5, 4.0, #4 Camalot*

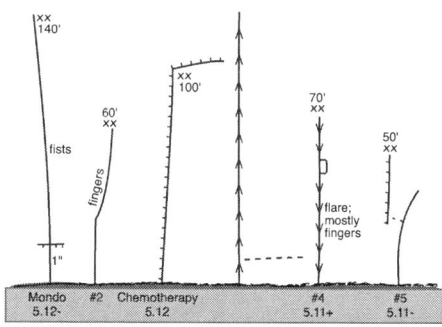

Broken Tooth 1

Broken Tooth

__7__ **Unnamed 5.11- 120'**
One of the better hand-crack corners at the Creek. Goes through several small roofs. *(1)1.5, (1)2.0, (4)2.5, (7)3.0, (4)3.5, (1)* **#4 Camalot**

__8__ **Dental Floss Tycoon 5.11- 150'**
A long and varied right-facing corner to the left of the most prominent pillar.

Var. From halfway up the previous route, traverse right to gain a splitter with a pod (150'). *(1)0.75, (1)1.0, (1)1.5, (1)2.0, (2)2.5, (7)3.0, (4)3.5, (1)* **#4 Camalot**

__9__ **Ukranian Root Canal 5.10+ 160'**
Go behind the prominent pillar from the right. Climb a steep hand crack on the overhanging face of the pillar, turn the roof (what—no anchors?) and continue up a long chimney system that forms the left side of the pillar. *2.0–5.0, extra runners, double ropes useful*

__10__ **The Pussy Wuss Crack (a.k.a. Sucker Crack) 5.10+ 70'**
Climb the deceptively difficult wide crack over a roof on the prominent pillar at the top of the trail. *(1)3.5, (3)* **#4 Camalots**, *(1)* **#4.5 Camalot**

__11__ **Heat Searcher 5.10/5.11+ 120'/65'**
A two-pitch Petro/Royster masterpiece.

Pitch 1: Climb behind the pillar to reach twin stemming cracks.

Pitch 2: Climb a stunning off-fingers/thin hands splitter. *(2)0.75, (2)1.0, (3)1.5, (3)2.0, (2)2.5, (2)3.0, (1)3.5, (1)4.0*

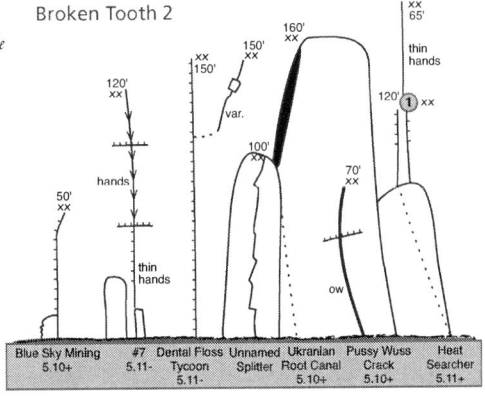

118

Steve Su on **Root Canal** 5.11+   Photograph by Andrew Burr

Broken Tooth

12 **Rock Lobster 5.11 110'**
An all-time favorite! An ever-narrowing splitter, from hands on down. Seventy-meter rope useful for toproping. Same goes for **Inflictor** and **Polygrip**. (2)1.0, (3)1.5, (2)2.0, (1)2.5, (4)3.0, (1)3.5

13 **Inflictor 5.12- 110'**
One of the few fingers/tips cracks with footholds. A thin crux. Shares anchor with **Polygrip**. (1)0.33, (4)0.4, (3)0.5, (2)0.75, (2)1.0, (1)1.5, nuts

14 **Polygrip 5.11+ 105'**
Excellent three-part climb. An easier version of **Bad Cat**. Offset thin hands, fingers in a varnished corner (the route's namesake), pull a roof and finish with a few moves of rattly fingers. (7)0.75, (4)1.0, (4)1.5, (3)2.0

15 **Rhythm Method 5.12 55'**
Tips splitter. (1)0.33, (3)0.4, (7)0.5, (3)0.75

16 **Root Canal 5.11+ 120'**
Difficult offwidth to a fists roof (Hard-to-see anchors). 3.0–? Heavy on the big stuff

17 **Gingivitis 5.10 50'/60'**
Pitch 1: Climb past a flake on the right side of a pillar, belay on a ledge.

Pitch 2: Climb a flake to the right of a right-facing corner.

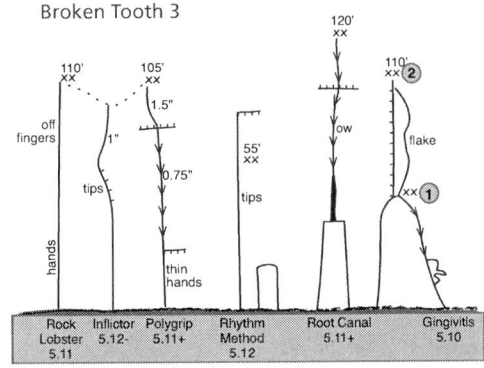

Broken Tooth 3

120

David Bloom on **Inflictor** 5.12-   Photograph by Nils Davis

Broken Tooth

18 Broken Tooth 5.12- 100'
Named for the feature that forms the roof halfway up the climb. Incredible from beginning to end! Thin hands in a flare, pull around the broken tooth, finish up a pumpy offset. *(3) each 1.0–3.5 and (1) #4 or #4.5 Camalot*

19 The Dentist's Chair 5.11+ 150'
Offwidth splitter with pods on the inside wall left of **Unbelievable**. *3.5–7.0, heavy on the big stuff*

20 Unbelievable 5.12 90'
Incredibly unbelievable classic varnished right-facing corner in a shady corridor. Layback and jam hands to off-fingers then punch the thin stemming crux. *(1)0.4, (3)0.75, (5)1.0, (4)1.5, (2)2.0, (2)2.5, (1)3.0, (1)3.5*

21 Insoluble 5.12 70'
A thin crack that emerges out of the corridor to the right of **Unbelievable**. *Many 0.5s*

22 The Tooth Fairy 5.11- 120'
Grueling offwidth in a clean flare. *(1) each 1.0–3.5, (4) #4 Camalots, (2) #4.5, (2) #5 Camalots, nuts*

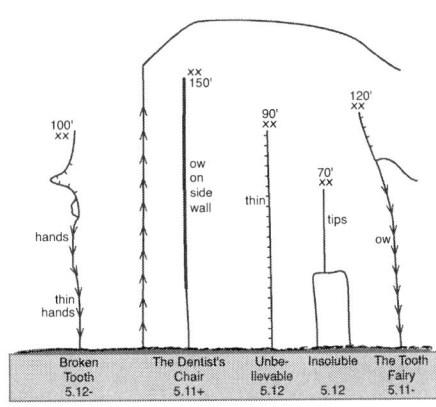

Desiree Westfall on **Rock Lobster** 5.11   Photograph by Joe Auer

The Fin

The Fin Overview

The Fin

If long, clean dihedrals are your bag then The Fin will not disappoint. There are many quality corners on this long buttress, and many of them go into the shade by early afternoon, making it a good warm-weather destination. The Fin is also known for its stout ratings, and its off-size cracks. You'll find just about everything here except a perfect hand crack. Same parking as Broken Tooth, but follow the trail to the west.

__1 **Third World Lover 5.10 70'**
Offset thin hands to fingers in nicely varnished rock. Try using just the righthand crack, for a 5.11+ pump. (2)1.5, (1)2.0, (3)2.5, (3)3.0, (2)3.5

__2 **Shivering Sheep 5.10+ 70'**
Visible anchors.

__3 **Unnamed 5.11 140'**
Fingers in a right-facing corner.

__4 **Crappucino 5.10 130'**
Hands in a right-facing corner, then jog left to a fingers splitter.

__5 **Fintastic 5.10- 50'**
Fingers in a right-facing corner, just right of a hands splitter.

__6 **Hot Fun Sunday 5.11 70'**
Thin hands in a shallow offset corner. 1.5–3.5

__7 **Flight Time 5.12- 50'**
Starts on a ledge left of a big block. A short, but quality splitter finger crack.

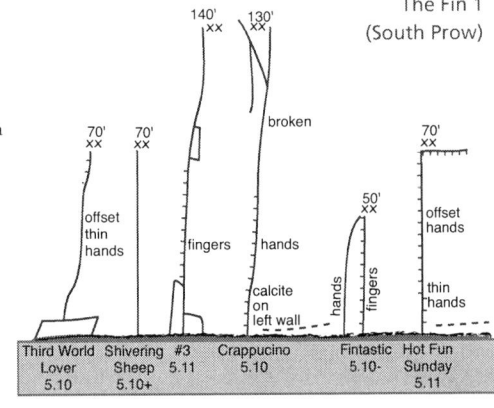

124

Renan Ozturk on **Hot Fun Sunday** 5.11   Photograph by Andrew Burr

The Fin

The Fin 2

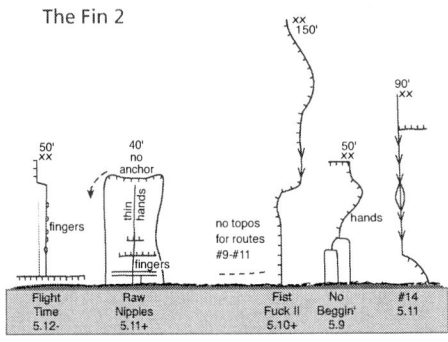

__8__ **Raw Nipples 5.11+ 40'**
An exciting little route through a couple of roofs. No anchor; downclimb to the left.

__9__ **Unknown 50'**
Climb a straight-in crack to hands in a changing corner. Traverse right on ledge to anchor.

__10__ **Unnamed 5.10 50'**
Climb a flake to a short right-facing corner. Shares anchor with previous route.

__11__ **Unknown 5.10 ?'**
This is a 5.10 corner right of the previous route.

__12__ **Fist Fuck II 5.10+ 150'**
A nice fist splitter that goes through a roof. The original name of this route is not known. The original F.F. is on the far right side of The Fin.

__13__ **No Beggin' 5.9 50'**
Right-facing hands.

__14__ **Unnamed 5.11 90'**
Left of a pillar is this right-facing corner that enters a large pod.

__15__ **Jewel of Denial 5.11- 90'**
Left-facing crack up to right-facing crack.

__16__ **Unknown ? 80'/150'**
A two-pitch splitter, just right of a pillar. The first pitch has probably gone free, but not the second.

__17__ **Walkin' Talkin' Bob 5.10- 50'**
Start on top of some stacked blocks and climb hands in a right-facing flake.

__18__ **Midget Gem 5.11 50'**
Climb a very thin crack to the **Walkin' Talkin' Bob** anchors. *#00 Aliens*

__19__ **Brother From Another Planet 5.12- 80'**
Climb a widening right-facing corner, to an offwidth flare through a roof. Vicious!

__20__ **Skid Row 5.11+ 90'**
Sustained off-fingers in a right-facing corner. Pulls a roof. The climb is named for the fine layer of sand on the wall under the roof. (1)0.5, (1)0.75, (8)1.0, (3)1.5, (1)2.5

__21__ **The Felcher 5.11- 95'**
This does not suck. A straight-in corner through a roof to off-fingers in a left-facing corner. (1)0.33, (1)0.4, (2)1.0, (7)1.5, (1)2.5

__22__ **Nagasaki 5.10+ 120'**
A great warm-up for the routes to the right, but still a little bit of a sandbag. A long right-facing corner, fingers to wide hands. (2)0.75, (3)1.0, (4)1.5, (6)2.0, (4)3.0, (1)3.5

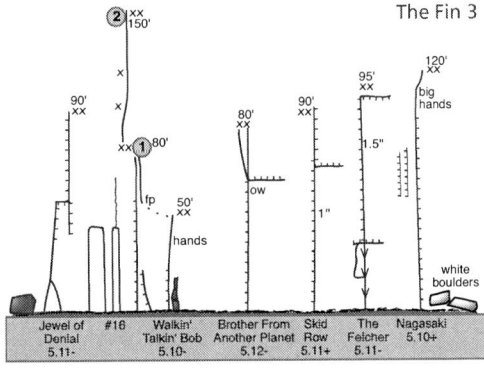

Ari Menitove on **Brother From Another Planet** 5.12- Photograph by Andrew Burr

The Fin

23 Unnamed 5.11 80'
Fingers and thin hands in a clean right-facing corner. One of the best climbs at Indian Creek without a name. *(1)0.5, (1)0.75(1)1.0, (4)1.5, (1)2.0, (1)2.5*

24 Double Trouble 5.11- 120'
Mega-classic twin cracks in a right-facing corner. *(2)0.75, (4)1.0, (4)1.5, (2)2.0, (3)2.5*

25 Beauty and the Beast 5.12- 60'
An excellent Petro/Gnade find. Tight fingers in an ebony varnished right-facing corner. *(2)0.5, (7)0.75*

26 Strike and Dip 5.12- 140'
Originally rated 5.11, it may still be a sandbag at the present grade. Unrelenting big fingers and strenuous liebacking. Sometimes sandy, as the route does not get done often. *(12)1.0, (9)1.5, (1) each 2.0–3.0*

27 Demolition 5.11 150'
This fine Petro/Gnade route was once guarded by a large loose block. Clean off-fingers and hands in a right-facing corner leads to a short offwidth at the top. *(2)1.0, (4)1.5, (1)2.0, (3)2.5, (2)3.0, (2)3.5, (1) #4.5 Camalot*

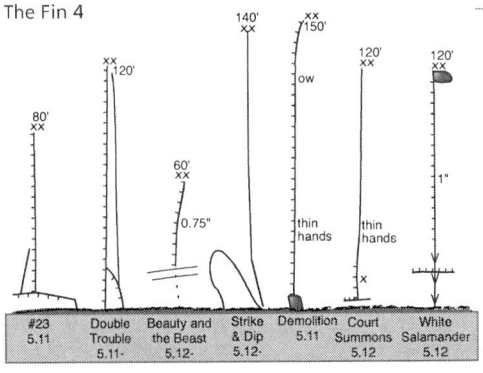

__28__ **Court Summons 5.12 120'**
Bouldery moves in a small right-facing corner, past a bolt, leads to a good thin-hands splitter. Another great find by Petro/Gnade. *(1)0.5, (2) each 1.0–2.0, (1) each 2.5–4.0*

__29__ **White Salamander 5.12 120'**
Difficult stemming start over a small roof. Ultra-sustained big fingers in a varnished right-facing corner. *(1)0.4, (3)0.5, (6)0.75, (9)1.0, (1) each 1.5–3.5*

__30__ **Virgin Voyage 5.10+ 60'**
A nice finger crack for the grade. *(3) each 0.4–0.75*

__31__ **Hail Bopp 5.11+ 100'**
Face climbing to interesting, varied climbing. A Greg Child route. *Many tiny TCUs*

__32__ **F.F. 5.11 130'**
Hands to overhanging fists in a dramatic right-facing corner. *3.0–4.0*

__33__ **Force It In 5.12 60'**
An unrelenting tips lieback in a varnished right-facing corner. *(3)0.4, (4) blue Aliens, (1)0.5*

The Fin 5

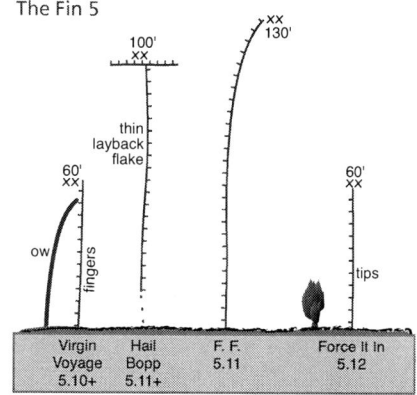

Public Service Wall

This is the west face of The Fin and contains over a dozen routes spread out along the length of the wall.

__1__ **Unknown ? ?'**
Climb a right-facing dihedral past a bolt, to a straight-in crack.

__2__ **Demolition Man 5.10+ ?'**
This route has two pitches.

__3__ **Unnamed 5.10 ?'**
Two pitches up a right-facing corner. Looks good!

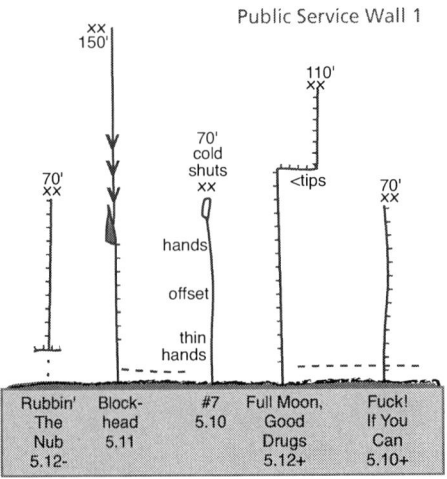

__4__ **Nineric ? ?'**
This takes a straight-in crack.

__5__ **Rubbin' the Nub 5.12- 70'**
Sustained fingers lieback in a varnished right-facing corner. (2)0.5, (6)0.75, (4)1.0, (1)1.5, (1)3.0

__6__ **Blockhead 5.11 150'**
A broken start leads to fingers in a left-facing offset and over a huge chockstone (The Blockhead). Long, varied and physical. (1)0.5, (2)0.75, (2)1.0, (3)1.5, (3)2.0, (1)2.5, (2)3.0, (2)3.5, (1)4.0, (1) #4 Camalot

__7__ **Unnamed 5.10 70'**
Thin-hands splitter to offset hands and a cold-shut anchor. (1)2.0, (1)2.5, (2)3.0, (3)3.5

__8__ **Full Moon, Good Drugs 5.12+ 110'**
The crag testpiece. Climb the awesome right-facing corner, with technical stemming over a less-than-tips roof. (6)0.33, (5)0.4, (1)0.5, (2)0.75, (1) each 1.0–3.0

_9_ **Fuck! If You Can 5.10+ 70'**
Left-facing. *0.75–3.0*

_10_ **Repo Man 5.11- 60'**
Big fingers to offwidth in an offset splitter. *1.0–5.0*

_11_ **Go Drown in a Lake of Diet Coke, Fucker! 5.11- 130'**
Thin hands in a flare and through a roof. *(2)1.0, (6)2.0, (3)2.5, (2)3.0, (1) each #4, #4.5 Camalots*

_12_ **Not Too Spicy 5.12 80'**
A thin start to some pods, followed by a crazy mantel to a flare finale. *(3)0.33, (4)0.4, (1)3.5, (1) #4 Camalot*

_13_ **Rabid Animal 5.11+ 150'**
Thin hands in a right-facing varnished flake.

_14_ **Hands Up 5.10 ?'**
Mostly big hands in a right-facing dihedral. *TCUs, (2) #0.75 Camalots, (2)2.0, (2)2.5, (2) #2 Camalots, (2)3.0, (2) #3 Camalots, (1) #3.5 Camalot*

_15_ **Morning Wood 5.11 90'**
Off-fingers to thin-hands splitter that angles left to a right-facing fingers corner. Starts right of some stacked blocks.

_16_ **Unknown ? 40'**
Hands in a left-facing corner. Located where the west face and south face converge.

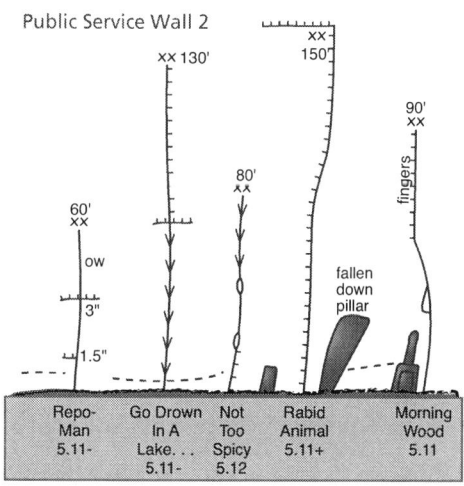

Public Service Wall 2

Six Star Wall

Six Star Wall
Take a right turn on the first dirt road past the Broken Tooth/Fin access road. Drive down this road as far as your car will allow. The wall to your right is the back side of The Fin and is known as Public Service Wall. This wall stays in the shade until the late afternoon. The wall to your left is the extreme right side of Disappointment Cliffs. Straight ahead is Six Star Wall. The first two routes are to the left on the prominent prow on the left (Six Star Left), and all the other routes are found on a separate section (Six Star Center) to the right.

Six Star Left
1 **Trundle Alley 5.12 60'**
Tips in a small corner to a ledge, climb a slot to the right, move back left to a tips splitter. *(2)0.4, (8)0.5, (1)0.75, (1)1.0, (1)1.5, Lowe Balls*

2 **Six Star Crack 5.12/5.13- 130'/100'**
The second pitch of this amazing route defies description.

Pitch 1: 0.5–3.0, 3 bolts
Pitch 2: (3)1.0, (5)1.5, (7)2.0, (3)2.25 (red Camalots)

3 **Drugstore Cowboy 5.10 60'**
Fingers to a slot to fingers. Look for calcite on the left wall.

Six Star Center
4 **Unnamed ? 60'**
Right-facing flake with cupped hands. *(2) #0.5 Camalots, (2) #0.75 Camalots, (2)3.0, (3)3.5, (1) #5 Camalot*

5 **Big Rig 5.11 ?'**
Right-facing offwidth to squeeze.

6 **Adrenaline 5.12- 100'**
Thin hands splitter out a roof.

7 **Unnamed 5.11- ?'**
Cupped hands out a roof.

8 **Pile of Puppies 5.11 120'**
Wide crack to bulging corner to flare.

9 **Egg Burglar 5.10 ?'**
Wide hands.

10 **Unnamed 5.10 ?'**
Left-facing black corner to chimney. *(1)1.0, (2)1.5, (3)2.0, (1)2.5, (3)3.0*

11 **Scarab 5.11 ?'**
Thin hands to a flake. *1.0–2.5*

12 **You Found It 5.12 ?'**
Two pitches.

Disappointment Cliffs

Disappointment Cliffs

Disappointment Cliffs

The longest buttress at The Creek, but with relatively few routes. There are some gems however, including the 1992 Jonny Woodward masterpiece, **Winner Takes All**, and the short-but-quality **The Angry Inch**. Most of the routes are clustered at the ends of the buttress. For climbs on the right side, park as for Six Star Wall. For routes on the left side drive a short ways up the Meat Walls road and hike up and right.

The following 11 climbs are on the far left (west) side of the wall.

1 **Unknown ? 120'**
Left-facing corner.

2 **Unknown ? 40'**
Left-facing fingers corner.

3 **Unknown ? 50'**
Right-facing thin-hands corner.

4 **Dis That 5.12- 120'**
Starts on a ledge. Stembox to splitter.

5 **Eat a File 5.12- 120'**
Overhanging straight-in corner.

6 **Plaque Wars 5.11- 140'**
Broken start to a left-facing wide-hands corner.

7 **Unknown 2 pitches**
Pitch 1: A bolt ladder.

Pitch 2: An undone splitter.

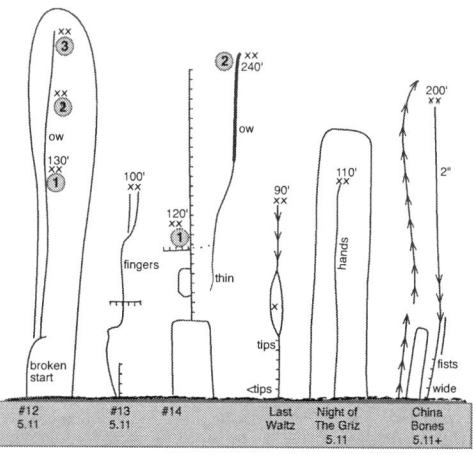
Disappointment Cliffs 1 (SE Face)

133

Disappointment Cliffs

8 Drop Shipment 5.11 100'
Broken start to fingers in a clean low-angle corner. (2)0.5, (5)0.75, (3)1.0, (3)1.5, (1) each red and blue Lowe Balls

9 Winner Takes All 5.13- 80'
Makes **Tricks** look like a pile! A small left-facing corner leads to a roof and then steep splitter fingers and finally a leftwards traverse. 0.5–1.5, with (6)0.75, (6)1.0

10 Remote Control 5.12- 100'
A broken start to a right-facing lieback corner. Pumpy! (1)1.0, (8)1.5, (4)2.0, (1)2.5, (1)3.5, (1) #4 Camalot

11 Teri's Lieback 5.11 100'
This climb is located somewhere in the middle of the cliff across from the old landing strip. (5)1.0, (6)1.5, (5)2.0, (2)2.5, (1)3.0

The following climbs are on the right (east) side of the cliff.

12 Unnamed 5.11 3 pitches
Ascend a crack system up a pillar.

13 Unnamed 5.11 100'
Fingers.

14 Unknown ? 2 pitches
The second pitch is offwidth.

15 Last Waltz ? 90'
A less-than–tips start.

16 Night of the Griz 5.11 110'
Varied cracks to a steep hands splitter on the front of a large pillar.

17 China Bones 5.11+ 200'
Climb a straight-in corner that goes from wide to fists, up broken twin cracks, then a two-inch splitter forever. Two pitches.

18 Unknown ? 100'
A chossy start gives way to varnished thin hands in a right-facing corner.

Disappointment Cliffs 2

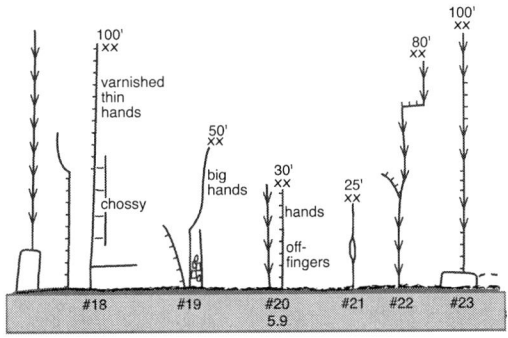

19 **Unknown ? 50'**
Climb over chockstones in a short slot, then up splitter wide hands.

20 **Unnamed 5.9 30'**
Short layback to hands in a right-facing corner. 1.5–3.0

21 **Unknown ? 25'**
A short aid seam with a pod down low.

22 **Unknown ? 80'**
A straight-in corner through a small roof.

23 **Unknown ? 100'**
Starts on top of a block in a right-facing corner.

24 **Dangerous Lesion 5.13- 90'**
A steep tips splitter, and classic Woodward wordplay. Located to the right of a large pillar with a chimney on its right side.

25 **Unknown ? 80'**
A hands-to-fists splitter through some soft rock.

26 **The Angry Inch 5.12+ 45'**
Pure splitter. *Many 1.0*

27 **Unknown ? 45'**
Hands to fists in a red right-facing corner just right of The Angry Inch.

28 **Unknown ? 90'**
The last route on the right side of the Disappointment Cliffs is this aid route that starts less-than-tips in a right-facing corner and passes a bolt in a slot.

Disappointment Cliffs 3

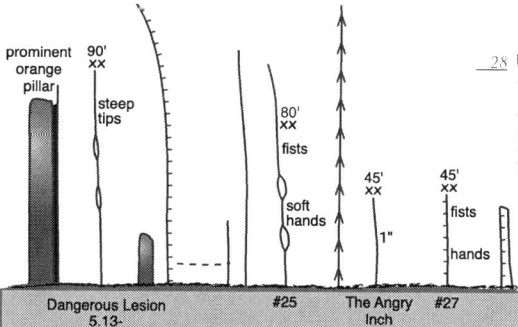

ACCESS: IT'S EVERY ONE'S CONCERN

The Access Fund is a national non-profit climbers' organization working to keep climbing areas open and conserve the climbing environment. Need help with a climbing related issue? Call us and please consider the principles below when climbing.

• **ASPIRE TO CLIMB WITHOUT LEAVING A TRACE:** Especially in environmentally sensitive areas like caves. Chalk can be a significant impact. Pick up litter and leave trees and plants intact.

• **DISPOSE OF HUMAN WASTE PROPERLY:** Use toilets whenever possible. If toilets are not available, dig a "cat hole" at least six inches deep and 200 feet from any water, trails, campsites, or the base of climbs. Always pack out toilet paper. Use a "poop tube" on big wall routes.

• **USE EXISTING TRAILS:** Cutting switchbacks causes erosion. When walking off-trail, tread lightly, especially in the desert on cryptogamic soils.

• **BE DISCRETE WITH FIXED ANCHORS:** Bolts are controversial and are not a convenience. Avoid placing unless they are absolutely necessary. Camouflage all anchors and remove unsightly slings from rappel stations.

• **RESPECT THE RULES:** Speak up when other climbers do not. Expect restrictions in designated wilderness areas, rock art sites, and caves. Power drills are illegal in wilderness and all national parks.

• **PARK AND CAMP IN DESIGNATED AREAS:** Some climbing areas require a permit for overnight camping.

• **MAINTAIN A LOW PROFILE**

• **RESPECT PRIVATE PROPERTY:** Be courteous to land owners.

• **JOIN THE ACCESS FUND:** To become a member, make a tax-deductible donation of $35.

PO Box 17010
Boulder, CO 80308
303.545.6772

your climbing future
www.accessfund.org

4 Meat Walls, etc.

John Varco on **Carnivore** 5.12-   Photograph by Eric Draper

First Meat Wall

Area Overview
The First Meat Wall to the Beef Basin Crags

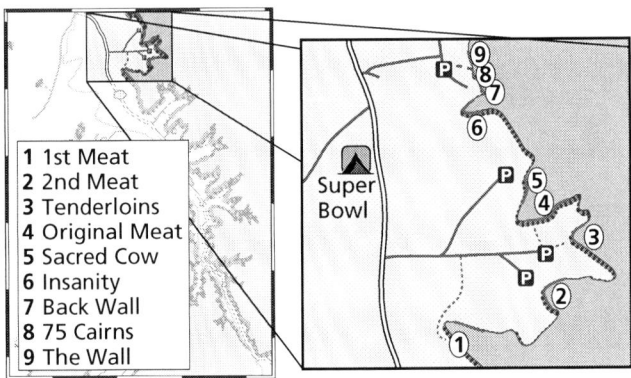

1. 1st Meat
2. 2nd Meat
3. Tenderloins
4. Original Meat
5. Sacred Cow
6. Insanity
7. Back Wall
8. 75 Cairns
9. The Wall

First Meat Wall

First Meat Wall
This seldom-visited cliff is an extension of the left side of The Disappointment Cliffs. It is almost always in the shade.

Photograph by Richard Durnan

___1 **Unnamed 5.12 ?'**
Splitter crack.

___2 **Here's the Beef ? ?'**
Right-facing dihedral.

___3 **Orpio 5.11 ?'**
Straight-in crack. The plaque is broken, but most likely the name is supposed to be Scorpio. TCUs to tight-hands size gear

___4 **Beef Soda 5.10+ 70'**
Tight hands in a right-facing dihedral. *(3) #0.75 Camalots, (3)2.0, (2) #1 Camalot, (1) #2 Camalot, (1)3.0, (1) #3 Camalot*

___5 **Short Loin 5.10 50'**
Tight hands in a left-facing dihedral to the top of a pillar.

___6 **Braised Ribs 5.12 50'**
This straight-in tips crack gains the other side of the same pillar. Can be toproped after doing Short Loin.

___7 **Unknown ? ?'**
Big hands and fists.

The next three routes are on the prow, just before reaching Disappointment Cliffs.

___8 **Unknown ? 2 pitches**
First pitch looks to be killer hands, second is a variety of sizes.

___9 **Unknown ? ?'**
Fingers in a left-facing dihedral.

___10 **Unnamed 5.10+ 70'**
Off-fingers to tight hands in a right-facing dihedral.

139

Karl Kelley

Creek Freaks

"Are you boys crazy?" A typical response in the climbing community around Moab. "The Creek for half a day? The creek in August?" The word obsessed comes to mind...

It has been a crazy night at work, busy as hell, and it's now midnight. The last seven hours at work in a 120 degree kitchen, sweat soaked chef coats. "C'mon man, prep list, get on it! Let's get out of here, my house 7AM."

Power nap.

"Get in the truck, let's go, every body got every thing?" A quick stop at the Shell on the way out for gas , red bulls and horrific smelling egg sandwiches, a true gift in the culinary world. "Man, do you guys really have to eat that crap in my truck?" After the morning ritual of vying for the front seat, we head on down Hwy 191 South. That is one straight road! 95 mph gets you to the heart of the Creek in 40 minutes, and then it's: "Where do guys want to climb?"

"Does it really matter, it's all killer, let's go to a wall we haven't been to."

As we head up to the cliff, Dylan's excited, "Yeah, look at that killer splitter ahead of us!" "Damn Dylan, that looks like 2 Friends again (my nemesis)," I reply as he looks back at me and smiles, knowing it means gobies for me. "How about that long corner to the right?" I ask. Dylan looks back and says, "It looks like open 3 Camalots. That gives me huge gobies!" I look at him, smile and say, "Yeah, looks killer! Who's making the salsa tonight?" Jay is quick on the "Not It!", knowing all too well that working with lime juice is no fun with gobies.

Indian Creek must have been the incentive to invent the Gri Gri. As I belay Dylan up the future gobie climb, it is hard not to look around in awe. My mind wanders taking in the incredible landscape around me. So much beauty, so many cliffs, colors and smells, so much tranquility, and so much history...what an amazing place! My thoughts are interrupted as Dylan reaches the top and asks to be lowered. Now it's my turn. As I get on the climb, everything around me disappears and all my attention is focused on trying to figure out how the hell I'm going to ascend this nemesis size; will I ever figure it out? Who cares, I tell myself, its all part of the attraction. After a few more pitches, I look at my watch in a panic, "Hey you guys, we're way late! We have to go! Shoot, we didn't get to that roof crack, you guys want to come back tomorrow?" "Oh yeah!"

The Creek is a special place. It is such a vast area, that I can go with my wife or friends and be totally by ourselves if we choose. In the spring, the cacti bloom with bright yellows and pinks. The summer months are spent honing your shade chasing and hydration skills. The fall foliage with bright yellows up against the red cliffs is nothing short of spectacular, and that's coming from a guy born and raised in New England. The winter months are spent on south facing cliffs in a t-shirt or light weight Capiline. The Creek is a true 5-star area throughout the year.

Be warned, however, The Creek is also a wild place. We have seen rattlers, bears, lynx and ranchers with guns. Please be respectful to all of their spaces. I'm sure you're concerned about your own crag, so please bring that concern to ours while visiting. Happy climbing and exploring!

Karl Kelley

Second Meat Wall

Second Meat Wall

Second Meat Wall

The filet mignon of the Meat Wall group. This wall may have been the original Meat Wall, but everyone has since reassigned it to second-meat status. The cliff is shaped like a semi-circle, so it is possible to follow the shade or sun, depending on the season. Turn right on the first dirt road after Six Star Canyon. See Meat Walls map (page 138) for Second Meat parking.

__1__ **Unknown ? 90'**
Thin hands in a red right-facing corner to a flake.

__2__ **Green Eggs and Ham 5.10 70'**
A twin-crack start to fists and offwidth in a right-facing flake.

__3__ **Unknown ? 110'**
Starts left of a large pinyon pine. Long right-facing flake, offwidth to thin hands.

__4__ **Unknown ? 130'**
A left-facing corner through two roofs.

__5__ **Swedish Meatballs 5.11 130'**
Climb a pillar (wide on the right side), and the long left-facing corner above it, passing a fixed pin. *0.75–3.5*

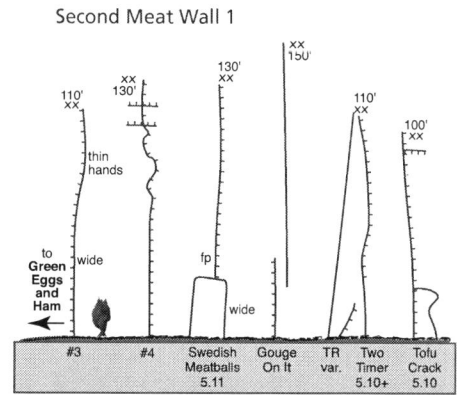

Second Meat Wall 1

Second Meat Wall

6 Gouge On It ? 150'
Climb a short right-facing corner, then move right to a long splitter.

7 Two Timer 5.10+ 110'
A good left-facing corner. For added fun, toprope the 5.12- fingers splitter left of **Two Timer**, known as **Two Timer II**. This pitch shares the same anchor.

8 Tofu Crack 5.10 100'
A quality left-facing corner. Starts to the left of a prominent group of junipers.

9 The Pastafarian 5.12 80'
Start above a pillar, then stem wildly past thin offset twin cracks and two bolts. Serve it up al dente.

10 Top Sirloin 5.11 100'
Start on a ledge. Sustained, quality thin hands in a steep left-facing corner. *(1)2.0, (8)2.5 (#1 Camalots work best), (1)3.5*

11 X-tra Lean 5.11+ 65'
Climb a slightly broken off-fingers splitter to a ledge. Delicately jam, layback and stem through a thin section to the anchor. *(2)0.4, (3)0.5, (3)0.75, (2)1.0*

12 Unknown ?' 130'
A left-facing corner through a roof, with a super-thin start.

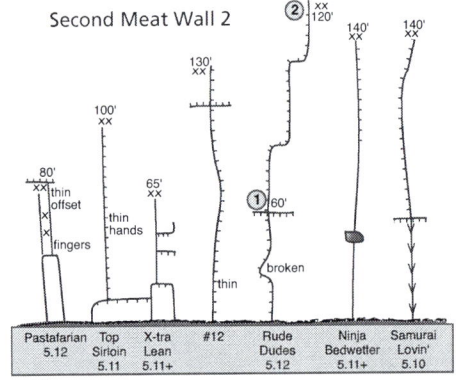

142

13 **Rude Dudes 5.12 60'/120'**
Pitch 1: Climb broken flakes to a ledge.

Pitch 2: Start with a hollow flake and then climb a stunning right-facing corner through a couple of large roofs.

14 **Ninja Bedwetter 5.11+ 140'**
Splitter through a pod and into a left-facing corner. *0.4–#4 Camalot with (3)0.5, (4)0.75*

15 **Samurai Loving 5.10 140'**
Start left of a dead snag. Climb broken rock to a right-facing thin-hands corner.

16 **Meat Ya Later 5.11+ 70'**
Start above a pillar, climb past a bolt and up to a 15' hand crack out a roof.

17 **Free Range 5.12+ 130'**
Fingers and tips left of **Sesh One Cooking**.

18 **Sesh One Cooking 5.11- 120'**
Climb the left side of a pillar, to thin hands in a right-facing corner. *(1)1.0, (2)1.5, (7)2.0, (2)2.5*

19 **Soylent Green ? 100'**
A left-facing corner through a pod.

20 **T-Bones Tonight 5.12- 100'**
Don't hesitate to get on this enduring classic, even if you are a vegetarian. Quality thin hands in a black left-facing corner and a wild big-hands roof. There is a second pitch, 110' long—the grade is unknown. *(1)0.5, (2)0.75, (2)1.5, (5)2.0, (2)2.5, (1)3.0, (2)3.5, (1) #4 Camalot*

21 **Tube Steaks Tomorrow 5.10+ 90'**
A fingery crux, but mainly good hands in a left-facing corner. *(1)1.0, (1)1.5, (2)2.0, (3)2.5, (3)3.0, (1)3.5*

22 **Carnivore 5.12- 90'**
The long-sought-after second pitch to **Tube Steaks** is truly a vegan's nightmare. Offwidth. *(2)3.5, (1)4.0, (5) #4 Camalots, (2) #4.5 Camalots, (1) #5 Camalot*

23 **At Your Cervix 5.11- 110'**
A difficult start gives way to an excellent fingers/off-fingers lieback. *(5)1.0, (7)1.5, (1)2.0, (4)2.5*

24 **Pleased to Meat Ya 5.12- 70'**
A thin left-facing corner in featured rock. *0.4–0.75*

Second Meat Wall 3

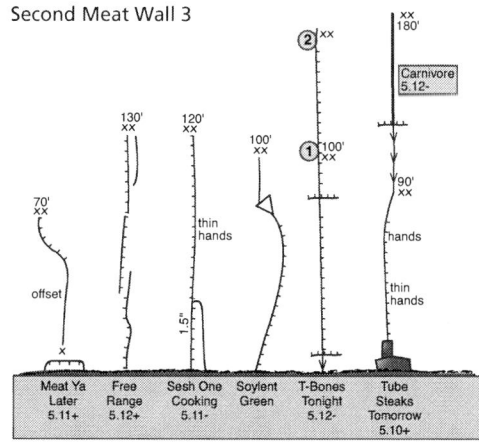

143

Second Meat Wall

<u>25</u> **Humble Pie (a.k.a. Raw) 5.12+ 80'**
Very thin.

<u>26</u> **The Butcher's Dog 5.11- 150'**
A long, varied, broken left-facing corner. Watch your ropes when rapping.

<u>27</u> **Meat Your Maker 5.12 80'**

<u>28</u> **Unknown ? 70'**
A left-facing corner goes to thin hands in a straight-in corner and finishes with twin cracks to a one-bolt anchor.

<u>29</u> **Camping Under The Influence 5.12- 95'**
Start in a flare on the right side of a pillar, make a crack switch, then up a right-slanting off-fingers crack. Desperate just before the anchor. (4)0.75, (4)1.0, (5)1.5, (2)2.0, (2)2.5, (1)3.0

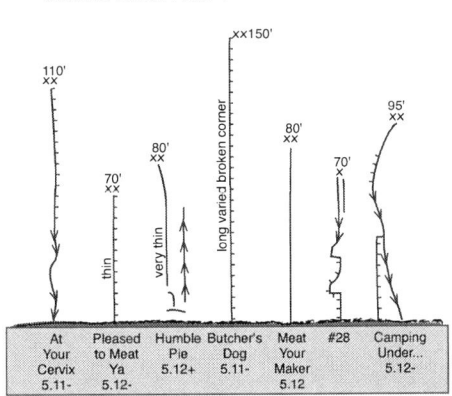

Second Meat Wall 4

Justin Cassels on **Camping Under the Influence 5.12-**   Photograph by Eric Draper

Second Meat Wall

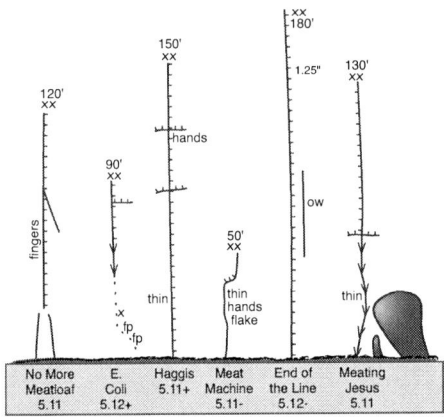

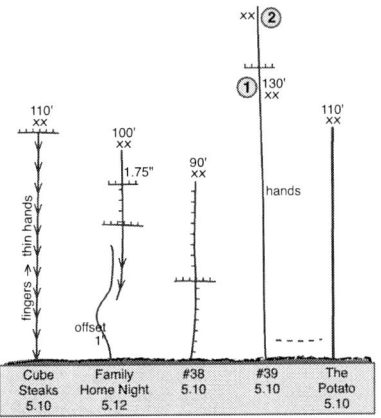

__30__ **No More Meatloaf
(a.k.a. Meatloaf in the Moonlite) 5.11 120'**
Fingers in a left-facing corner.

__31__ **E. Coli 5.12+ 90'**
Face climbing to steep fingers. Look for two fixed pins and a bolt.

__32__ **Haggis 5.11+ 150'**
Thin start in a left-facing corner, then out two roofs.

__33__ **Meat Machine 5.11- 50'**
A thin-hands flake to a tricky roof. 1.5–3.0

__34__ **End of the Line 5.12- 180'**
Off-fingers laybacking forever! (8)1.0, (8)1.5, (4)0.75 (1) each #3.0–#4.0 Camalots

__35__ **Meating Jesus 5.11 130'**
Start left of a very large boulder. A thin straight-in corner out a roof and up a right-facing corner.

__36__ **Cube Steaks 5.10 110'**
Fingers and thin hands in a straight-in corner. (2)0.75, (2)1.0, (6)1.5, (1)2.5

__37__ **Family Home Night 5.12 100'**
An off-fingers and thin-hands testpiece with some face climbing thrown in. Small nuts, (1)0.33, (1)0.4, (2)0.75, (6)1.0, (5)1.5, (4)2.0

__38__ **Unnamed 5.10 90'**
Off-fingers in a left-facing corner through a small roof and up a right-facing corner. (1)0.75, (1)1.5, (3)2.0, (3)2.5, (1)3.0

__39__ **Unnamed 5.10/5.11+ 130'**
Pitch 1: Splitter 5.10 crack. (1)0.75, (2)1.0, (2)2.0, (3)2.5, (1)3.5

Pitch 2: A sandy finger-stack roof to another splitter crack.

__40__ **The Potato 5.10 110'**
This offwidth is on the far right of the cliff.

Tenderloins

Tenderloins

Tenderloins Wall

This may be the smallest of the Meat Walls, but its lack of size is more than made up for by the quality of the routes. The cliff is set back from its neighbors; Original Meat on the left, and Second Meat on the right.

1 **Unnamed 5.11+ 90'**
Twin finger splitters to a right-facing thin-hands corner. There is a leaning pillar to the right and a juniper to the left of the start. *0.4–3.0*

2 **Unnamed 5.11+ 90'**
Climb a slot to an offset fingers splitter. *0.5–2.0*

3 **Unnamed 5.11+ 95'**
A splitter with two roofs, fingers to arching fists. *(1) each 0.75–3.0, (2)3.5, (3)4.0, (1) #4 Camalot*

4 **Hot Lunch 5.11 165'**
Start left of a bombay in a left-facing corner to a thin-hands and finger splitter. *0.5–2.5*

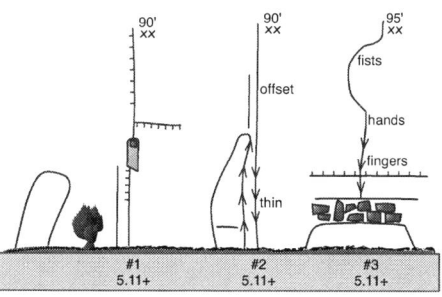

Tenderloins 1

Tenderloins

Tenderloins 2

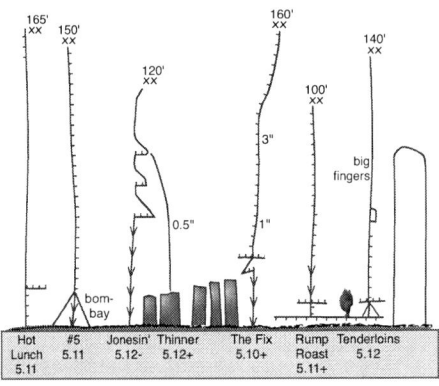

Tenderloins 3

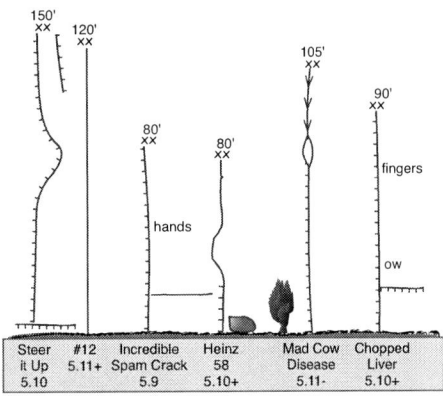

_5_ **Unnamed 5.11 150'**
A difficult bombay start to hands in a left-facing corner. *(1)0.4, (3)1.0, (3)2.0, (4)3.0, (1)3.5, (1)4.0*

_6_ **Jonesin' 5.12- 120'**
Make sure you've built up your endurance before trying this ultra-sustained corner, or you'll be jonesin'. *(2)0.4, (2)0.5, (10)0.75, (8)1.0, (3)1.5, (1) each 2.0–3.5*

_7_ **Thinner 5.12+ 120'**
The thinner direct start to **Jonesin'**. *Extra 0.5s*

_8_ **The Fix**
(a.k.a. The Slaughter House) 5.10+ 160'
Start in a small flare and climb over a small roof. Then fingers to hands in a long corner. Kind of a sandbag. *(2)0.75, (4)1.0, (2)1.5, (2)2.0, (3)2.5, (4)3.0, (1)3.5*

_9_ **Rump Roast 5.11+ 100'**
Start on a ledge, left of a pinyon. Off-fingers in a sustained right-facing corner. *(4)0.75, (2)1.0, (6)1.5, (3)2.0, (1)2.5*

_10_ **Tenderloins 5.12 140'**
A gorgeous off-fingers splitter on excellent rock. *(2)0.75, (6)1.0, (6)1.5, (2)2.0*

_11_ **Steer it Up 5.10 150'**
A long right-facing corner. *(2)1.0, (3)1.5, (1)2.0, (2)2.5, (6)3.0, (6)3.5, (3)4.0, (1) #4 Camalot, extra slings*

_12_ **Unnamed 5.11+ 120'**
Varied splitter, mostly thin hands.

_13_ **Incredible Spam Crack 5.9 80'**
Hands in a clean right-facing corner. *(3)2.5, (5)3.0, (1)3.5, (1)4.0*

_14_ **Heinz 58 5.10+ 80'**
Start in a right-facing corner and climb this cool flared fingers splitter.

_15_ **Mad Cow Disease 5.11- 105'**
Hands to wide hands in a right-facing corner; thin, cruxy finish. *(1)0.5, (2)1.0, (2)1.5, (2)2.0, (3)2.5, (4)3.0, (2)3.5, (1)4.0, (1) #4 Camalot*

_16_ **Chopped Liver 5.10+ 90'**
Offwidth to fingers in a right-facing corner.

Original Meat Wall

Original Meat Wall

Original Meat Wall

The wall for people who think that #3.5 Friends are perfect hands. Same parking as Tenderloins, but a separate trail. A good amount of afternoon shade at this crag. It is possible to combine two walls in a day (Sacred Cow and Original Meat) by walking along the base of the cliff.

1 Unknown ? 140'
Big hands in a changing corner and through a roof. Starts above broken pillars.

2 Unknown ? 100'
Wavy left-angling thin-hands splitter above some broken ledges. A few hundred feet left of #3.

3 Unknown ? 80'
A thin left-facing corner.

4 The Streets of Delhi 5.11+ 150'
Straight-in corner to a squeeze and into a long right-facing corner. 0.75–4.0

Original Meat Wall

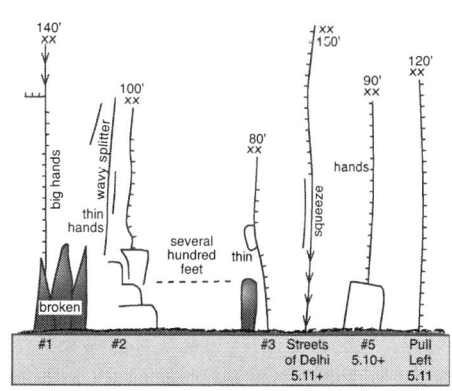

Original Meat Wall

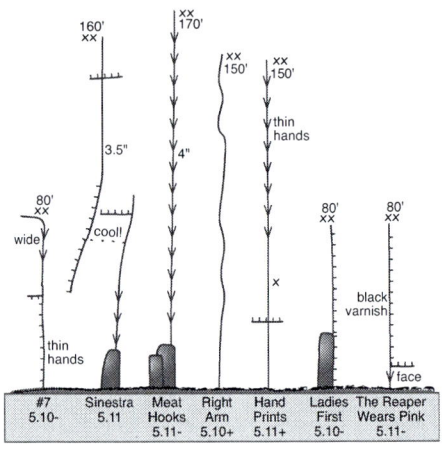

Original Meat Wall 2

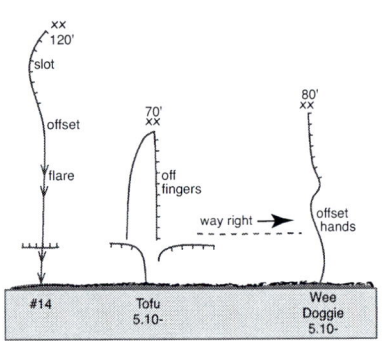

Original Meat Wall 3

__5__ **Unnamed 5.10+ 90'**
Hands in a left-facing corner. Start above a small pillar. *(2)2.0, (5)2.5, (2)3.0, (2)3.5*

__6__ **Pull Left 5.11 120'**
Left-facing corner with a fixed piton.

__7__ **Unnamed 5.10- 80'**
Thin hands to offwidth.

__8__ **Sinestra 5.11 160'**
Funky hands to an outrageous traverse, then a big-hands splitter and a roof. Quality all the way. *(1)2.0, (3)2.5, (6)3.0, (6)3.5, (2)4.0, extra slings*

__9__ **Meat Hooks 5.11- 170'**
Unless your hands are the size of meat hooks, this beautiful corner is pretty brutal! *(1)2.5, (9)3.5, (5)4.0, (2) #4 Camalot*

__10__ **Right Arm 5.10+ 150'**
A great and varied offset splitter. *(1)1.0, (2)1.5, (3)2.0, (6)2.5, (3)3.0, (3)3.5, (1)4.0*

__11__ **Hand Prints 5.11+ 150'**
Climb past a small roof, pass a bolt and finish with quality thin hands. *(1)0.4, (1)0.5, (3)1.0, (4)1.5, (6)2.0, (1)2.5, (2)3.0, (1) #4 Camalot*

__12__ **Ladies First 5.10- 80'**
A straight-in fingers corner. *(1)0.4, (1)0.5, (2) each 0.75–3.0*

__13__ **The Reaper Wears Pink 5.11- 80'**
Varnished layback in a left-facing corner. *Nuts, (2) each 1.0–3.5*

__14__ **Unknown ? 120'**
Flare to offset flake with a squeeze at the top.

__15__ **Tofu 5.10- 70'**
Off-fingers layback in a left-facing corner.

__16__ **Wee Doggie 5.10- 80'**
A mostly hands splitter to a left-facing corner. This is a long walk to the right. *(1)1.0, (1)1.5, (1)2.0, (3)2.5, (2)3.0, (1)3.5*

Sacred Cow

Sacred Cow   Original Meat Wall

Sacred Cow
A stellar wall with something for everyone, and lots of morning shade. Turn right on the Meat Walls road, but at the first fork in the road turn left, and drive until the road ends. Hike up and left to meet the trail.

__1__ **Unknown ? 120'**
Varied corner.

__2__ **The Milk Box 5.12- 60'**
Stem wildly, pull a roof, and finish with fingertips in a corner. *Medium nuts, (1)0.5, (3)0.75, (4)1.0*

__3__ **Sacred Cow 5.12 160'**
Thin hands in a corner, pull a roof, rest. Charge up the unrelenting finger-stacking splitter. May feel harder if your hands are not pretty small. *(1)1.0, (5)1.5 (green Camalots work best), (8)2.0, (1)2.5, (1)3.0*

__4__ **Twin Cam 5.12 160'**
Sacred Cow's twin brother. *(3)0.75, (2)1.0, (10)1.5, (6)2.0*

Sacred Cow   Tenderloins   Second Meat Wall

Sacred Cow

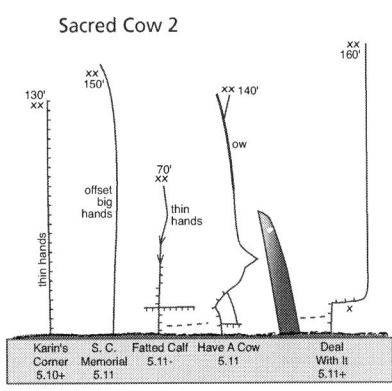

__5__ **Vegetarian Corner 5.10+ 100'**
A nicely varied meat alternative. *(3)2.0, (4)2.5, (3)3.0, (2)3.5, (2)4.0, (1) #4 Camalot*

__6__ **Sample the Sausage 5.11- 110'**
Cool stemming and varied jamming. *(1)0.4, (4)0.5, (1)0.75, (3)1.0, (2) each 1.5–2.5, (2)3.0, (2)3.5, (1) #4 Camalot*

__7__ **Signe Du Taureau 5.12+ 100'**
A recent Stevie Haston contribution. Start in a right-facing dihedral, make hard face moves right to gain a very steep widening splitter. *Lowe Balls, small Aliens, wires, (4)1.0, (4)1.5*

__8__ **Cowch Potato 5.11- 70'**
Splitter hands to a difficult flake. *(1)1.0, (3) each 1.5–3.0*

__9__ **Karin's Corner 5.10+ 130'**
Beautiful thin-hands corner, really hard for the grade! *(1)0.75, (2)1.0, (5)1.5, (7)2.0, (1)2.5, (1)3.5*

__10__ **Steve Carruthers Memorial (a.k.a S.C. Memorial) 5.11 150'**
Never-ending cupped-hands splitter. *(2)2.5, (5)3.0, (9)3.5*

__11__ **Fatted Calf 5.11- 70'**
Excellent thin-hands splitter. The **Scarface** of Sacred Cow. Harder for big hands. *(3)1.5, (4)2.0, (4)2.5*

__12__ **Have A Cow 5.11 140'**
A zigzagging thin-hands to fingers splitter, that widens to splitter offwidth. *1.5–5.0*

__13__ **Deal With It 5.11+ 160'**
Start in a very thin right-facing corner and stem past a bolt (a little sporty) and under a roof, to reach this very long fingers to cupped-hands splitter. *0.4–4.0*

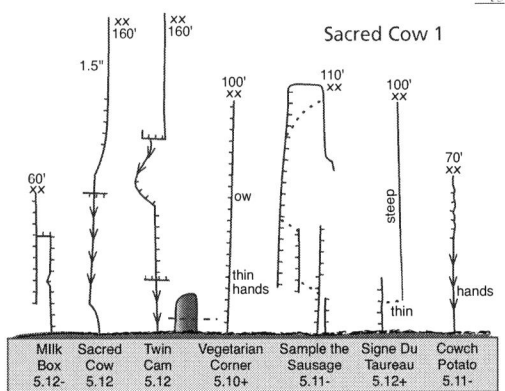

Stevie Haston on **Steve Carruthers Memorial** 5.11 Photograph by Laurence Gouault

Micah Dash

Pain for Pleasure

My internship in the climbing world began in the red desert of Indian Creek. A passionate apprentice I would spend day upon endless day climbing. Compelled by the stunning lines shooting like the contrails of rockets, I would climb until I had nothing left.

David, Heavy Duty, and Keith were my Indian Creek mentors. They were adamant that taping was merely a form of cheating, not quite aid climbing, but not good style. Thus, over the years I have managed to leave a little piece of myself at nearly every crag in The Creek. Like a monkey possessed I would climb until my hands and fingers would be mere appendages, tender, swollen and oozing, a physical example of my madness and obsession. Each piece of skin, each drop of blood, has been rubbed into the Wingate sandstone and left as a modern day pictograph.

Together the four of us spent endless days walking the cliffs, looking for first ascents, and plaques at the base of old routes to add to Dave's guidebook. Heavy searched for his nemesis, two-inch cracks. Dave and I sought splitter one-inch finger cracks, the sort that could only be found in the desert of Indian Creek. After finding the line that inspired me the most or that scared me worst, I would rack up slowly, with butterflies running through my belly. At the base, staring at my small hands I knew that I would only have one attempt. Any more would surely result in a severe lose of skin and blood. I wouldn't dare ask my partners for tape knowing that they would deem me "light duty." Wounds from the days and weeks before were still oozing and tender. Thoughts of cramming them into a crack seemed sadistic. The first few jams would hurt, but once on lead the endorphins would kick in and the pain would be exchanged for power.

At the end of the day we would retire, running down the steep talus cone to camp below Bridger Jack Butte. There inside my 1978 Toyota Winnebago I would sit with my friends and share the day's adventures, each of us comparing our new open battle wounds. Alan and I would prepare dinner for a crew of our hungry, weary, tired friends. Heavy would ask me to slice up a collection of onions and limes. Cutting the acidic fruits and vegetables into fine pieces would burn the exposed tissue of my hands and fingers. I would be forced to stop with my chores for a moment as the pain would occasionally spike. At night I would lay with my hands above my head, suspended in the air so that in my dreams I wouldn't be awakened by the uncomfortable task of peeling the open tender tissue from my pillow.

Photograph of Micah Dash by John Dickey

Cliffs of Insanity

Cliffs of Insanity   Photograph by Richard Durnan

The Cliffs of Insanity

The most extreme crag at The Creek. It takes a bit more effort to get motivated to climb at this insane cliff—but you will be rewarded. The cliff has a very obvious prow which significantly dictates climbing conditions. To the right are the mega-classic **Wiggins I** and **Wiggins II**, long splitters of incomparable beauty. This is the sunny side of the cliff and is best visited on a clear winter day. To the left of the prow are several splitter testpieces that are best done on those days when you just have to climb in the shade. Whichever side you choose be prepared for a 45-minute uphill slog.

Drive 1.3 miles past the Meat Wall turn-off. Turn right on a gated dirt road, and drive 1.2 miles on dirt to a small primitive parking spot. Head up to the west face. An alternate approach, if you are planning on mainly climbing on the right side, is to park as for Sacred Cow and walk up and left to the Wiggins area. Either way it's a hump.

Cliffs of Insanity

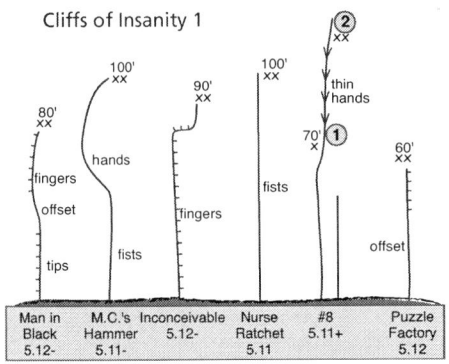

The first three routes are on the far left of the wall. Not shown on topo.

1 Unnamed 5.10+ 130'
Awesome splitter hand crack, which goes over a small roof near the top. This is a five-minute walk left from **Man in Black**.

2 Unknown ? 2 pitches
First pitch is a chossy offwidth by a pillar. The second looks like a hand crack. Hidden anchors.

3 Unknown ? ?'
Straight-in fingers to hands to fists.

4 Man in Black 5.12- 80'
Right-facing offset tips to fingers.

5 M.C.'s Hammer 5.11- 100'
A proud fist to off-fingers splitter. *0.75–5.0*

6 Inconceivable 5.12- 90'
Sustained fingers in a left-facing corner to a small roof. *Mostly 1.0 and 1.5*

7 Nurse Ratchet 5.11 100'
Offset fists.

**8 Unnamed 5.11/5.11+
2 pitches**
Pitch 1: Climb past thin broken cracks with some face moves (70', 5.11).

Pitch 2: Really tight hands splitter through a sandy bulge (5.11+, *0.5–3.5*).

9 Puzzle Factory 5.12 60'
A Scott Carson classic. Offset off-fingers splitter. *(2)1.0, (8)1.5, (1)3.5, (1)4.0*

10 Mini Cave 5.11 45'
Short cave crack in a right-facing dihedral. Not shown on topo. *(3)1.5*

11 Prepare to Die 5.10 60'
This is some distance to the right of **Puzzle Factory**. *(1)1.0, (1)1.5, (3)2.0, (1)2.5, (1)3.0, (1)3.5*

12 Unknown ? 140'
Long left-facing corner; thin down low past a fixed piece, and with a slot up high.

13 Unnamed 5.10 120'
Long right-facing corner, thin hands down low.

14 Unnamed 5.11 100'
This north-facing splitter starts down and right, up a ramp. Steep hands to a difficult pod. *(3)0.75, (4)1.0, (4)1.5, (3)2.0, (3)2.5*

Tommy Caldwell on **Puzzle Factory** 5.12 Photograph by Topher Donahue

Cliffs of Insanity

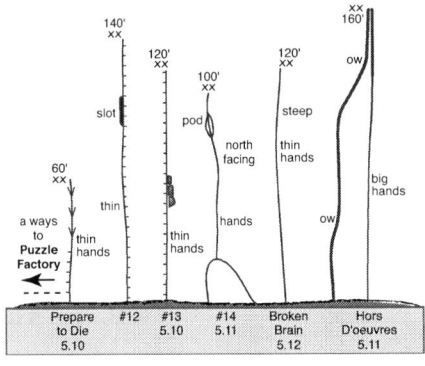
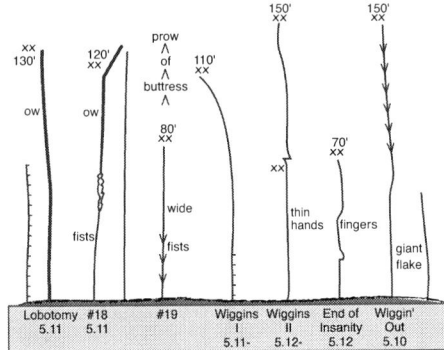

15 **Broken Brain 5.12 120'**
This mind-blowing thin-hands splitter was made famous by a poster of a young Tommy Caldwell taking a monstrous whipper. *(1)1.0, (3)1.5, (6)2.0, (6)2.5, (1)3.0, bolt*

16 **Hors D'oeuvres 5.11 160'**
Excellent thin-hands splitter to a wide crack in a featured flake. A wee bit scary. *(1)1.5, (2)2.0, (3)2.5, (4)3.0, (5)3.5, (1)4.0, (1) each #4, #4.5, #5 Camalot*

17 **Lobotomy 5.11 130'**
Stunning offwidth.

18 **Unnamed 5.11 120'**
Fists in a flare, to offwidth splitter.

19 **Unknown ? 80'**
Fists in a flare to offset offwidth on prow of Cliffs of Insanity.

20 **Wiggins I 5.11- 110'**
Either a dream climb or a nightmare, depending on your hand size. Hands to off-fist splitter forever. Earl was "The Man." *(2)3.5, (4)4.0, (4) #4 Camalots*

21 **Wiggin II 5.12- 150'**
Splitter thin hands narrowing to tips. Intermediate fairy rap station. Although attributed to Wiggins, this enduro crack was first climbed by Leonard "The Egg with Legs" Coyne. *(2)0.5, (1)0.75, (3)1.0, (5)1.5, (5)2.0, (4)2.5, (1)3.0*

22 **End of Insanity 5.12 70'**
Fingers splitter. *0.4–2.0, heavy on the 1.0*

23 **Wiggin' Out 5.10 150'**
Giant flare to corner. *3.5–7.0 with (5) #4 Camalots*

The next climb is some distance to the right.

24 **Calling All Units 5.11- ?'**
This is the only known climb on the wall to the right of Cliffs of Insanity (and left of Sacred Cow).

Craig Luebben on **Wiggins** I 5.11- Photograph by Topher Donahue

Back Wall and 75 Cairns Wall

The Back Wall

The Back Wall and 75 Cairns Wall

The Back Wall is located behind the Cliffs of Insanity and houses a few relatively unvisited routes, which are not described here. Seventy-Five Cairns Wall is located around the corner to the left on a prominent buttress. Approach by hiking past the Cliffs of Insanity, or as for The Wall (see facing page). All the routes described here are on 75 Cairns Wall.

75 Cairns Wall

1 **Dangling Chad ? ?'**
Tight-hands flake.

2 **Unknown ? ?'**
Right-facing dihedral.

3 **Unknown ? ?'**
Flake.

4 **Unknown ? ?'**
Big-hands slot.

5 **Imagine ? ?'**
Seam to fingers.

6 **Unknown ? ?'**
Hands.

7 **In and Out 5.10 ?'**
Left-facing dihedral.

8 **Unknown ? ?'**
Right-facing dihedral. Hands and fingers.

9 **Chota Boy ? ?'**
Splitter.

10 **Unknown ? ?'**
Left-facing corner. Fingers.

11 **Pistol ? ?'**
Splitter hands to left-facing tight-hands dihedral. Two pitches.

12 **Unknown ? ?'**
Fingers and hands.

13 **Unknown ? ?'**
Right-facing dihedral. Fists and hands.

14 **Unknown ? ?'**
Right-facing dihedral. Thin to off-fingers. *Heavy on the 2.0*

The Wall

The Wall

The Wall

The Wall is a pretty new development at Indian Creek, and is located left of 75 Cairns Wall. Drive 13.5 miles from Newspaper Rock to a right turn off the main road. Be sure to close any gates after you. Go one tenth of a mile to a left turn. Go 1.6 miles to a right turn on a road cutting across a field towards the obvious forming arch. Park as you start to go uphill, just before the mine. From here the trail goes directly left to right and dumps you out on the left side of the photo above, a little ways left of **The Trial** (look for cairns).

__1 **The Trial 5.10 80'**
Right-facing dihedral with a bulge. (2) 0.5, (1) 1.0, (1) 1.5, (1) 2.0, (2) 2.5, (1) 3.0

__2 **Run Like Hell 5.10 85'**
Splitter. (1) 2.0, (3) 2.5, (3)3.5, (1) 4.0

__3 **Goodbye Cruel World 5.12- 60'**
Left-facing dihedral. (2) #1 TCU, (6) #0.4 Camalots, (3) #3 TCU, (1) #4.5 Camalot

__4 **Comfortably Numb 5.10 160'**
Hands in a left-facing dihedral. (1)1.0, (1)2.5, (3)3.0, (3)3.5, (2) #3.5 Camalots, (1) #4.5 Camalot

__5 **Pigs on the Wing 5.11 90'**
Splitter with a crack switch. TCUs, (1)1.0, (2)1.5, (4)2.0, (4)2.5, (2)3.0

__6 **Brain Damage 5.10+ 110'**
Switching corners. (2)1.0, (3)1.5, (7)2.0, (1)2.5, (1)3.0, (1)3.5, (1) #4.5 Camalot

Suburbia

Suburbia
This cliff is located rather left of The Wall. Expect a pretty long hike. Not much information is known about this area. We hope to update this page as new information is available. No topo.

There has been some recent development on the cliffs beyond Suburbia. Collectively this area is known as New Suburbia. Beyond this, the cliffs bend around into Hart's Draw. Hart's Draw is the next canyon system north of Indian Creek, with just a few established routes. Access is difficult, mostly from various dirt roads on the mesa-tops northeast of Indian Creek. Happy exploring!

__1 **Unknown ? ?'**
A chimney, with an anchor.

__2 **Killer 5.12- 140'**
(4)0.75, (6)1.0, (9)1.5, (6)2.0, (1)3.5

__3 **Cowboys in Control 5.10 140'**
1.0–3.0

__4 **Manifest Destiny 5.10 80'**
A right-facing dihedral. (1) each #2.5 Friend, #3 & #4.5 Camalot, (2) each #1, #3.5, #4 Camalots

__5 **Despo 5.12+ 100'**
A flake. (1)0.4, (2)1.5, (2)2.0, (1)3.0, (2)3.5, (2)4.0

__6 **Nomadic Alternative 5.9 50'**
2.5–3.0

The last climb is around the corner to the right.

__7 **Long Way From Suburbia 5.10 50'**
2.5–3.0

Sharp End Publishing
Authentic Guides From Core Climbers

www.SharpEndBooks.com

.FREE Vacation Planner
.Guide Book Previews
.Monthly Specials

Right: Colorado Bouldering 2

5 Six Shooters and Bridger Jack Area

Achey on the first ascent of Learning to Crawl (5.11) on Thumbelina. Photograph by Ed Webster

Timmy O'Neill

Sacred Party

Alan rang me out of the blue. His message was emphatic, garbled, until Justin grabbed the phone, "…bring you, Glory, some of those organic Boulderite turkeys and get your asses to the Creek for the 4th annual fest…beep." The machine cut Justin off as Alan's frantic voice, rising an octave, shouted not to worry about the hormones and drugs in the turkeys, as he had plenty. Excited curiosity and the opportunity to gather together with the tribe in the crisp, sage-scented autumn desert had us packing and on our way in a few hours. The mexi-shaggin' wagon puttered up the Continental Divide, the crux section of the approach to the Creek, and with no heat and sleeping bags stuffed around our feet, the turkeys arrived frozen stiffer than Walt Disney's head.

Thanksgiving, the annual bloating of the belly, is typically celebrated in the radiant warmth of the family home with the extended clan seated around a blessed table. That is, unless you celebrate Turkey Day with a gaggle of blissed out, desert dirt bags and their sand-caked dogs, all baying in unison under a star filled night to the spittle filled exclamations of a tweaking expatriate Brit. It's the day to express gratitude for the climber's good fortune: sunshine, stone, friendship, respiration, and for some, pale ale and kind nugs. Welcome to Indian Creek on a special "Climbing Family" holiday for a heartfelt sacred party.

The fun and games had already commenced when we pulled in. As we drove down the undulating, berm-lined Beef Basin road, we could see a silhouetted figure walking a taut line of one-inch webbing, five hundred feet up, between the Kings of Pain. Pure pleasure came to mind. Other figures on the landscape were perched atop Easter Island's nub of a summit; a dust devil rose from the footsteps of a party descending the Bridger Jack's super-chunk talus cone. Before we could race off to the nearest escarpment of Wingate we had to locate Heavy Duty's beached trailer and check in with our unassuming Master of Ceremonies. We found him in the midst of preparing his yearly banquet for sixty of his closest friends: elbow deep in a bucket of stuffing, a percolating vat of primo onion soup, a virtual garden of fresh salad, all fixed by hand, a pair of unwashed, scab covered hands at that. If Mr. Duty, the epitome of kinetic energy, could attain the alchemist's art of turning his spastic intensity into gold he'd be a walking Fort Knox.

Several desert denizens tended to a twelve pack under the auspices of stoking the fire. They were amassing the coals required to fill an earthen oven holding four plump foil-covered gobblers. Most dinner guests have never cooked in the ground, usually reserving the terra firma for the baking of post-digestive loaves but Alan is a maverick chef, not one to be satisfied within the confines of the status quo kitchen. As he finished mincing turkey gizzards, we listened to his Cockney accented ramblings of the latest ticks of desert test pieces, peppered with techno sound bites and obscene lines from Eminem. His fingers, covered with bird bits, pointed towards a truck hood festooned with a dozen homemade fruit pies. He assuredly pledged that, "this is going to be the most awesome party The Creek has ever seen."

Photograph of Timmy O'Neill by John Dickey

164

Heavy Duty (with turkey) and Keith Reynolds prepare for the festivities.
Photograph by John Dickey

The sun slowly dropped behind a ribbon of accordion cracked sandstone buttresses. The sky changed from blue, to orange red, to gunmetal gray, eventually painting itself black. It was time to kickoff our Dionysian soiree. As the final stragglers returned from a satisfied thrashing on the world's finest sandy splitters, the last of the headlights rolled in from Moab.

Alan inaugurated the dinner with a sincere blessing of the food and all those present, "Enjoy it my friends and may we gather together until we are old and gray." Someone teasingly shouted, "...too late, you're already old and gray." A chop licking chow line assembled alongside a cornucopia of outrageously tasty food arranged atop the desert sands. Laughter and the smacking of ravenous lips accompanied the gangster rhythms of Tu Pac. More wood was thrown on the fire including a massive tree trunk hefted overhead by Keith, the crowned "Strongest Man of Indian Creek", which sent a swarm of firefly-like coals into the night. The flames checked the evening chill and danced across the animated faces of people simply alive in the glorious moment.

Eventually the marauding dogs were free to pick through the carcasses, growling their delight. A harvest medley of fresh fruit pie was carted through the crowd and sweet-tooth inspired hands snatched it from the splintered plywood tray. Melted ice cream dripped down fingers, smeared onto ember-pocked fleece. Justin increased the decibel on the trance music and "Heavy's" eyes rolled into the back of his lolling head as he began to gyrate. The assembled climbing riff-raff followed his lead and evoked the primal magic of this place—hands held aloft towards the opalescent moon, legs rooted deeply like the sturdy cottonwood, and eyes opened wide peering into the wild, ancient landscape. Alan's words echoed through the night, "We might as well dance hard, as we've only one life to live, right Timmy?" The camaraderie and vitality of this sacred party will course through our veins until our next desert reunion.

Timmy O'Neill (on the bass drum), Michael Vladeck, and a complete stranger have an improvisational jam session.
Photograph by John Dickey

North Six Shooter Peak

Area Overview
North Six Shooter to Optimator Wall

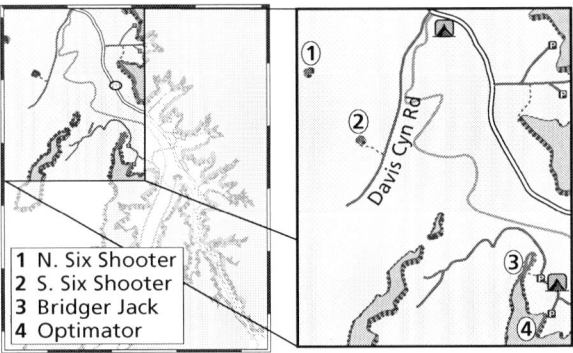

1 N. Six Shooter
2 S. Six Shooter
3 Bridger Jack
4 Optimator

North Six Shooter Peak

The southeast face of this classic desert spire is host to two of the desert's best tower routes, **Lightning Bolt Cracks** and **Liquid Sky**. The west face is home to a couple of really old, really wide classics. The peak is visible to the west about 12 miles past Newspaper Rock on Highway 211.

Turn left on Davis Canyon Road and drive as close as you can without destroying any vegetation. An alternate approach is to turn left on the next road after Davis Canyon Road. Allow 1–1.5 hours for the approach.

North Six Shooter south face   Photograph by Steve "Crusher" Bartlett

1 Lightning Bolt Cracks 5.11-

3 or 4 pitches

Pitch 1: Climb the right of the two obvious splitters on the southeast face. The fingers start is the technical crux of the route (5.11-). After a wide move traverse left to a sloping belay.

Pitch 2: Slightly right of the belay, climb fingers to fists through a small roof (5.10).

Pitch 3: Work left to an overhanging bombay corner (hands in the back), and turn the roof (5.10). One may belay here, or with good use of long runners, continue up the unprotected squeeze chimney to the summit.

Rappel off the west face with one 70-meter rope or two 50-meter ropes. One 60-meter rope will get you within 10 feet of a ledge, and a slightly sketchy downclimb.

Nuts, (1)0.4, (2) each 1.0–3.0, (3)3.5, (1) each #4 and #4.5 Camalot

2 Liquid Sky 5.11+ 3 pitches

Lightning Bolt's evil twin brother. The mother of all squeeze chimneys. The crux third pitch has one tunneling through an offwidth roof 200 feet off the deck. Much harder for rotund torsos.

Pitch 1: Climb the splitter finger crack to the left of **Lightning Bolt**'s first pitch (5.11).

Pitch 2: Climb a wide slot straight up from the belay (5.9).

Pitch 3: Move right and climb a left-facing offwidth corner (#5 Camalots) to the obvious roof. This is as far as many people get. If you are not afraid squeeze up inside the roof and find the path of least resistance to emerge well above the roof. Regular chimneying will see you to the top (5.11 squeeze).

The following two routes are on the west face of North Six Shooter Peak.

3 Shadows Route (a.k.a. Lightning Bolt Crack's Analog) 5.10+ 2 pitches

Pitch 1: Climb the analog crack; traverse left under a roof, up a block, left again and up a chimney. This is known as the "Road Warriors in Action Pitch."

Pitch 2: Climb the long squeeze chimney, passing several bolts. This is the "Sleeping Bag Simulator Pitch."

2.0–4.0 and offwidth gear

4 Pratt-Robinson 5.10-, A0 2 pitches

Pitch 1: The long offwidth to the right of the **Shadows** route (5.10-).

Pitch 2: Some free climbing and some aid past fixed protection to the summit (5.7, A0).

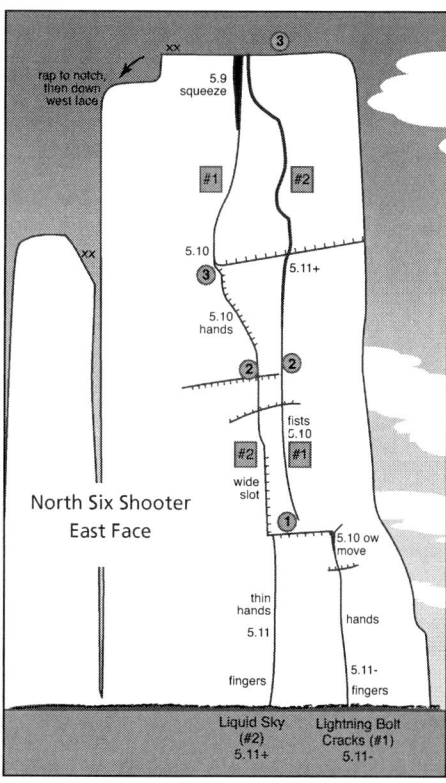

North Six Shooter East Face

South Six Shooter Peak

Not quite as impressive as its big brother to the north, this peak offers a half-dozen fun moderate climbs in the 5.7–5.10 range. All are 1–3 pitches in length.

Approach from the Davis Canyon Road. Hike up the talus from its southeastern-most point, close to where the road skirts the base (only high clearance vehicles will get this far). Look for cairns, and a faint trail. The trail wanders through the lowest rock bands, winds round to the left at the flat area, then (more cairns) heads straight up the south side of the formation.

✓1 South Face 5.7 3 pitches

This popular route begins on the far left side of the south face. The route summits the left of the two highest pillars. Rope up just where the ground dives down and left.

Pitch 1: Angle up and left on easy ledges into a shallow alcove (there is a petroglyph high up on the left wall) and continue up a short 5.5 chimney to a ledge.

Pitch 2: Head through a notch behind a pillar, and traverse thirty feet to the final pitch (which ascends an obvious dihedral with a bolt). You can do this traverse high (easier), or take a lower line and climb a short but quality left-facing 5.7 layback crack, to gain the same belay ledge. There is a set of rap slings just below this ledge.

Pitch 3: Cruise to the poorly-protected crux mantel. Once above this, clip a bolt and finish on steep jugs. (2) *each 1.0–3.0*

South and North Six Shooter Peaks   Photograph by Richard Durnan

Var. The right summit is a little harder. Climb an unprotectable 5.8 flake/rib on the left side of the south face. At the horizontal break, place a cam, and move right (easier) to finish.

Descend with one 60m rope, or two shorter ropes. Rap from the summit to the slings just below the second belay. Rap from here to the ground.

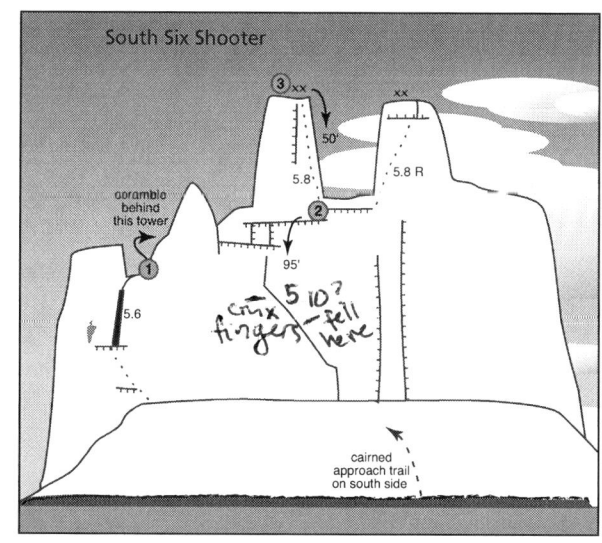

Bridger Jack Mesa

Bridger Jack Mesa

If you get tired of cragging and have the urge to climb a few pitches in a row and actually summit, then check out some of the quality offerings in the Bridger Jack group.

Thumbelina

1 Learning to Crawl 5.11 165'

Located on the leftmost spire (as viewed from the east) known as Thumbelina. A unique bolted arete climb. Can be done as a very long pitch or with a short approach pitch and a belay. *Quickdraws, nuts, 1 set TCUs, (1)2.0, (1)2.5, 6 bolts*

Sparkling Touch

2 Sparkling Touch 5.11- 165' 2 pitches

Pitch 1: Twin cracks, mostly hands, in a long pitch to a belay ledge (5.10-).

Pitch 2: Step across to the summit block and face climb up and right past two old bolts (5.11-) *(2) each 0.75–3.5, (1)4.0, extra runners.*

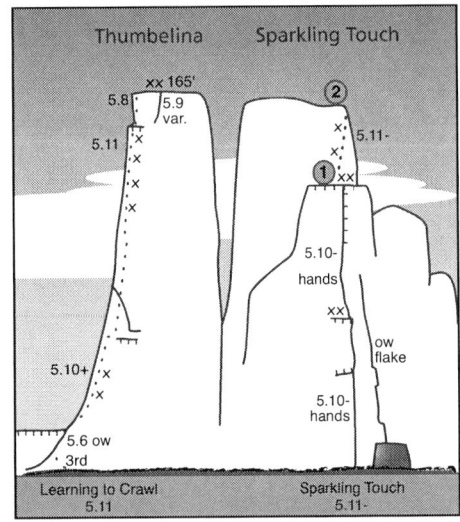

Easter Island
Thunderbolts 5.10 2 pitches
Located on the smallest and last-to-be-climbed spire known as Easter Island.

Pitch 1: Climb a 5.8 wide-hands crack on the east face to a ledge. Step right around a pillar and scramble up and around to a belay on the west face.

Pitch 2: Fun face climbing (5.10) past seven bolts on the west face. Pitch 2 is a little more sustained since the helpful Volkswagen-sized chockstone fell off the start of the pitch on, believe it or not, Easter Sunday 2002.

Var. Pitch 1: Climb splitter fingers to tips in a corner, just right of the standard start (5.11+).

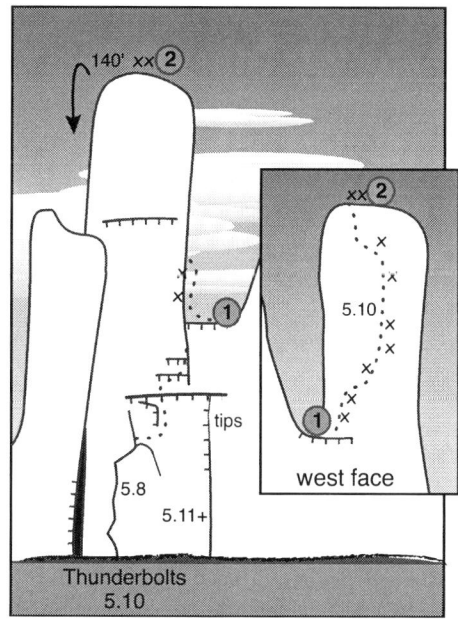

Bridger Jack Mesa

Sunflower Tower

4 East Face 5.10+ 3 pitches

Pitch 1: Awkward hands to a stembox (5.10-, 90').

Pitch 2: Splitter thin hands to fingers in a left-facing corner (5.10+, 90').

Pitch 3: Traverse left onto the west face passing old fixed protection, and then up a loose crack past one more bolt. The bolts on this pitch are ancient Star-Drives and should not be trusted (5.8, 50').

Rap the route with one 60-meter rope. *(1)0.75, (2)1.0, (3)1.5, (2)2.0, (2)2.5, (1)3.0, (1)3.5*

5 The Way of Friends 5.11 3 pitches

Pitch 1: Start with hands in a left-facing corner to the right of the **East Face**. There are offwidths and fixed protection on pitches 2 and 3. Pitch 2 is located on the left side of the Sunflower/Hummingbird notch and the third pitch takes an obvious wide diagonal crack on the east face of the summit block on Sunflower. No topo.

Hummingbird Spire

6 Wild West Show 5.10, A1 4 pitches

Pitch 1: A short slab crack.

Pitches 2 and 3: Follow a long left-facing corner.

Pitch 4: Follow a diagonal crack system that passes drilled pitons (A1), and then head up a corner to the summit of Hummingbird Spire.

7 Hoop Dancer 5.11 2 or 3 pitches

The hallmark of this route is the overhanging hand crack on the north face that takes you to the summit of Hummingbird Spire. There are two ways to start the route. The original line climbs the ugly first pitch of **Sacred Space**.

Var. A better (but much harder) alternative is to climb the clean left-facing corner of **Egg Drop Soup** to the right of **Sacred Space** in 2 pitches. Rappel **Wild West Show**. *Extra 2.0–3.0*

King of Pain

8 Sacred Space 5.11 2 pitches

The only route that gains the south summit. A Jeff Achey classic.

Pitch 1: Climb a broken blocky crack system straight up to the Hummingbird/King of Pain notch (5.9R).

Pitch 2: A steep fist to offwidth splitter on the south face of King of Pain (5.11). This burly pitch receives stunning afternoon light.

Rappel **Wild Flower**. *Mostly 5.0–7.0 on pitch 2*

9 Egg Drop Soup 5.12 80'

This is the beautiful left-facing corner just right of **Sacred Space**. 5.12 off-finger laybacking gains a two-bolt anchor, and 5.10 hands and the notch. The route is a good way of reaching **Hoop Dancer's** or **Sacred Space's** second pitches. *(2)0.5, (3)0.75, (4)1.0, (5)1.5, (3)2.0*

10 Vision Quest 5.10+ 4 pitches

A burly route on the east face of King of Pain.

Pitch 1: Fingers in a right-facing corner to hands and fists up the left side of a large block (5.10).

Pitch 2: Through a slot, then up a classic hands-and-fist corner to a second slot. The first slot is easier and better protected and more fun than it appears, the second is not (5.10).

Pitch 3: A short offwidth to good fists to overhanging hands. Belay in an alcove (5.10+).

Pitch 4: Hands and jugs up the steep groove, to a large ledge. Stem between the summits, and finish on unlikely face moves (5.9+).

Rappel **Wild Flower**. *(1)0.5, (2)0.75, (2)1.0, (1) each 1.5–3.0, (3)3.5, (1) each 4.0, #4 Camalot, #5 Camalot*

11 Ziji 5.12 4 pitches

A Tibetan word for "monumental elegance." Definitely the line to do on Bridger Jack if you're up for it. Starts just uphill and right of **Vision Quest**.

Pitch 1: Hard stemming, face, and groove climbing past two drilled pitons, and up a strenuous flare (5.11).

Pitch 2: Sustained big-fingers splitter and a hard face move past a pin (5.12).

Pitch 3: Tight fingers in a right-facing corner, past a silly drilled piton (5.12-).

Pitch 4: Thin hands in a left-facing corner to an exciting traverse left, and loose face climbing to the summit (5.10).

Rappel **Wild Flower**. *(1)0.4, (2)0.5, (5)0.75, (9)1.0, (3)1.5, (2)2.0, Small nuts. For Pitch 1: (1) #2.5, (1) #4.0, (1) #4.5 Camalot*

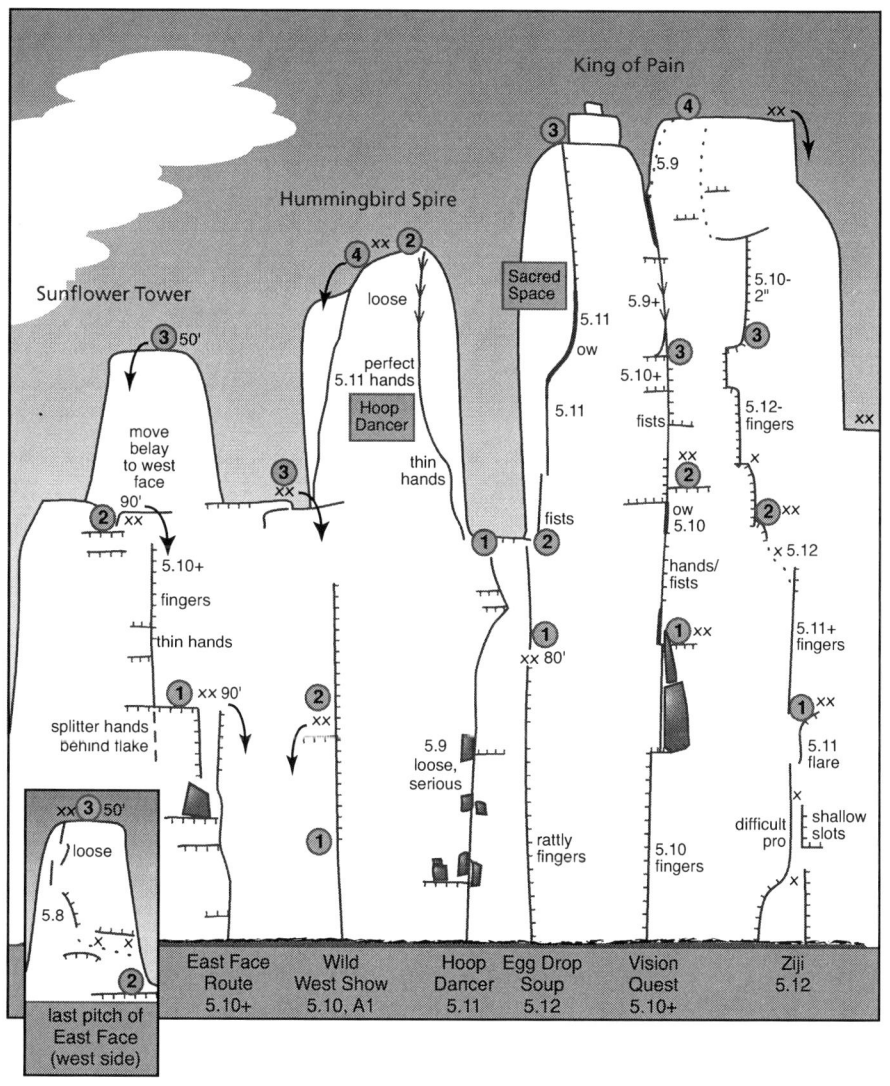

Bridger Jack Mesa

12 Rites of Passage 5.11+ 5 pitches
Climbs the only clean corner system on the west side of King of Pain. A good exercise in off-sizes. Start on the west side of the tower.

Pitch 1: A broken left-facing corner (5.9).

Pitch 2: Up and right past a drilled pin, to 1.5" splitter (5.11+).

Pitch 3: Fist and offwidth to a cave belay. (1)0.5 and (1)2.0 for belay (5.10).

Pitch 4: Climb up to a bolt and out a fist crack in the roof of the cave (5.11+).

Pitch 5: Climb a 5.10 offwidth, face traverse left and up a straight-in corner.

Rappel **Wild Flower**. (2)0.75, (2)1.0, (3)1.5, (3)2.0, (2) each 2.5–3.5, (1)4.0, (2) #4 Camalots

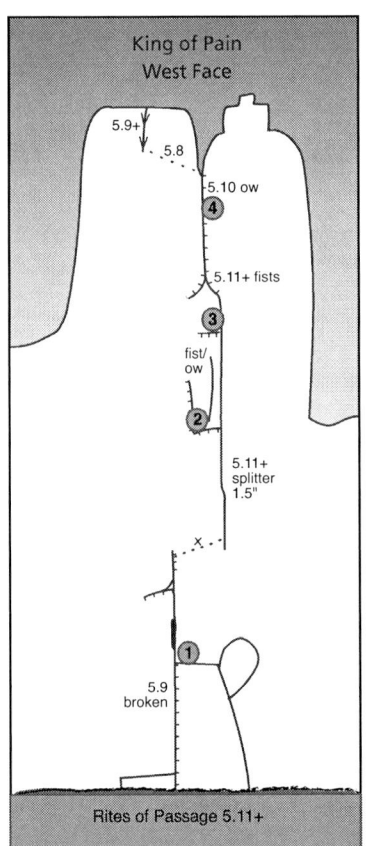

Bridger Jack Butte
13 Wild Flower 5.10 3 pitches
The first route to be climbed on Bridger Jack Mesa. The standard rappel for all Bridger Jack Butte, and King of Pain routes. None of the bolts on the route were placed on the first ascent. Start below the notch separating King of Pain and Bridger Jack Butte.

Pitch 1: A long pitch of lower-angle cracks and corners past one bolt (5.9).

Pitch 2: Hands past one bolt (5.10-).

Pitch 3: Climb the steep flare past two bolts on the south face of Bridger Jack Mesa (5.10 offwidth).

Rappel the route. (1)0.5, (2) each 0.75–3.5, (1) #4.5 Camalot, (2) #5 Camalots

14 Basket Case 5.11- 4 pitches
This route follows a crack system on the right side of a huge (200') pillar that is left of **Powders**...

Pitch 1: A left-facing corner with a drilled piton, to a straight-in corner. Two-bolt belay.

Pitch 2: Continue up the corner to a two-bolt belay.

Pitches 3–4: Up cracks/corner to the summit.

15 Jack in the Box 5.13-(?) 70'
This so-far-unsent project features wild stemming up to a roof, and a merciless finger-stacking splitter. *0.4–1.5, heavy on the 1.0 (0.5 Camalots)*

16 Unnamed 5.12, A1 4 pitches
Several attempts to free this amazing line were made by Seth Shaw before his untimely death in 2000.

Pitch 1: Splitter fingers to a two-bolt belay (5.12?).

Pitch 2: Traverse right to a shallow right-facing corner and up a thin splitter (A1).

Pitch 3: Splitter through several roofs.

Pitch 4: Up cracks to summit.

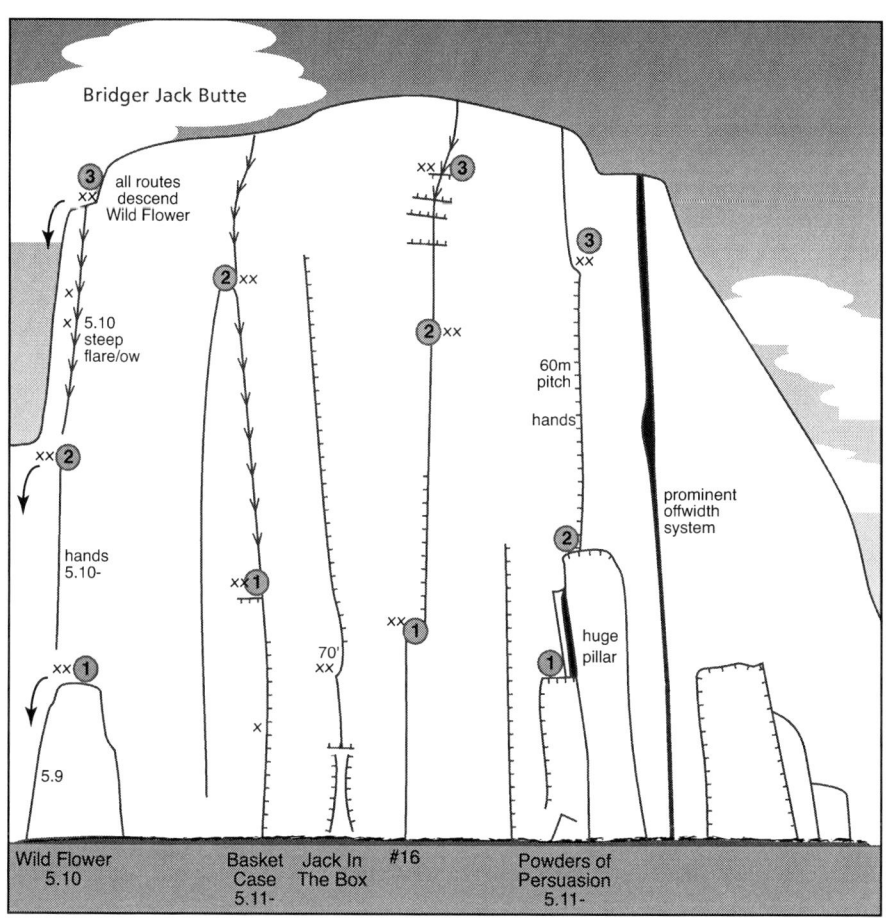

17 **Powders of Persuasion 5.11- 4 pitches**

Pitch 1: Climb a crack left of a cave, belay in chimney (5.9).

Pitch 2: Chimney to offwidth, belay at the base of the huge left-facing dihedral (5.11-).

Pitch 3: Incredible 60-meter wide-hands to thin-hands left-facing corner (5.10+).

Pitch 4: Traverse left under a roof and up cracks to summit (5.9).
(1)0.75, (1)1.0, (1)1.5, (1)2.0, (2)2.5, (6)3.0, (3)3.5, (1) each #4, #5 Camalot

18 **Hydrophobic Coyote 5.10- 3 pitches**

Climbs the north buttress of Bridger Jack Butte.

Pitch 1: Start in a right-facing corner, traverse right to an overhanging fist crack passing two drilled pitons and up to a ledge.

Pitch 2: Climb a loose chimney to a ledge.

Pitch 3: Hand crack to the summit.

You will need (2)4.0 for the first pitch in addition to a standard rack.

Bridger Jack Mesa

_19_ **The Round-up Route ? ?'**
Climb fists for two pitches in a left-facing corner, left of #18, and join the third pitch of that route.

_20_ **Death Pitches 5.11 3 pitches**
A scary crack system on the northwest ridge of Bridger Jack Butte.

_21_ **Rimshot 5.11- 5 pitches**
A really fun, varied route on the west face of the butte, put up by Bret Ruckman and Marco Cornacchione.

Pitch 1: Splitter hands to belay in a pod (5.10).

Pitch 2: Thin crack out of the pod, and traverse left across the face (5.10+).

Pitch 3: Chimney behind a flake to a splitter, then a thin-hands stembox. Super cool (5.10)!

Pitch 4: Thin hands to fists in a right-facing corner (5.11-).

Pitch 5: Traverse right to a steep 5.9 hands splitter.

Rappel **Wild Flower**. *(1)0.4, (1)0.5, (2) each 0.75–3.5, (3)2.5, (1) #4 Camalot, (1) #4.5 Camalot, medium nuts*

Bridger Jack Mesa-West Face
_22_ **Friendly Corner 5.11 4 pitches**
Located to the right of **Rites of Passage**, on the west face, just right of **Thumbelina**.

Pitch 1: Wide hands and fists, left of a gray corner, to a two-bolt belay (5.11-).

Pitch 2: Fists to fingers to two-bolt belay (5.10).

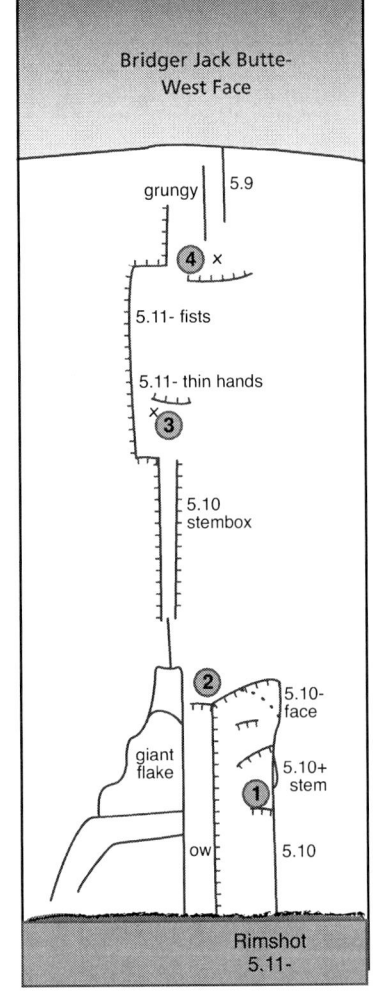

Jeff Achey on the first ascent of Vision Quest.   Photograph by Ed Webster

Jeff Achey

Wide, Wide Weekend
First ascents of Sacred Space and Liquid Sky

November 1984, Chip Chace and I drive over the passes from Boulder toward Indian Creek. We philosophize—not only to pass the miles but in hopes of letting our coming drama on the sandstone give us some sort of a clue. Why do men and women climb desert spires? Because it makes us *be there*.

If a desert crack has never felt a climber's hand, does it have an exact size? There is no way to prove so, and so we decide not, decide that the universe could vary in response to our rock karma, could help us along or repel us. Fingers or stacks, fist or offwidth—our attitude might determine which. We drive west through the night with our motivation burning like juniper, hot and clean and bright. If our superstition changes nothing in the stone, at least it keeps us awake and entertained.

At midnight we pull in to the old ranch road and throw bivi sacks out in a field. The Bridger Jack Spires loom somewhere above us, obscured in chill clouds. Overnight it snows, and we awake frosted white along with the cactus and sage, one with the land. The morning, bitter at first, slowly warms, so we hike to the rocks.

The crack we've come to try splits what might be the steepest wall in Indian Creek, the 200-foot south face of King of Pain. A pitch through scary blocks puts us below the notch with Hummingbird Spire. From here the crack looks ... wide. The first 30-foot section is a Supercrack-style splitter, which might be hands, but when I get to its base I laugh out loud. My fist rattles uselessly. At the time, my knowledge of "Leavittation" is limited to a stunt I read about, performed in an underground parking garage in California. In other words, I have absolutely no idea how to climb this crack.

But I have one piece of gear that fits, so before giving up I slot a big Tri-cam overhead, grasp the crack's edges in textbook Gaston Rebuffat style, and wriggle my leg in. My knee wedges perfectly. I can sit on it and drop both hands. Incredulous, up I go for 30 feet, Gastoning the edges, sliding my leg up, pushing the wobbly Tri-cam ahead of me. I can't tell if I'm climbing 5.11 or 5.2.

The rest of the pitch is classic, burly, tower-crack terrain, hands to fists, with varied, zigzagging cracks that end—just before my strength does—in a sandy hand traverse. I belay in a slot below a knife-slash squeeze chimney that shoots toward the summit, flawless except for a chockstone that blocks the exit.

Chip leads up with no pro, lizard-like, unhesitating. He's burrowed into the depths, but 60 feet of rope still hangs free of the crack. If he blows it passing the chockstone he'll go 200 feet directly onto my belay. But he doesn't fall because...well, that would be giving it away.

Next morning we're tired but game, and head up to North Six Shooter to look at another wide crack. I've seen it from the Lightning Bolts and the crucial section looks like a yes/no question, moderate or impossible. Crack size will determine all.

The first pitch starts in a perfect finger crack left of the Lightning Bolts, perfect but ordinary, previously climbed. Above, we cross over right to a crack that has not been climbed, for good reason: varying from six to 12 inches, it leads up to and over one of the biggest roofs in the Canyonlands.

Chip bails in the face of a seven-inch section around a small roof that he can't protect. I'm sure I won't fare any better, but if I don't go up to his highpoint I'll second-guess all the way back to Boulder and beyond. Toproped through a tube chock I lieback the lower offwidth, and my free-flying position gives me a completely different perspective than Chip had, wedged in the crack. It looks like I could just keep liebacking—if I had the courage. At the end of the roof is a big foothold that Chip could not see.

Wide, Wide Weekend

Minutes pass, and I huddle near the high pro, think about the drive home, and finally I go for the hold, figuring I can probably retreat from there. At the foothold I can cock one leg in the offwidth and get a no-hands stance. Magic. I'm now 10 feet out from the tube.

I could drill, maybe, but don't want to. Instead, I rest and ponder. I lean left and finger the edge of the seven-inch crack, finding it crisp and positive, perfect for liebacking. The wall is featureless. I try to clear my mind to match. A moment arrives—of inspiration or recklessness—and I launch out for the alcove 30 feet higher.

The climbing above looks ridiculous: a 15-foot roof, much too wide and flared to jam. I drill a bolt for the belay and bring up Chip. Above me, the crack's interior looks right on the line between chimney and offwidth. Moderate or impossible. In my mind's eye I can see its width wavering on karmic currents.

Chip takes only a couple of pieces of gear as he passes me. In a minute flat he is up in the slot, squirming horizontally out. All I can see are his feet, heel-toeing and T-stacking just above the flare. The run of the rope is crazy—from my hands it makes a gentle arc straight out, then up into the crack. The arc grows longer and more frightening as he moves outward. The rope sways back and forth in the breeze, with the desert floor and South Six Shooter spire far below and behind. In minutes, Chip has finished the pitch and joined the final chimney of the Lighting Bolts.

As I worm into the appallingly exposed hole I soon realize I'm thicker around the chest than Chip. Much thicker. Where he slithered and squirmed, I wedge. Finally I orient myself at a 45-degree angle so my hips and chest follow the same subtle path through the squeeze. Once I begin I can't turn my head, so I choose to look down at the talus, instead of up into the depths of the spire. For nearly the next hour I am locked in a hideous struggle, and only my fierce determination to share in Chip's fantastic pitch shields me from utter panic. Years later, when I do the Harding Slot on Astroman, it will seem positively spacious.

The wide, wide weekend proved it: our karma definitely affected crack size. Only thing I can't figure is whether we'd been good boys or bad.

Jeff Achey

Jeff Achey 1984
Photograph by Ed Webster

Optimator Wall

The Optimator Wall

The Optimator Wall

Named after the Jose Pereyra off-fingers testpiece **The Optimator**. This wall has seen a recent surge of development in a wide range of grades. Not to be missed is the unique **Anunnaki**, which stays dry in the rain. Lots of afternoon shade.

1 **Jews on Crack 5.11 130'**
You don't have to be Jewish to torture yourself on this strenuous cupped hands roof, but it helps if you have experience in suffering. *(2)2.0, (2)2.5, (3)3.0, (5)3.5, (4)4.0, (2) #4 Camalots*

2 **Sardikar 5.10+ 130'**
A nicely varied left-facing corner. *(2)0.5, (3)1.0, (3)1.5, (2)2.0, (2)2.5, (3)3.0, (2)3.5*

3 **Soul Fire 5.11- 90'**
A thin-hands splitter left of a left-facing corner. *(1)1.5, (6)2.0, (4)2.5*

4 **Chick Flick 5.10 130'**
A clean left-facing corner, fingers to offwidth. *0.75–6.0*

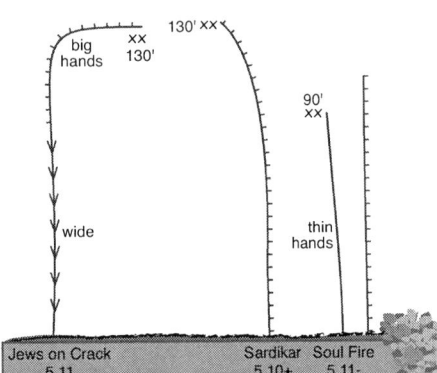

Optimator 2

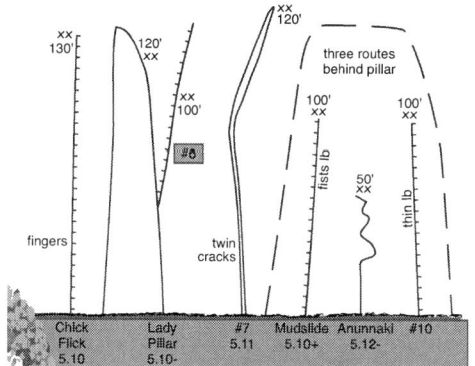

Optimator 3

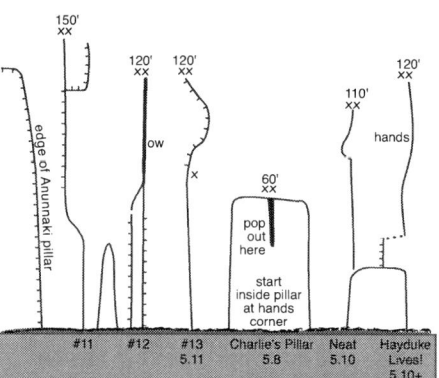

___5 **Lady Pillar 5.10- 120'**
A left-leaning crack, mostly fingers, on the right side of a pillar. (2)0.5, (2)0.75, (2)1.0, (1)2.0, (2)3.0, (1)3.5

___6 **Long Island Ice Ted 5.10+ 100'**
Same start as **Lady Pillar** but go right and climb the right-leaning hands-to-tips crack.

___7 **Unnamed 5.11 120'**
Twin cracks to a pod.

___8 **Anunnaki 5.12- 50'**
An overhanging hands-to-fingers zigzagging splitter on the underneath side of a fallen pillar. Not to be missed! (2)0.75, (1)1.0, (2)1.5, (2)2.0, (1) each 2.5–3.5

___9 **Mudslide 5.10+ 100'**
Behind the pillar are two layback climbs. This is the wider one on the left.

___10 **Unknown ? 100'**
The thinner layback on the right.

___11 **Unknown ? 150'**
Fingers to hands in a right-facing corner, to the right of the **Anunnaki** pillar.

___12 **Unknown ? 120'**
A stemming start to an offset offwidth crack.

___13 **Unknown 5.11 120'**
Climb a crack past a bolt and up a sandy right-facing corner.

___14 **Charlie's Pillar 5.8 60'**
Climb a crack system inside a pillar and pop out the front side up high.

___15 **Neat 5.10 110'**
Technical thin start to splitter hands. Good warm-up. (1)0.5, (1)1.0, (1)1.5, (2)2.0, (3)2.5, (4)3.0

___16 **Hayduke Lives! 5.10+ 120'**
Start as for **Neat**, then traverse right along a thin seam to a good hands splitter. (2)0.33, (1)1.5, (1)2.0, (1)2.5, (6)3.0, (2)3.5

___17 **Unnamed 5.11+ 100'**
A very difficult flare.

___18 **Gunning for Gonzo 5.11 100'**
Strenuous flare to fists in a corner. Starts just right of some petroglyphs. *Heavy on the 4.0*

___19 **Two Scoops 5.12 50'**
Very thin climbing past an unnecessary bolt to offset fingers. 0.33–1.0

181

Optimator Wall

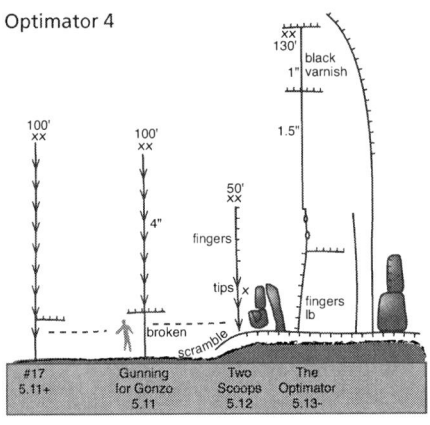
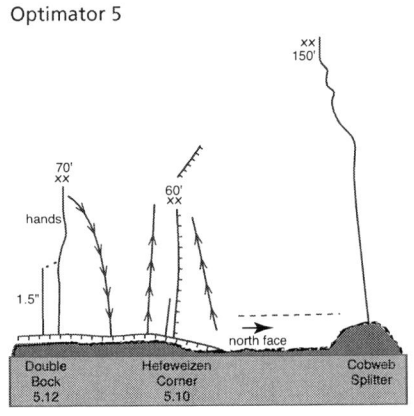

20 **The Optimator 5.13- 130'**
Tight fingers in a shallow right-facing corner will warm you up for 80' of steep off-fingers splitter. Simply stunning! (5)0.75, (5)1.0, (10)1.5, (3)2.0, (2)2.5

21 **Double Bock 5.12 70'**
Beautiful twin cracks. Hard size and hard crack switch. Access from the right side of the ledge system. (1)0.5, (2)0.75, (2)1.0, (3)1.5, (2)2.5, (1)3.0

22 **Hefeweizen Corner 5.10 60'**
A left-facing corner with a twin-crack start.

23 **Cobweb Splitter ? 150'**
A zigzagging splitter around on the north face.

801.484.8073

3265 E. 3300 S. Salt Lake City, UT 84109

6 Cottonwood West

Matt Pesce on **Golden Eye** 5.10 on the Technicolor Wall Photograph by Steve "Crusher" Bartlett

4x4 Area

Area Overview
Cottonwood West: 4 X 4 Wall to Critic's Choice

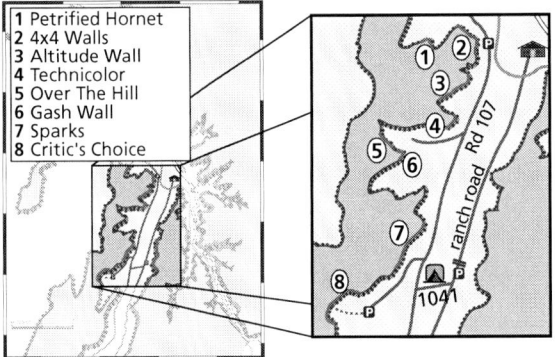

1 Petrified Hornet
2 4x4 Walls
3 Altitude Wall
4 Technicolor
5 Over The Hill
6 Gash Wall
7 Sparks
8 Critic's Choice

The west side of Cottonwood Canyon is home to the well-established 4x4 Wall but also contains an abundance of newer routes. In the golden age of Indian Creek climbing, the walls on this side of the canyon were difficult to reach, as the only road was the now off-limits road that cut through the Dugout Ranch property. The hike from this road involved cutting through vegetated and uneven terrain—if you were lucky enough to get across the creek in your vehicle. As a result, the walls on the west side still contain some untapped potential, though Moab locals have been rapidly scooping up the remaining gems.

Routes are listed from left to right, though the walls are listed from right to left as one approaches them on Road 107 when coming from Highway 211.

Petrified Hornet Wall

Petrified Hornet Wall

Petrified Hornet Wall
This newly developed and often shady wall is the far right side of the 4X4 cliff. It's definitely worth a visit by those looking for something new.

1 **Sabbath, Bloody Sabbath 5.12- 100'**
Left-facing dihedral through roofs.

2 **Kiefer Ari 5.11- 80'**
Splitter.

3 **Mad Hatter 5.12- 100'**
Right-facing dihedral that ends in a cave.

4 **Unknown Corner ? ?'**
Bouldery thin start to a great looking corner.

5 **Crescent Corner 5.10 50'**
Just left of **Petrified Hornet** is this hand to fist crack.

6 **Petrified Hornet 5.10+ 90'**
Quality. A bouldery start leads to great hands in a right-facing dihedral. Reminiscent of **Think Pink** on Battle of the Bulge.

7 **Unknown ? ?'**
Splitter.

4x4 Wall

4x4 Wall

4x4 Wall

One of the few north-facing walls at The Creek. Save it for those sweltering days. A few testpieces reside here, as well as many quality 5.11s. From the junction of Highway 211 and Beef Basin Road, drive 1.2 miles to the third cattle guard on the road. Park in a small turnoff on the left. The trail angles up and right, and emerges near the climb **4x4**. There is a smaller trail that cuts left once you are close to the base to access climbs to the left of **4x4**.

_1_ **Destination Paris 5.10+ 100'**
This nicely varied climb starts fingers and thin hands in a right-facing corner, and finishes with some face climbing to reach the belay. It is located several hundred feet left of the routes on the main north face.

_2_ **Unknown ? 150'**
A huge left-facing offwidth corner.

_3_ **Marshmallow Safari 5.10 70'**
Hands to wide-hands corner. *(1)2.5, (3)3.0, (3)3.5, (1) #4 Camalot*

_4_ **Unnamed 5.11 150'**
Fingers to hands in a long corner.

_5_ **Salt Lake Special 5.12+ 60'**
A Dean Potter finger crack in black rock. *0.4–1.0*

_6_ **4x4 5.11- 80'**
Gorgeous cupped hands in a corner to fists out a roof. Harder for small hands. *(2)3.0, (4)3.5, (2)4.0*

_7_ **Hydraulic Pump 5.12+ 80'**
Unrelenting difficultly-sized liebacks in a changing corner define this Steve Hong classic. The difficulty is slightly dependent on the number of cams you place. *(1)0.75, (3)1.0, (8)1.5*

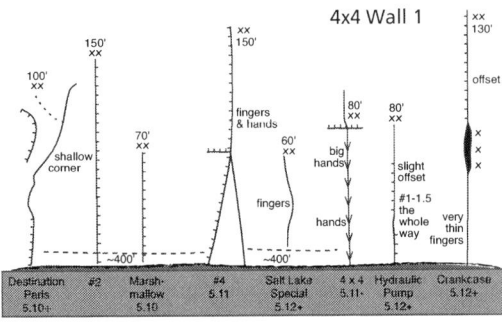

4x4 Wall 2

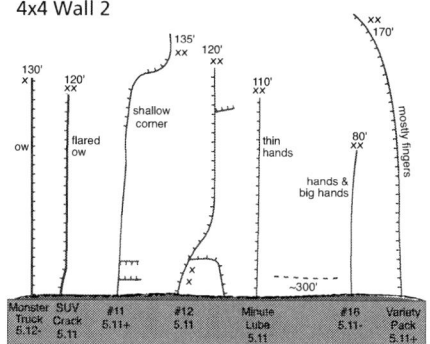

_8_ Crankcase 5.12+ 130'

You'll find every size of finger crack in the first 50 feet of this route, as well as five corner switches to go with it. The middle contains a strenuous bolted offwidth leading to a finish with thin hands in a right-facing corner. You might have to replace some parts after struggling up this Carruthers classic! *(2) each 0.5–1.0, (5)1.5, (3)2.0, (1)2.5, bolts*

_9_ Monster Truck 5.12- 130'

Offwidth in left-facing corner. A Seth Shaw route. Shares anchor with **Crankcase**.

_10_ SUV Crack 5.11 120'

A right-facing offwidth.

_11_ Unnamed 5.11+ 135'

Thin face start, to steep hands and a thin-hands/off-fingers finish. Highly recommended. *(2)0.4, (1)0.5, (4)1.5, (5)2.0, (5)2.5, (3)3.0, (1) 3 5*

_12_ Unnamed 5.11 120'

Difficult face moves past two bolts (second one hard to clip) to sustained thin hands. Another quality unnamed route. *(1)0.75, (5)1.5, (7)2.0, bolts*

_13_ Minute Lube 5.11 110'

Fingers and thin hands in a right-facing corner. Hard start, sometimes sandy. *(2)0.5, (1)0.75, (4)1.0, (7)1.5, (1)2.5, (1)3.0*

_14_ Unknown ? 80'

Hands in a flare, anchor inside pod. Not on topo.

_15_ Unnamed 5.10- 80'

Hands splitter to wide left-facing corner to roof. Not on topo.

_16_ Unnamed 5.11- 80'

Splitter hands to wide hands and a short off-width. *(1)2.0, (4)2.5, (4)3.0, (1) #4 Camalot*

_17_ Variety Pack 5.11+ 170'

One of the longest and most sustained pitches at the grade. Mostly fingers. *(1)0.5, (8)0.75, (8)1.0, (4)1.5, (3)2.0, (2)2.5*

_18_ Unnamed 5.10+ 70'

Thin hands in a shallow right-facing corner. Shares anchor with the following route. *1.0–3.0, mostly 1.5–2.0*

_19_ Unnamed 5.10 70'

Offset hands. A good warm-up. *(2)2.0, (4)2.5, (2)3.0*

_20_ Unnamed 5.11- 150'

Fingers to thin hands out two roofs. This and the next route are pretty far to the right on the west face. *1.0–2.5*

_21_ Unnamed 5.11 100'

1.0–1.5

Altitude Wall and 4x4 Left

Altitude Wall and 4x4 Left

These two walls are located left of 4x4 Wall. The 4x4 Left Wall is the immediate continuation of the cliff of 4x4 Wall (to the left, around the prow). Altitude Wall is a separate cliff a little ways further left again.

1 **Altitude Sickness 5.10+ 60'**
Left-facing dihedral through a tight-hands roof. *(1)1.0, (2)1.5, (1) each #1, #2, #5 Camalots, long runners for roof*

2 **Cruising Altitude 5.10 75'**
Left-facing dihedral. *TCUs, (1)2.0, (1)2.5, (1) #2 Camalot, (3) #3 Camalots*

3 **Bad Boy ? ?'**
Flake to V-Slot.

4 **OW Boulder ? ?'**

The following routes are on 4x4 Left. They are best approached from the road or the 4x4 Wall.

5 **Unknown 5.11 ?'**
Right-facing dihedral. *TCUs*

6 **3D 5.10+ ?'**
An awesome route that tackles a splitter up the front of a leaning pillar. Continue past the top of the pillar to anchors.

7 **Unknown ? ?'**
Splitter.

8 **Unknown ? ?'**
Splitter. Tight hands to tips. Faces up the Beef Basin Road.

9 **Unknown 5.10+ 150'**
Left-facing corner. This route should go to the top if it doesn't already. *(2)1.0, (2)1.5, (6)2.0, (2)2.5, (4)3.0, (4) #3 Camalots, (2) #3.5 Camalots, (1) #4 Camalot*

10 **Destination Paris**
This is the leftmost route on the 4x4 Wall (see page 186 for description).

Technicolor Wall

Technicolor Wall south face

Technicolor Wall

This seldom-visited wall has a few scattered gems for the curious. Continue 1.2 miles past the 4X4 cattle guard and park on the right. There are three faces; a sunny south face to the left, an east face (directly above your car; look for the prominent square pillar), and a shady north face around to the right. Immediately under the south face is a rough road leading back to a fire ring, at the back of a large amphitheater. **The Gash** and **Over The Hill** are located on the left side of this amphitheater. Note: The trails in this area can be difficult to follow.

The following two climbs are on the left side of the south face, near the back of the amphitheater. Park at the fire ring, and head up and left.

1 Colorblind 5.11 120'
A left facing dihedral.

2 Golden Eye 5.10 120'
This stellar route climbs a large left-facing dihedral located directly under a prominent tower on the upper cliffband. There is a caramel-looking rock wall to its left. Starts fingers, slowly widens to hands, then gradually pinches back to fingers. A 70 meter rope barely returns you to terra firma. (3)1.0, (3)1.5, (2)2.0, (2)2.5, (3)3.0, (1)3.5

The next two routes are close together about 300 hundred yards to the right. Park about halfway down the rough road, and hike uphill.

3 Unnamed 5.10 65'
A left-facing corner. Starts hands, goes to rattly fists. (2)3.5, (2)4.0, (2) #3.5 Camalots, (2) #4 Camalots

4 Unnamed 5.10- 85'
This unusual route is easier (and much more fun) than it appears. It follows a well-protected chimney, with just a couple tricky moves. A worthy Indian Creek moderate. (2)0.5, (1)1.0, (2)4.0, (1) #3.5 Camalot, (1) #4 Camalot, wires

Technicolor Wall

The next few routes are on the front face.

5 Dualing Exits 5.10/5.9+/5.10+/5.11 90'
Pitch 1: Climb a right-facing dihedral then step up and across to a left-facing dihedral.

Pitch 2: Short 5.9+ face.

Pitch 3: Splitter to offwidth.

Pitch 4: Left facing dihedral.
Pitch one gear: (1)1.5, (4)2.0, (2)2.5, (1)3.0, (1)4.0, (1) #3.5 Camalot, (1) #5 Camalot. Remainder of route: Hand to offwidth gear. From the anchors on pitch 2 it is possible to toprope a difficult offwidth route to the left

6 On the Up and Up 5.10 70'
Left of the prominent pillar is this big-hands splitter. *(2)2.5, (3)3.0, (3)3.5*

7 Unnamed 5.12- 60'
Immediately to the right is this often-sandy off-fingers splitter. *0.75–2.0, heavy on the 1.5*

8 Unnamed 5.9 60'
Hands in a corner. Shares anchor with previous route.

9 Whale's Back 5.11- 120'
One of the best hand cracks in a corner for those with big hands. Located to the right of the prominent pillar. *(6)3.0, (5)3.5*

10 Carruthers 5.10+ 140'
Double cracks, mostly hands, leads to a ledge. A 25-foot thin-hands splitter leads to the anchor.

11 Technicolor 5.11+ 100'
This beautiful right-facing corner is several hundred feet to the right, on the north face. The only thing this route suffers from is loneliness. Somebody please replace the ancient anchor. *(2)0.75, (1)1.0, (1)1.5, (5)2.0, (1)2.5, (4)3.0*

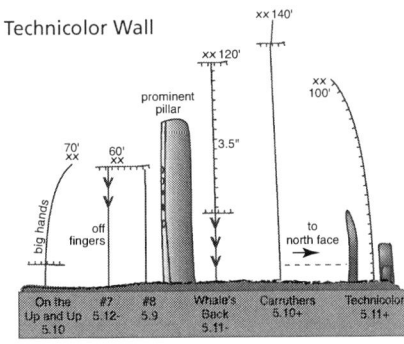

Joe Slansky on #3 Unnamed 5.10   Photograph by Steve "Crusher" Bartlett

Over the Hill

Over the Hill
This shady crag faces across to the south face of Technicolor Wall. It is home to four known climbs. Drive into the amphitheater (described in the Technicolor Wall introduction) and park at the campsite/fire ring.

1 **Over the Hill 5.11+ 90'**
Bouldery start to bulging hands. *(1) set TCUs, (3) 1.0, (1) 1.5, (2)2.5, (3) 3.0, (3) #3 Camalots*

2 **Unknown ? ?'**

3 **Jahmon 5.11+ ?'**
Left-facing dihedral. Fists at top. *(2) 2.5, (1) 3.0, (1) 3.5 (4) #3.5 Camalots, (2) #4 Camalots*

4 **Switching ? ?'**
Straight-in crack.

Photograph by David Vaughan

The Gash

The Gash
This crag faces across to the south face of Technicolor Wall, and is located left of Over the Hill. Like Over the Hill it is a nice venue on a hot day. Park on the amphitheater road opposite the crag, and hike directly up.

___1 **Hot Dogs 5.10 75'**
Right-facing dihedral. (2) 2.0, (1)3.0, (4) 3.5, (2) #3.5 Camalots, (1) #4 Camalot

___2 **Inset Pillar 5.11 100'**
TCUs, (1) 1.5, (5) 2.0, (2) 2.5, (2) 3.0, (3) #3.5 Camalots, (2) #4 Camalots

___3 **Jutting Flake 5.10 85'**
Boulder up a jutting flake into a left-facing dihedral. High quality. (2) 1.5, (3)2.0, (4)2.5, (2) 3.0, (2) #3 Camalots, (1) #5 Camalot

___4 **Unknown 5.10 ?'**
Splitter.

___5 **Unknown ? 100'**
Splitter off-fingers.

The following two routes are on the left side of the cove, just left of a recess.

___6 **The Gash 5.11- 65'**
A right-facing corner. Perfect hands leads to an offwidth section, protected by a bolt. (2) 2.0, (1) 2.5, (1) 3.0, (3) #3 Camalots, (2) #3.5 Camalots, (2) #4 Camalots, (1) quickdraw

___7 **Hollow Man 5.9 115'**
The rock in this innocent-looking dihedral sounds disconcertingly hollow. *Mostly hand-size gear*

Sparks Wall

Sparks Wall

Sparks Wall

This compact wall is actually the northernmost extension of Critic's Choice Wall. There are a baker's dozen of routes, but they are all long and of good quality. They can be sandy, however, as this cliff does not see much action. Park on the right 2.4 miles past the 4x4 cattle guard. The wall is fairly close to the road, and receives afternoon shade.

_1 **Spark it up Sparky 5.11- 65'**
On the far left side of the wall. Just off the photo.

_2 **Sparks of the Tempest 5.11+ 100'**
Cool starting moves gain a sustained thin-hands corner, which leads to a fun roof and a great finish. *(1)0.4, (1)0.5, (1)0.75, (2)1.0, (3)1.5, (2)2.0, (6)2.5*

_3 **Sparking Spurs 5.12 140'**
The gem of the cliff. Thin hands (5.11+) to the first set of anchors at 70'. A fat-fingers frenzy to the second anchor.

_4 **Low Spark 5.11 140', Two Pitches**
Thin-hands splitter to hands in a slot. There is a short second pitch (5.10). *(1)1.0, (1)1.5, (4)2.0, (5)2.5, (5)3.0, (3)3.5*

_5 **Go Sparky Go 5.11+ 70'**
Hands to a leaning fingers offset. *(1)0.75, (1)1.0, (2)2.0, (2)2.5, (2)3.0*

_6 **Old Sparky 5.12- 160'**
Offset fingers splitter to a long left-facing corner through roofs.

_7 **Sparkling Gefilte Fish 5.10 65'**
Hands to fists in a right-facing offset on the front of a pillar. *(2)2.5, (2)3.0, (2)3.5, (2)4.0*

_8 **Sparkling Schnitzel 5.11- 70'**
Just right of **Sparkling Gefilte Fish**, on the right side of the pillar, is this offwidth. *(1)3.0, (1)3.5, (3)4.0, (2) #4 Camalots*

On the north face are five more climbs.

_9_ **Rowdy 5.10 90'**
This big-hands right-arching splitter shares an anchor with the next route.

_10_ **Unnamed 5.10+ 90'**
The right crack. Offwidth.

_11_ **Scenic Line 5.10 60'**
A shallow left-facing corner that slants from right to left. *(1)1.0, (2)1.5, (7)2.0, (2)3.0*

_12_ **Stiff Line 5.10 60'**
Right-facing dihedral. *TCUs, (1)1.5, (2)2.0, (1)2.5*

_13_ **Flat Line 5.11+ 60'**
A left-facing dihedral. This route shares anchors with **Stiff Line**. *(2)0.75, (1)1.0, (1)1.5, (1) 2.0 (1)2.5, (1)3.0, (1) #3.5 Camalot*

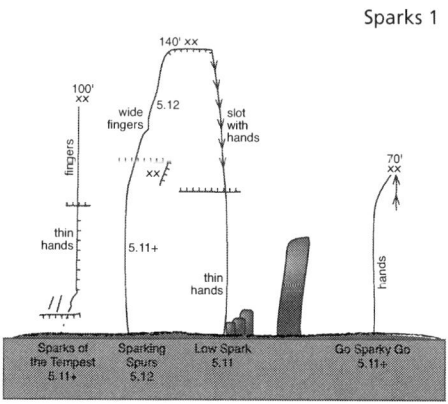

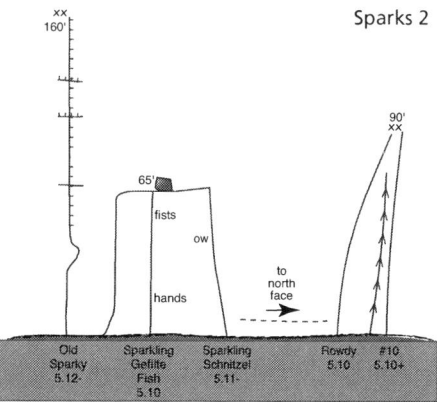

Critic's Choice

Critic's Choice

Critic's Choice

This is the last major wall on the west side of Beef Basin Road. There is a huge arch forming in the middle of the wall. **Bunny Slope** is left of the arch. **Belly Full of Bad Berries** is the left dihedral of the arch. The classic splitter **Critic's Choice** is to the right of the arch. From the beginning of Beef Basin Road, drive 4.3 miles (at this point you will have just crossed your fifth cattle guard) immediately turn right and parallel an old barbed wire fence, then veer left and drive as close to the arch as your car allows. There is no obvious trail, but head up in the vicinity of the arch as shown on the photo.

1 **Cryptogamic Sole 5.10+ ?'**
This route is located 0.25 miles left of the arch. This dihedral—with a less-than-perfect appearance—is actually a decent climb.

2 **Ragin' Mofo 5.11+ 160'**
Somewhere left of **Ruby Flame**.

3 **Ruby Flame 5.11 90'**
Twin crack start to splitter offwidth.

4 **Bunny Slope 5.9+ 160'**
Thin hands with a little looseness to gorgeous hands in a long right-facing corner. Many #2 Camalots (about 10-15) OR *(1) 2.0, (5) 2.5, (7) 3.0*

5 **Blue Square 5.10 ?'**
Big hands to offwidth.

6 **Ed's World 5.10- 60'**
A slabby fingers to thin-hands splitter. Starts left of a large juniper.

7 **Belly Full of Bad Berries 5.13- 70'**
This stunning line, first led by Brad Jackson, received international acclaim in a 2001 issue of *Rock and Ice* featuring the infamous male model John Varco posing on this brutal overhanging offwidth. *(1) each 2.0–3.5, (2) #4 Camalots, (2) #4.5 Camalots, (1) #5 Camalot*

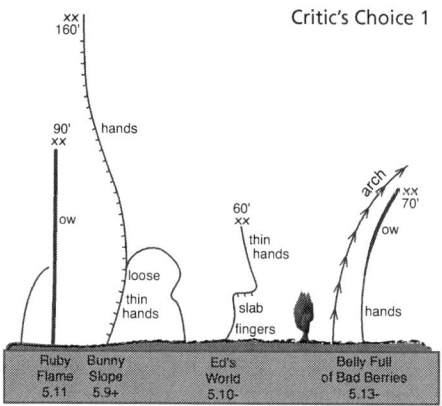

Critic's Choice 1

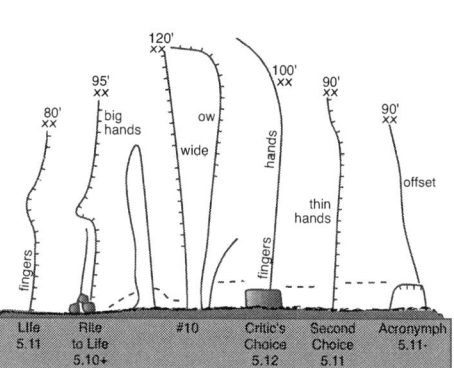

Critic's Choice 2

__8__ **Life 5.11 80'**
The first route to the right of the arch is this sweet finger crack in a left-facing corner. *(2)0.4, (2)0.5, (4)0.75, (3)1.0, (2)1.5*

__9__ **Rite to Life 5.10+ 95'**
A twin-crack start above some boulders to burly wide hands in a steep left-facing corner. *(1)0.75, (4)2.5, (3)3.0, (3)3.5*

__10__ **Unknown ? 120'**
A wide crack in a right-facing corner.

__11__ **Critic's Choice 5.12 100'**
Words cannot describe the magnificence of this classic splitter—a Ruckman Brothers classic. Sometimes sandy. *(1)0.5, (6)0.75, (2)1.0, (2)1.5, (4)2.5, (1)3.0*

__12__ **Second Choice 5.11 90'**
Quality thin hands in a clean left-facing corner. *(5)1.0, (5)1.5, (2)2.0*

__13__ **Acronymph 5.11- 90'**
This climb is a few hundred feet to the right, and starts on a ledge. It is an interesting left-angling offset splitter. *0.75–2.5, mainly fingers*

__14__ **Unnamed 5.10 90'**
Right-facing dihedral. *2.5–3.0*

197

Bret Ruckman

Indefatigable Youth

My earliest visit to Indian Creek was part of a family vacation to the Needles District of Canyonlands National Park, when my brother Stuart and I were both skinny teenagers. Accustomed to the granite slabs of Little Cottonwood Canyon, we craned our necks up at Supercrack Buttress, amazed by the impossible-looking cracks. We owned one #2 Friend. With it, we tried to get up a scrappy crack on the far left side of Supercrack Buttress but ended up climbing slabs by Newspaper Rock.

Several years later, bigger, "badder," and armed with huge racks of cams (pooled with other friends from SLC), we were able to make it up some of those stellar routes. Eventually we turned our attention to what we termed the "outback." In our minds, the outback was anything beyond the Fringe of Death Canyon. Quickly we realized that "others" (Hong and Budding, et al.) had been there before us, picking off nearly all the five-star climbs. And these routes were truly awesome—long, sweeping lines up aesthetic, varnished Wingate, with a single-bolt anchor a full rope-length up. We gradually visited most of those outback cliffs, cleaning up the leftovers, and sometimes even managed to get up an established climb here and there.

Indian Creek climbing was a perfect outlet for our twenty-something energy. I would wake up before dawn to walk a cliff, and return to camp so psyched to climb I could hardly make it through breakfast. We would throw together huge packs of gear, and hump them up the talus. Shouldering daunting racks of cams and pulling the weight of a lead line and a trail line, the leader would tackle cracks that were so long, demanding, and often painful, that he would arrive at the anchors quivering with fatigue, or worse. The belay on "Atomic Indian" a.k.a. "Atomic Chunks" (on the now-closed Paragon Prow Wall), was christened in spectacular fashion by my brother, after a particularly demanding offwidth. Following the sun or the shade, we would often visit several cliffs in a day, and if there happened to be any light left after climbing, we would drive along, scoping the cliffs with binoculars, hoping to spy that perfect splitter crack.

For me, there is an enduring image of Indian Creek: we sit, depleted at last, at the base of the cliffs, watching the sunset. Above us the varnished sandstone is glowing a brilliant red/orange as we rip the tattered athletic tape off our hands. It is very quiet and still, only the sound of the occasional car, the distant cow, or the lone crow drifting along the rim above us. It's been another exhausting day, full of adventure, stuck ropes, rattlesnakes and other surprises. My body is filthy and dehydrated, my fingers swollen and bloody. I should feel like a wreck, but I feel great, and completely satisfied. We take heaps of gear and shove them into our packs, and head down the talus in fading light, to our camp beneath the golden cottonwoods. We have earned our beer and chips again, and can't wait to do the same thing again tomorrow.

Bret Ruckman

Bret and Stuart Ruckman atop Pistol Whipped after the FA.

7 Cottonwood East

David Bloom on **Layaway Plan** 5.11+ — Photograph by John Dickey

Pistol Whipped

Area Overview
Pistol Whipped to Tricks Wall

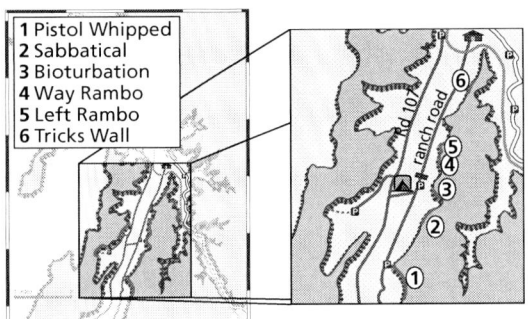

1 Pistol Whipped
2 Sabbatical
3 Bioturbation
4 Way Rambo
5 Left Rambo
6 Tricks Wall

Pistol Whipped

Shorter routes and some shade add to the popularity of this fine cliff. Don't miss the three-pitch classic the cliff is named for.

Drive 4.8 miles down Beef Basin Road to the junction of 107 (Beef Basin Road) and County Road 1041. Turn left on 1041, cross over Cottonwood Creek, and turn right, go 1.5 miles and park on the right.

__1__ **Hijinx in the Desert 5.11- 90'**
Fingers to thin hands up a right-facing offset.

__2__ **Dusty Trails to Nowhere 5.10 50'**
Hands in a right-facing corner, 30' right of Hijinx. (2)2.5, (3)3.0

__3__ **Wolf's Ear 5.11+ 80'**
Right-facing corner with a wide slot, to steep hands.

__4__ **Rump Roast II 5.11 70'**
Beautiful wide-fingers and thin-hands splitter. (1)0.4, (1)0.75, (2)1.0, (5)1.5, (4)2.0

__5__ **Coyote Essence 5.11- 50'**
Steep fingers and hands in a small left-facing corner, just left of a huge detached flake. (2)1.0, (2)1.5, (1)2.0, (2)2.5, (1)3.0

__6__ **Unnamed 5.11-R 100'**
Fingers in a shallow corner. Very thin at the top.

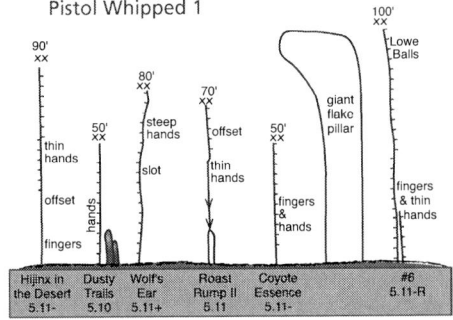

_7_ **Unknown ? 80'**
Tips splitter past a bolt.

_8_ **Coyne Crack Simulator 5.11- 40'**
Nice fingers to thin-hands splitter to small left-facing corner. *(1)1.0, (1)1.5, (2)2.0, (1)2.5, (1)3.0, (1)3.5*

_9_ **Wounded Knee 5.10+ 75'**
Twin crack start, fingers/thin hands to a small left-facing corner. *(2)2.0, (2)2.5, (3)3.0, (2)3.5*

_10_ **Spaghetti Western 5.11 120'**
Gorgeous striped right-facing corner. A fingers start to sustained thin hands and hands. *(1)0.75, (1)1.0, (2)1.5, (1)2.0, (3)2.5, (5)3.0, (1)4.0*

_11_ **Revenge of the Rock Gods 5.10+ 70'**
Fingers and hands. Starts in a shallow right-facing corner. *(1)0.75, (2)1.0, (2)1.5, (2)2.0, (2)3.0, (1)3.5*

_12_ **Steve's Wimpout 5.10 40'**
Fingers in a left-facing corner through a small roof. *(2)0.75, (3)1.0, (1)1.5, (1)2.5*

_13_ **Pinyon Pining 5.10 3 pitches**
The route follows a right-facing offwidth corner.

Pitch 1: Broken rock (5.7).

Pitch 2: Climb wide 5.10 past a bolt.

Pitch 3: 5.yuck
(1)0.75, (1)1.5, (4)3.0, (3)3.5, (3)4.0, (1) #4 Camalot, fixed pro

Pistol Whipped 2

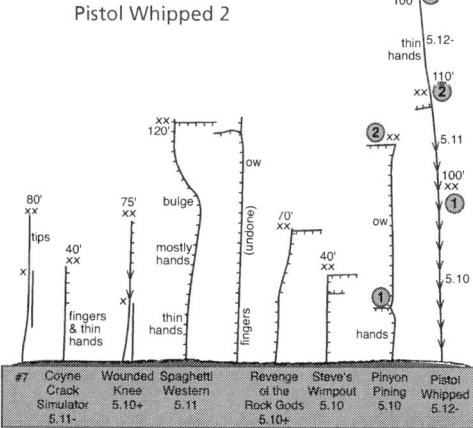

Pistol Whipped

_14_ Pistol Whipped 5.12- 3 pitches
Pitch 1: A broken dihedral that gets thin at the top, 5.10, 100'.

Pitch 2: Come out of the slot and up thin hands and hands in a left-facing corner, 5.11, 100'.

Pitch 3: Amazing thin-hands splitter, 5.12-, 100'. *(1)0.5, (3) each 0.5-1.5, (4)2.0, (5)2.5, (3)3.0, (1) #4 Camalot*

_15_ Unnamed 5.13- 60'
Fingers to tips splitter. Desperate! *(2)0.65, (7)0.75, (2)1.0*

_16_ Chambered Round 5.10 90'
Chimney behind a pillar to left-facing corner.

_17_ Skidmarks 5.10 35'
Wavy fingers in a left-facing corner. *(3)0.5, (1)0.5, (1)1.5, (1)2.5*

_18_ Short and Stupid 5.8+ 25'
Thin hands in a left-facing corner. *(2)2.0, (1)2.5*

_19_ Unknown ? 120'
Hands on left side of pillar to wide slot.

_20_ Sig Saur 5.12- 60'
Fingers splitter. *(6)0.75, (3)1.0, (1)1.5, (1)3.0*

_21_ Jolly Rancher 5.10 150'
Splitter hands to wide hands. *(1) each 0.75–2.0, (2)2.5, (1)3.0, (8)3.5*

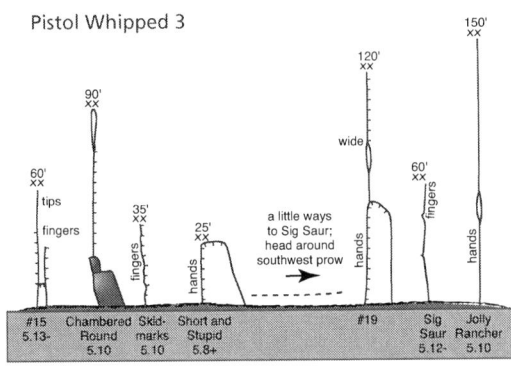

Fred Knapp on **Wounded Knee** 5.10+   Photograph by Stewart M. Green

Sabbatical Wall

Sabbatical Wall

Sabbatical Wall

This wall lies between Bioturbation and Pistol Whipped. It is also referred to as the Pregnant Woman Wall. Thanks to Karl Kelley for info.

1 **Pregnant Woman Grazing 5.10 ?'**
A straight-in offwidth crack. The anchors, up where the crack thins down to fingers and the angle eases back, are hard to see. Look for plaque, directly across from the road junction.

2 **Double Time 5.10 110'**
Splitter to left-facing dihedral. *(1)2.5, (3) #3 Camalots, (4) #3.5 Camalots*

3 **Holiday Pay 5.10- 60'**
Left-facing dihedral. *TCUs, (1)1.0, (2)3.5, (3)4.0, (2) #4 Camalots*

4 **Lichen Vacation 5.10 125'**
Left-facing dihedral. *(3)2.0, (2)2.5, (2)3.0, (1)3.5, (2)4.0, (2) #4 Camalots*

5 **E.T.O. 5.hard 105'**
Ethical time out. Stemming corner. *Seven draws and TCUs*

6 **Workin' Man 5.11- 65'**
Right-facing dihedral.

7 **Make it a Triple 5.10/5.10+/5.10+**
This three-pitch route takes a right-facing corner. *(2)1.5, (1)2.0, (4)3.0, (4) #3.5 Camalots, (1) #4 Camalot*

8 **Bon Voyage 5.11 125'**
Open book. *(5)1.5, (4)2.0, (5) #1 Camalots, (1) #3.5 Camalot*

9 **Sabbatical 36 5.10 155'**
This Karl Kelley route is about a 10-minutes walk to the right of **Pregnant Woman Grazing**. A right-facing corner. *(2) #0.5 Camalots, (1) #0.75 Camalot, (3) #1 Camalots, (3) #2 Camalots, (3)3.0, (3) #3 Camalots, (1) #3.5 Camalot, (1) #5 Camalot*

10 **The Toss 5.10 40'**
This finger/hand crack is to the right of **Sabbatical 36**. *Mostly yellow TCUs, #0.75 Camalots, #1 Camalots*

11 **Finger Fun 5.10/5.11 2 pitches**
This two-pitch route heads up a Bunny Slope-like ramp feature, to within about 30 feet of the rim. *P1: mostly blue and yellow TCUs, P2: mostly purple and blue TCUs*

Photograph of Fred Knapp on Fist Fight by Steve "Crusher" Bartlett

Treat Your Belayer to The Desert Bistro

Desert Bistro
92 E. Center St.
Moab, UT 84532
435-259-0756
www.desertbistro.com

The Desert Bistro uses the freshest ingredients possible, and makes everything on premises. All entrées & sauces are made to

Marco Cornacchione

Rimshot

At 7AM the mercury was already pushing 80, so by the time Bret and I parked for the Bridger Jack approach it was well over 90. Oh well, nothing like a sweltering desert hike across cow pastures to warm one up for a day of crack climbing. Our objective was Ponders of Persuasion, or Powders, and at that time no road led to what is now one of the lighter talus cones in The Creek. Instead, we wandered in from the paved road throwing our monstrous-as-ever packs over numerous gateless barbwire fences. Dodging one rattlesnake, we arrived at the base an hour or so later thinking that those past trips of freezing our butts off weren't so bad after all. The southeast-facing crux corner shone in the sun like those glorious hands over in Salt Lake—equally welcoming for the unaware.

Having never succeeded on an Indian Creek 5.11+ in friendly conditions, I gave only the obligatory "well, *we* could do this if *you* lead the crux" when Bret suggested a look around on the shady side of the mesa. Dodging the serpent again (I've seen it or its kin every time I've rounded the prow of Bridger Jack in warm weather) we ventured into the more forgiving shade of the west side. From our best reading of *Desert Rock*, there were no routes on this side so we set about finding something to climb that might take us to the top.

The route we found, **Rimshot**, proved a fine adventure with exciting climbing. Indeed, it was an adventure that solidified a friendship which would get us up many future routes, from desert towers to the Black Canyon and Rocky Mountain National Park. But on this day we still needed to get down. It was late when we signed the summit register, a trend that would also be a trademark of our long routes together. There were, I think, about four or five entries. All were new routes.

The first rap went well, then pulling the rope on the second rap the knot stuck. No rope flicking tricks worked so Bret prusiked up and saved the day. At the end of the next rap I stood comfortably on a ledge as I threaded the two faded slings of the American Triangle (climbers pretended to be too cheap in those days to add webbing or biners to rappels). As Bret rapped down to me, I realized in the waning light that abrasion had reduced one spot of the anchor slings to a few measly threads. My heart stopped as I thanked my luck and cursed my tiredness. Quickly I clipped to the star drive and began revamping the anchor.

It was dark by the time we had chiseled the all-important route plaque, but our closest call still awaited us. As we tromped in the moonlight along a short section of road crossing Indian Creek and connecting two of the fields I started to kick the blob of tumbleweed in front of me. Luckily, it got out of the way. Turning on our lamps we chuckled as a rather large porcupine waddled off toward the creek....

For the Wingate cliffs of Indian Creek, this little adventure happened as I write this, but in climbing time it happened before humans overran the earth. When I compiled 200 Classic Indian Creek Climbs I had seen a total of 8, yes, 8 people at crags other than Supercrack. Now, climbers overrun Indian Creek. My initial anger at seeing the crowds come, my embarrassment at some of the errors in the book, and my remorse at ever having written it have mellowed. Indian Creek is still one of the finest experiences climbing has to offer, yet it seems that each year there are new warnings, from the BLM and from the Nature Conservancy, about getting our environmental act together. We'll all be using this guide for many years, having memorable adventures with close friends, if we choose to do so.

Marco Cornacchione

Bioturbation Wall

Bioturbation Wall

Bioturbation Wall

The Bioturbation Wall refers to the cliffs to the right of Way Rambo. **Chest Full of Kind** is not too far right of Way Rambo. A recent flurry of activity adds to the old Ruckman classic **Repose**. Drive east on the Road 1041, and park somewhere near the junction with the ranch road, south of the cattle guard. The route **Bioturbation** is more or less right in front of you.

_1_ **Chest Full of Kind 5.10 45'**
This entertaining route takes the left-facing dihedral in the forming arch. The everyman's **Belly Full of Bad Berries.** (1)2.0, (2)2.5, (2)3.0, (1)3.5, (1)4.0

_2_ **Cups 5.10 50'**
This route is located about 100 yards right of **Chest Full of Kind**, and takes a left-facing corner through some bulges. Mostly big hands.
(3) #3 Camalots, (3) #3.5 Camalots, (1) #4 Camalot

_3_ **Scrunch 5.12 ?'**
Fingers splitter with three bolts.

_4_ **Lifer 5.11 80'**
This stellar route is about 30 or 40 yards right again. Look for a left-facing dihedral leading to an undercling flake.
(2)1.5, (9)2.0, (3)2.5

_5_ **Regime Change 5.12 ?'**
Straight in tips with four bolts.

_6_ **Unknown ? ?'**
A tight-hands right-facing dihedral that ends beneath a roof.

_7_ **Repose 5.10R/X 170'**
A very clean left-facing corner. The twin parallel cracks of the route are close enough together as to make the pro a little questionable.

Dylan Warren on **Chest Full of Kind**   Photograph by Leslie Warren

Bioturbation Wall

Bioturbation Wall

8 Unnamed 5.11 70'
Good off-fingers splitter with a loose start. *(2)1.0, (4)1.5, (2)2.0, (1)2.5*

9 Unknown ? 70'
A stembox with two bolts. Anchors on left wall under a roof.

10 Bioturbation 5.10+ 65'
Fingers in a left-facing corner. *(1)0.5, (2)0.75, (2)1.0, (4)1.5, (2)2.0, (1)2.5*

11 Unknown ? 100'
Right-facing flake, red webbing on anchors. This may be 5.9, called **Rayne**.

12 Unknown ? 120'
Big hands in a left-facing corner.

Way Rambo

Way Rambo

Way Rambo

A stellar cliff that has seen some recent development. Turn left on County Road 1041, cross the creek, and turn left on the road which leads to the Dugout Ranch. You will soon encounter a cattle guard (under Bioturbation). In the past, climbers have driven and parked beyond this cattle guard. To preserve good relations with the ranchers, please park just before (south of) the Bioturbation cattle guard. Walk up the road a little ways and go right up a large drainage with junipers. The trail comes out at **Rochambeau**.

1 Wishbone Suspension 5.11- 70'
This is just left of **Coppertone**, and indeed looks something like an upside-down wishbone.

2 Coppertone 5.10 110'
A few hundred feet to the left of **Layaway Plan**, left of a large juniper, and right next to some pictographs. A short strenuous layback leads to triple cracks up high. This route was established at a time when protecting Indian artifacts was less of a concern. In the interests of protecting both this cultural heritage, and climbing access to Indian Creek, please do not climb this route.

3 The Cockometer 5.10- 60'
Soft start to nicely varied splitter. Do you measure up? (1)0.5, (1)0.75, (1)1.5, (3)2.0, (2)2.5, (2)3.0, (1)3.5

4 Good Times 5.11- 150'
Long offwidth, mostly five-inch.

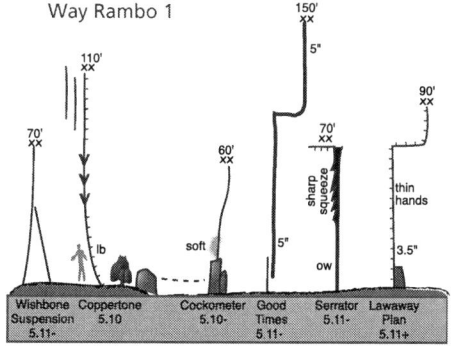

209

Way Rambo

_5 **The Serrator 5.11- 70'**
Splitter off-fists offwidth to a razor-thin squeeze. Watch your rope on the edge! *(1) #4 Camalot, (2) #4.5 Camalots, (2) #6 Friends*

_6 **Layaway Plan 5.11+ 90'**
Sustained thin hands in a left-facing corner to a wild tight-hands roof. Some people jam the roof, others try the layaway plan. *(1)1.0, (1)1.5, (7)2.0, (3)2.5, (2)3.5*

_7 **Slice and Dice 5.12 60'**
Very steep and sustained finger stacks through a small roof. Featured on the cover of *Climbing* #128. *(1)0.75, (1)1.0, (8)1.5 (green Camalots), (1)2.0*

_8 **Unnamed 5.10 90'**
Hands and wide hands up a two-tiered right-facing corner. *(1)2.5, (4)3.0, (3)3.5, (2)4.0, (1) #4 Camalot*

_9 **The Monk 5.10 80'**
Hands to fingers. *(2)1.5, (1)2.0, (1)2.5, (3)3.0, (2)3.5, (1)4.0*

Way Rambo 2

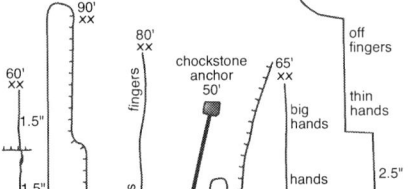

_10 **Way Nutter 5.9 50'**
A fun offwidth crack, left of a pillar. *(1)3.0, (2)3.5, (1)4.0, (1) #4 Camalot, (1) #4.5 Camalot, (1) #5 Camalot*

_11 **Blue Sun 5.10 65'**
Killer splitter hands and big hands. *(5)3.0, (3)3.5*

_12 **Way Rambo 5.12- 100'**
Superb hands to off-fingers splitter, sprint left to the anchors. *(1)1.0, (2)1.5, (3)2.0, (4)2.5*

√ _13 **Rochambeau 5.9 75'** FUN!
A little bit of everything in this featured right-facing corner. *(2)1.0, (1)1.5, (2)2.0, (1)2.5, (2)3.0, (2)3.5*

Chris Hackarth on **Way Rambo** 5.12-   Photograph by John Dickey

Way Rambo

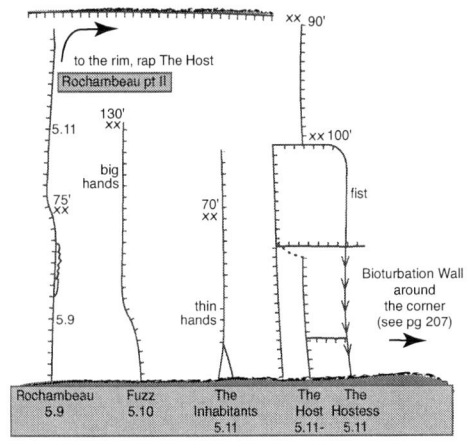

14 Rochambeau, Part II 5.11 130'
This is the second pitch of **Rochambeau**, included separately because it is considerably harder. This tops out on the rim, from where you rap from a juniper, located to the right, then down **The Host**.

15 Fuzz 5.10 130'
A long, ever-steepening hands and big-hands left-facing corner. *(1)1.0, (1)2.0, (2)2.5, (4)3.0, (3)3.5, (1)4.0*

16 The Inhabitants 5.11 70'
Stout thin hands in a varnished changing corner. *(1)1.5, (5)2.0, (1)2.5, (1)3.0, (2)3.5*

17 The Host 5.11- 100'
Stemming start to cool roof, to clean left-facing corner. There is a second pitch starting from the middle of the big ledge atop **The Host** and **The Hostess**. This takes a left-facing corner, and is a burly 5.10. *(1) each 0.5–1.0, (2)1.5, (3)2.0, (2)3.0, (1)3.5, (1) #4 Camalot*

18 The Hostess 5.11 100'
Same start as **The Host**, squeeze through the roof on the right, and up the really burly splitter. Find out who wears the pants in this family. *(2)0.75, (2)1.0, (1)1.5, (1)2.0, (1)2.5, (5)3.0, (2)3.5, (2)4.0, (1) #4 Camalot, (1) #4.5 Camalot*

On the right side of the photo above, the obvious forming arch feature houses **Chest Full of Kind**, on the far left end of Bioturbation Wall.

Left Rambo

Left Rambo

Left Rambo

The left side of Way Rambo. It is probably easiest to approach these climbs by walking further up the road from Way Rambo and up the talus slope.

_1_ Unknown 5.10 90'
A clean left-facing corner left of a large boulder.

_2_ Marathon Gasp 5.12 200'
A thin start in a left-facing corner, to an offset splitter.

_3_ Unknown 140'
A wavy thin-hands splitter.

_4_ 38 Special 5.12 80'
Tight fingers through a small roof. (1)0.4, (1)0.5, (8)0.75, (3)1.0

_5_ Unnamed 5.10+ 80'
Thin hands in a right-facing corner. Left of a large pillar.

_6_ Unknown ? 40'
Ugly aid seam.

_7_ Unnamed 5.11- 90'
Start above a small pillar and climb off-fingers to wide hands in a right-facing corner. 1.0–3.5

_8_ Fingers on a Landscape 5.11 120'
Fingers to thin hands in a left-facing corner. 0.5–2.0 with (8) 0.5

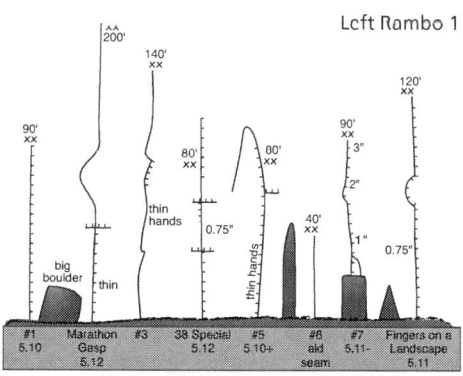

Left Rambo 1

213

Tricks Wall

Tricks Wall

Tricks Wall

This wall is actually the southern extension of Paragon Prow. It is the home of the route that is the archetype of Indian Creek climbing: **Tricks are for Kids**—an immaculate splitter, requiring mega-endurance and an armload of camming units. From the start of Beef Basin Road drive 2.2 miles and park on the left. Walk east across the sagebrush, cross Cottonwood Creek, and head straight towards a brown varnished wall with two long splitters and a bulbous-looking white top. This is slightly past the fourth cattle guard. There are several routes that have been climbed to the left of **Tricks** but they are not included here as they are in an access-sensitive area due to their proximity to the Dugout Ranch.

_1 **Tricks are for Kids 5.13 160'**
A Steve Hong classic. A full pitch of finger stacks. Guaranteed mega-pump. *0.5–2.5 with (6)1.0, (12)1.5*

_2 **Silly Rabbit 5.12+ 140'**
Splitter tips and fingers; a Steve Petro classic. *(7)0.5, (7)0.75, (1) each 2.0–4.0*

_3 **Cocoa Puffs 5.11 90'**
Mostly hands with a bolted offwidth section. A Melissa Quigley contribution. *(2) each 0.75–3.0*

8 New Walls

Karl Kelley on Fist Fight 5.10+   Photograph by Steve "Crusher" Bartlett

New Wall Area

Area Overview
The Fist Fight Wall/New Wall/Trick or Treat

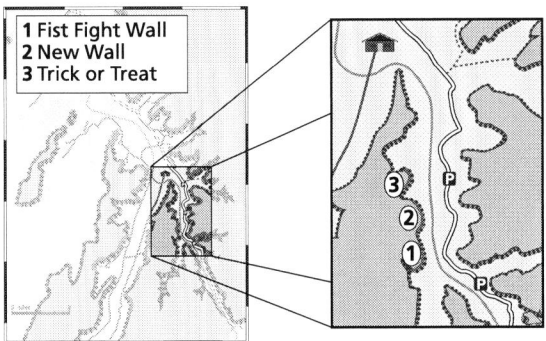

1 Fist Fight Wall
2 New Wall
3 Trick or Treat

The New Wall Area, comprising Fist Fight Wall, New Wall, and Trick Or Treat Wall offers good afternoon shade with its location on the south side of Highway 211, 1.0 mile west of the Donnelly Canyon parking area. The routes on these three adjacent walls are described from left to right (south to north).

Traditionally, the approach has been from the same parking as for **Scorpion Corner**, 5.12-, which is on the north side of the road. From there, climbers walked across a large open field and headed southwest to the cliffs. Problems with this approach, however, are becoming apparent, so climbers will need to find an alternative (see note below). Approaching from the Donnelly Canyon parking area still crosses ranch property, but is more discreet. As always, please keep out of the way of the ranchers and their cattle operation, and in particular keep dogs well away from cattle. It might be best to avoid these walls altogether until the access situation is finally figured out.

After recent (October 2003) meetings with the BLM, The Nature Conservancy, and Heidi Redd, Jason Keith of the Access Fund points out: "While those walls are on public property there's really no practical route to get to them and Heidi is starting to get fed up with climbers trespassing as they please across her (TNC's) property."

Fist Fight Wall

Fist Fight Wall

Fist Fight Wall

This wall is the leftmost of the three walls on the west side of the canyon, and faces directly across to Battle of the Bulge. Approach from the Donnelly Canyon parking area. This crag is little-visited. Watch for rattlesnakes during the warmer months.

__1__ **Unnamed 5.10 70'**
Shallow right-facing dihedral to a thin splitter.

__2__ **Unknown ? 110'**
Right-facing dihedral through roofs. All sizes.

__3__ **Roofus 5.10+ 110'**
Right-facing dihedral to a huge thin-hands roof. *(1)1.0, (2)2.0, (1)2.5, (3)3.0*

__4__ **Unknown ? 90'**
Splitter of various sizes.

__5__ **Unknown ? 120'**
Right-facing corner with bulges.

__6__ **Unnamed 5.10- 65'**
Right-facing corner starts off-fingers but widens to cups and fists. *(1)1.5, (1)2.0, (3) #3 Camalots, (2) #3.5 Camalots*

__7__ **Unknown ? ?'**
Right-facing dihedral with a suspect block at the top.

__8__ **Toprope Flake**
From the anchors of **Fist Fight** the wide flake just left can be toproped.

__9__ **Fist Fight 5.10+ 110'**
The best route on the wall! Leftward arching hands to big hands. *(1)2.0, (1)2.5, (3)3.0, (2)3.5, (3) #3 Camalots*

__10__ **Unknown ? ?'**
Shallow left-facing dihedral changes to straight-in tips.

217

New Wave Wall

New Wave Wall is the middle of the three New Walls. Nice afternoon shade. Approach from the Donnelly Canyon parking area.

New Wave Wall 1

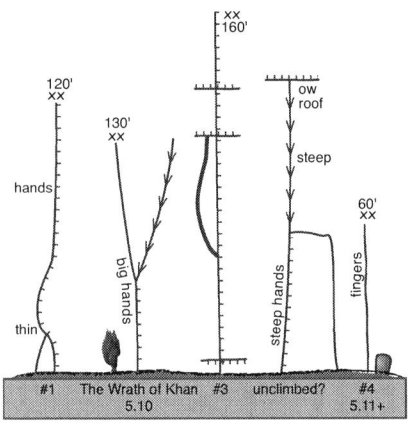

___1 **Unknown ? 120'**
Thin start to hands in a left-facing corner.

___2 **The Wrath of Khan 5.10 130'**
Big hands in a left-facing corner, splits left to a big-hands splitter. An old Bret/Stuart Ruckman route.

___3 **Unknown ? 160'**
Long left-facing corner through two big roofs.

___4 **Unnamed 5.11+ 60'**
Steep fingers splitter. *(1)0.5, (7)0.75, (2)1.0, (1)2.0, (1)3.0.*

___5 **Chalk Garden 5.11 165'**
Thin hands in a clean right-facing corner. Can be done in two pitches. *Pitch 1: (2)2.0, (4)2.5, (2)3.0.*

___6 **Unnamed 5.10 40'**
Good short warm-up. Fingers to thin hands in a left-facing corner. Please do not disturb the petroglyphs to your right! *(4)1.0, (1) each 1.5–2.5*

New Wave Wall 2

New Wave Wall 3

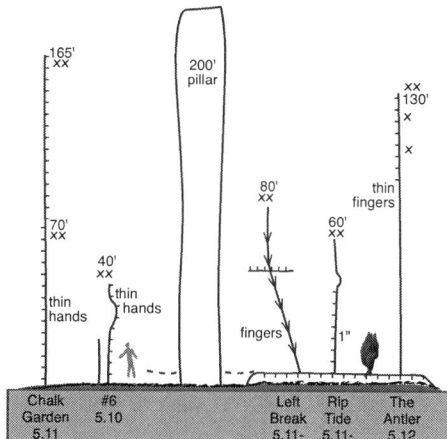
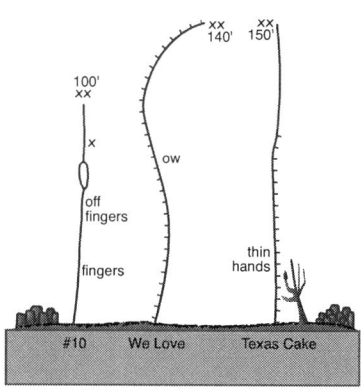

The following three routes start right of a 200' pillar, on a large ledge system.

_7_ **Left Break 5.11- 80'**
Left-leaning fingers dihedral to a roof. All sizes of jamming. *0.75–4.0*

_8_ **Rip Tide 5.11- 60'**
Fingers in a right-facing corner. *(3) each 0.75–1.5, (1) each 2.0–2.5*

_9_ **The Antler 5.12 130'**
Splitter off-fingers to a shallow right-facing corner, passing two bolts. *0.4–1.5, heavy on the 1.5*

_10_ **Unknown ? 100'**
Fingers to off-fingers splitter, bolt near the top. Located to the right of some Indian ruins.

_11_ **We Love ? 140'**
Offwidth in a right-facing corner.

_12_ **Texas Cake ? 150'**
Thin hands in a left-facing corner.

Trick or Treat

Trick or Treat Wall

Trick or Treat Wall

The furthest right (north) of the New Walls, this wall has some fine routes, however currently the access situation is rather problematic (see the New Walls introduction). Please do not approach directly from the road. Approach, if at all, from the Donnelly Canyon parking, skirting under the other New Wall cliffs. Do not climb any routes further right than the ones listed here.

__1 **Cow Crack 5.11+ 140'**
The crag classic. Climb a low-angle slab crack to an ever-steepening thin-hands splitter. Simply beautiful! This route is located left of an immense undone left-facing corner. *(3)0.75, (2)1.0, (2)1.5, (7)2.0, (3)2.5*

__2 **Unknown ? 85'**
An ugly vegetated start to a clean right-facing fingers and tips corner.

__3 **Unknown ? 100'**
Same ugly start then head right up an angling splitter to a left-facing corner.

__4 **Jimmy Dean 5.12 60'**
Very steep fat fingers in a changing corner. *(2)0.5, (2)0.75, (4)1.0, (2)1.5, (1)2.0*

__5 **Trick or Treat 5.11 100'**
Long and sustained right-facing corner. Goes through all the sizes. *(3)0.75, (2)1.0, (3)1.5, (4)2.0, (2)2.5, (2)3.0*

__6 **Hershey's Dark ? ?'**

__7 **Overthruster 5.11 80'**
This classic wavy thin-hands to cups splitter is way around to the right near the end of the north face. *2.0–3.5 with (5)2.5*

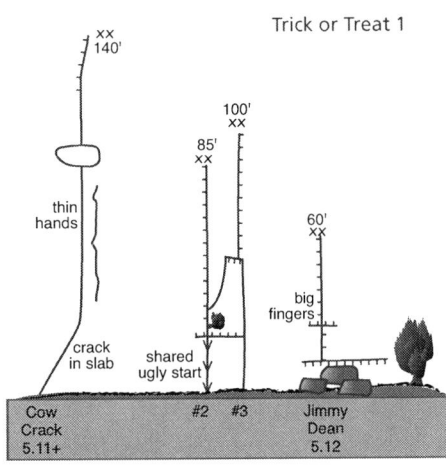

Trick or Treat 1

220

Trick or Treat

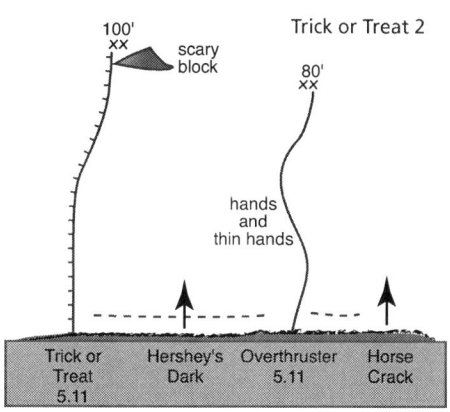

8 Horse Crack 5.11 130'
This route takes an inobvious obtuse corner leading to a small roof.

9 Q 5.10 65'
(2)2.0, (2)3.0, (2) #3.5 Camalots, (1) #4 Camalot

10 Zitz 5.10 75'
Left-facing dihedral. (1)1.5, (4)2.0, (2)2.5, (2)3.0

11 Vulcan Death Pinch 5.10 80'
Weird start to a handcrack in a right-facing dihedral.

12 Shucka-bro 5.11 145'
A Carruthers saying. This route is by itself on the far right. Starts with a 20' flake that leads to an obtuse corner. Mostly 1.5–2.0

Index

Symbols

1-900 5.10 88
38 Special 5.12 213
3D 5.10+ 188
4x4 5.11- 186
4x4 Left Wall 188
4x4 Wall 186
75 Cairns Wall 160
9 Lives 5.11+ 103

A

Acme Plaque Me 5.11 104
Acronymph 5.11- 197
Adrenaline 5.12- 132
Air Swedin 5.13R 65
Alley Cat 5.11+ 108
Alma Redd Corner 5.9/5.11+ 60'/100' 46
Altitude Sickness 5.10+ 188
Altitude Wall 188
Amaretto 5.9/5.11+ 46
Amaretto Corner 5.9/5.11+ 46
Anasazi 5.11- 47
Angry Inch, The 5.12+ 135
Antler, The 5.12 219
Anunnaki 5.12- 181
At Your Cervix 5.11- 143

B

Bachelor Party 5.11+ 113
Back Wall 160
Bad Boy ? 188
Bad Cat 5.12 112
Bar Exam 5.10+ 71
Basket Case 5.11- 174
Batteries Not Included 5.9+ 76
Battle of the Bulge 56
Battle of the Bulge 5.11 64
Beauty and the Beast 5.12- 128
Beef Soda 5.10+ 139
Belly Full of Bad Berries 5.13- 196
Big Baby, The 5.11 60
Big Fuckin' Cat 5.11+ 114
Big Guy 5.11- 84
Big Rig 5.11 132
Binou's Crack 5.9 52
Bioturbation 5.10+ 208
Bioturbation Wall 207
Black Corner, The 5.11 64
Black Uhuru 5.10+ 79
Blockhead 5.11 130
Blue Gramma 5.11 36
Blue Gramma Cliff 36
Blue Sky Mining 5.10+ 117
Blue Square 5.10 196
Blue Sun 5.10 210
Bon Voyage 5.11 204
Brain Damage 5.10+ 161
Braised Ribs 5.12 139
Bridger Jack Butte 174
Bridger Jack Mesa 170
Bridger Jack Mesa-West Face 176
Broken Brain 5.12 158
Broken Tooth 117
Broken Tooth 5.12- 122
Brother From Another Planet 5.12- 126
Buffalo Slots 5.10 43
Bunny Slope 5.9+ 196
Burl Dog 5.12+ 108
Butcher's Dog, The 5.11- 144

C

Cactus Flower 5.10+ 71
Cactus Flower Buttress 71
Cal and Andy's Route 5.10 62
Calling All Units 5.11- 158
Camping Under The Influence 5.12- 144
Carnivore 5.12- 143
Carruthers 5.10+ 190
Cat Burglar 5.12 112
Cat Man Do 5.10 113
Cat Paw 5.11 108
Cat Skills 5.11 105
Cat Touch This 5.12 114
Cat Walk 5.10+ 104
Cat Wall, The 103
Catastroph 5.11 113
Catastrophe 5.13- 114
Caterpillar 5.11 112
Cathedral of the Mad Feline 5.12+ 113
Catnap 5.11- 104
Cat's Cradle 5.12 114
Cattle Call 5.12- 104
Cave Route, The 5.10+ 62
Chalk Garden 5.11 218
Chambered Round 5.10 202
Charlie's Pillar 5.8 181
Chemotherapy 5.12 117
Cheshire Cat 5.11+ 114
Chest Full of Kind 5.10 207
Chick Flick 5.10 180
Child Abuse 5.11- 105
China Bones 5.11+ 134
Chocolate Corner 5.9 54
Chopped Liver 5.10+ 148
Chota Boy ? 160
Christmas Tree 5.12+ 59
Cliffs of Insanity, The 155
Cobweb Splitter ? 182
Cockometer , The 5.10- 209
Cocoa Puffs 5.11 214
Colorblind 5.11 189
Columbian Hit Man 5.11 83
Comfortably Numb 5.10 161
Comic Relief 5.12- 82
Coppertone 5.10 209
Court Summons 5.12 129
Cow Crack 5.11+ 220
Cowboys in Control 5.10 162
Cowch Potato 5.11- 152
Coyne Crack 5.11+ 44
Coyne Crack Simulator 5.11- 201
Coyote Essence 5.11- 200
Crack Attack 5.11- 58
Crankcase 5.12+ 187
Crappucino 5.10 124
Crescent Corner 5.10 185
Crewcut 5.11 113
Critic's Choice 5.12 197
Critic's Choice Wall 196
Cross Dihedral ? 83
Cruising Altitude 5.10 188
Cryptogamic Sole 5.10+ 196
Cube Steaks 5.10 146
Cups 5.10 207
Cure, The 96
Curiosity 5.11 111
Cyborg 5.12 94

D

Dangerous Lesion 5.13- 135
Dangling Chad ? 160

Dawn of an Age 5.10 36
Dead Crow 5.11+ 108
Deal With It 5.11+ 152
Death of a Cowboy 5.13- 83
Death Pitches 5.11 176
Deep Fat Fried 5.10+ 47
Demolition 5.11 128
Demolition Man 5.10+ 130
Dental Floss Tycoon 5.11- 118
Dentist's Chair, The 5.11+ 122
Deseret Moon 5.11+ 105
Desert Shield 5.12 82
Desert Storm 5.12 82
Desert Sunset 5.11 80
Desert Vuarnet 5.11+ 82
Despo 5.12+ 162
Destination Paris 5.10+ 186,188
Digital Readout 5.12 62
Dirt Cheap 5.10+ 83
Dis That 5.12- 133
Disappointment Cliffs 133
Disco Machine Gun 5.12 59
Doggie Go 5.11- 111
Dogs in Space 5.10 58
Donnelly Canyon 50
Dos Hermanos 5.11+ 54
Double Bock 5.12 182
Double Time 5.10 204
Double Trouble 5.11- 128
Dr. Carl 5.10 90
Drainpipe, The 5.10 55
Dreadasaurus 5.10+ 92
Drive-by Nailing A1+ 58
Drop Shipment 5.11 134
Drugstore Cowboy 5.10 132
Dualing Exits 5.10 190
Dunn's 5.10+ 72
Dusty Trails to Nowhere 5.10 200

E

E. Coli 5.12+ 146
E.T.O. 5.hard 204
East Face 5.10+ 172
Easter Island 171
Eat a File 5.12- 133
Ed's World 5.10- 196
Egg Burglar 5.10 132
Egg Drop Soup 5.12 172
Egg with Legs Crack, The 5.11+ 44
Elbow Vices 5.10 58
Electric 5.11+ 78
Elephant Ear 5.10+ 54
Elephant Man 5.10/5.11/5.11 54
End of Insanity 5.12 158
End of the Line 5.12- 146
Ernie Used to Box 5.11 92
Every Grapefruit For Himself 5.10 74
Excuse Station 5.11 89

F

F.F. 5.11 129
Family Home Night 5.12 146
Fantastic 5.12 94
Fat Boy Slim 5.11 58
Fat Cat 5.11- 113
Fatted Calf 5.11- 152
Felcher, The 5.11- 126
Felix 5.11 106
Fin, The 124
Finger Fun 5.10/5.11 204
Finger in a Corner ? 47

222

Index

Fingers in a Lightsocket 5.11+ 44
Fingers on a Landscape 5.11 213
Fintastic 5.10- 124
First Meat Wall 138
Fist Fight 5.10+ 217
Fist Fight Wall 217
Fix, The 5.10+ 148
Flat Line 5.11+ 195
Flesh and Bone 5.11 92
Flies Like Us 5.11+ 98
Flight Time 5.12- 124
Flower Power 5.10 76
For Dewey 5.12+ 84
Force It In 5.12 129
Formerly Aided 5.11 36
Fradie Cat 5.11-R 114
Free Berlin 5.11 113
Free Range 5.12+ 143
French Fried 5.11 94
Friction Slab 34
Friendly Corner 5.11 176
Fringe of Death 5.11+ 73
Fringe of Death Canyon 72
Fringe of Life 5.11 71
Fringe of Life Canyon 71
Fringe Walls, The 70
Frosted Flakes 5.12- 96
Fuck! If You Can 5.10+ 131
Fuel Injected Hard Body 5.12- 50
Full Moon, Good Drugs 5.12+ 130
Furr Ball 5.11 108
Fuzz 5.10 212

G

Gash, The 193
Gash, The 5.11- 193
Gato Negro 5.12- 105
Generic Crack 5.10- 50
Gingivitis 5.10 120
Go Drown in a Lake of Diet Coke, Fucker! 5.11- 131
Go Sparky Go 5.11+ 194
Goddamn 5.12- 98
Golden Eye 5.10 189
Good Times 5.11- 209
Goodbye Cruel World 5.12- 161
Gouge On It ? 142
Green Eggs and Ham 5.10 141
Grits Grunt 5.8 56
Gunning for Gonzo 5.11 181
Gurkha 5.12- 89

H

Haggis 5.11+ 146
Hail Bopp 5.11+ 129
Hair Bald 5.11+/5.10/5.12- 111
Hairball 5.11/5.10/5.12* 111
Ham on Rye 5.12 97
Hands Up 5.10 131
Have A Cow 5.11 152
Hayduke Lives! 5.10+ 181
Heat Searcher 5.10/5.11+ 118
Hefeweizen Corner 5.10 182
Heinz 58 5.10+ 148
Heir Apparent 5.10+ 71
Here's the Beef ? 139
Hershey's Dark ? 220
Hijinx in the Desert 5.11- 200
Hole in the Wall 5.11- 60
Holiday Pay 5.10- 204
Hollow Man 5.9 193
Hoop Dancer 5.11 172

Hors D'oeuvres 5.11 158
Horse Crack 5.11 221
Host, The 5.11- 212
Hostess, The 5.11 212
Hot Dogs 5.10 193
Hot Fun Sunday 5.11 124
Hot Lunch 5.11 147
Humble Pie 5.12+ 144
Hummingbird Spire 172
Hydraulic Pump 5.12+ 186
Hydrophobic Coyote 5.10- 175

I

Imagine ? 160
Immaculate Deception 5.10 74
In and Out 5.10 160
Inconceivable 5.12- 156
Incredible Hand Job ? 88
Incredible Spam Crack 5.9 148
Inflictor 5.12- 120
Inhabitants, The 5.11 212
Inset Pillar 5.11 193
Insoluble 5.12 122
International Affair 5.12 43
Into the Abyss Route 5.12- or 5.11 43

J

Jack in the Box 5.13-(?) 174
Jagged Wedge, The 5.10 62
Jahmon 5.11+ 192
Jane Fonda Total Body Workout 5.11- 60
Jewel of Denial 5.11- 126
Jews on Crack 5.11 180
Jimmy Dean 5.12 220
Johnny Cat 5.11+ 112
Jolly Rancher 5.10 202
Jonesin' 5.12- 148
Jutting Flake 5.10 193

K

Karin's Corner 5.10+ 152
Key Flake 5.10 44
Keyhole Flakes 5.10 44
Kiefer Ari 5.11- 185
Killer 5.12- 162
King Cat 5.11+ 111
King of Beasts 5.11+ 108
King of Pain 172
Kitten, The 5.11 114
Kitty Litter 5.10+ 108
Kool Cat 5.11 108

L

Ladies First 5.10- 150
Lady Pillar 5.10- 181
Last Battle 5.11 62
Last Waltz ? 134
Laurel 5.11 34
Layaway Plan 5.11+ 210
Learning to Crawl 5.11 170
Left Break 5.11- 219
Left Crack 5.12 94
Left Rambo 213
Left Side of Darkness, The 5.11+ 44
Less Than Zero 5.13 90
Let 'er Buck 5.12 52
Let's Dance 5.11 59
Lichen Vacation 5.10 204
Lieutenant Uhuru 5.11- 79
Life 5.11 197

Lifer 5.11 207
Lightning Bolt Cracks 5.11- 167
Line King, The 5.11- 108
Liquid Sky 5.11+ 167
Little Face Climb, The 5.11 46
Lobotomy 5.11 158
Long Crack 5.11 94
Long Island Ice Ted 5.10+ 181
Long Way From Suburbia 5.10 162
Look What Zog Do 5.11 106
Love Wall, The 88
Low Spark 5.11 194
Luxury Liner 5.10 46
Lynx 5.11- 108

M

M.C.'s Hammer 5.11- 156
Maceo 5.12- 103
Mad Cow Disease 5.11- 148
Mad Dog 5.11+ 111
Mad Hatter 5.12- 185
Make it a Triple 5.10/5.10+/5.10+ 204
Man in Black 5.12- 156
Manifest Destiny 5.10 162
Mantel Illness 5.11 84
Marathon Gasp 5.12 213
Marshmallow Safari 5.10 186
Marvelous 5.12 94
Meat Hooks 5.11- 150
Meat Machine 5.11- 146
Meat Ya Later 5.11+ 143
Meat Your Maker 5.12 144
Meating Jesus 5.11 146
Meatloaf in the Moonlite 5.11 146
Mega Bucks 5.11 89
Meow Mix 5.10+ 114
Middle Crack 5.12- 94
Midget Gem 5.11 126
Milk Box, The 5.12- 151
Mini Cave 5.11 156
Minute Lube 5.11 187
Mondo 5.12- 117
Monk, The 5.10 210
Monster Truck 5.12- 187
Moon Also Rises, The 5.11- 65
Moon Goddess Revenge 5.11- 36
More Power To You 5.11 78
Morning Wood 5.11 131
Mousetrap, The 5.12- 104
Mr. Peanut 5.11+ 52
Mudslide 5.10+ 181
Mystery Machine, The 5.10 65

N

Nagasaki 5.10+ 126
Naked and the Dead, The 5.8/5.10/? 50
Neutron Dance 5.10+ 71
New Wave Wall 218
Night of the Griz 5.11 134
Nineric ? 130
Ninja 5.11+ 89
Ninja Bedwetter 5.11+ 143
No Excuse 5.10+ 89
No More Meatloaf 5.11 146
Nomadic Alternative 5.9 162
North Six Shooter Peak 166
Not That Funny 5.12- 82
Not Too Spicy 5.12 131
Nubian Slave 5.11 80
Nuclear Waste 5.10 48
Nurse Ratchet 5.11 156

Index

O

Ocean Negro 5.9/5.12/5.12+ 54
Old Sparky 5.12- 194
On the Up and Up 5.10 190
One Eyed Poker 5.11+ 44
Optimator, The 5.13- 182
Optimator Wall, The 180
Original Meat Wall 149
Orion's Bow 5.10 36
Orpio 5.11 139
Our Piece of the Real Estate 5.11- 60
Over the Hill 192
Over the Hill 5.11+ 192
Overlook 5.11/5.12- 92
Overthruster 5.11 220
OW Boulder ? 188

P

Painted Pony 5.11 46
Pastafarian, The 5.12 142
Pat's Crack 5.12+ 96
Pecking Order 5.11 97
Pente 5.11- 90
Petrelli Motors 5.10 36
Petrified Hornet 5.10+ 185
Petrified Hornet Wall 185
Pigs in Space 5.10+ 58
Pigs on the Wing 5.11 161
Pile of Puppies 5.11 132
Pink Flamingo 5.13- 48
Pink Polypropylene Fantasy 5.11 46
Pinky Groovy 5.11- 112
Pinyon Pining 5.10 201
Pirate Treasure 5.10 94
Pistol ? 160
Pistol Whipped 200
Pistol Whipped 5.12- 202
Pit Bull Terror 5.11 113
Plaque Wars 5.11- 133
Pleased to Meat Ya 5.12- 143
Pods Wall, The 97
Polaris 5.10+ 83
Polygrip 5.11+ 120
Potato, The 5.10 146
Powders of Persuasion 5.11- 175
Power Line 5.12 75
Power of Love, The 5.13- 88
Power Paws 5.11 76
Power Play 5.11 76
Power Wall 75
Pratt- Robinson 5.10-, A0 167
Pregnant Woman Grazing 5.10 204
Prepare to Die 5.10 156
Pringles 5.12- or 5.11 43
Prospector 5.11 74
Public Service Wall 130
Pull Left 5.11 150
Puma 5.11+ 106
Pussy Cat 5.11 111
Pussy Galore 5.11- 113
Pussy Town 5.11+R 111
Pussy Whipped 5.11+ 103
Pussy Wuss Crack 5.10+ 118
Puzzle Factory 5.12 156

Q

Q 5.10 221
Quarter of a Man 5.11+ 62

R

Rabid Animal 5.11+ 131
Ragin' Mofo 5.11+ 196
Railroad Tracks 5.10- 65
Raja 5.11+ 89
Raw 5.12+ 144
Raw Nipples 5.11+ 126
Reaper Wears Pink, The 5.11- 150
Red Rain 5.11+ 83
Regime Change 5.12 207
Remote Control 5.12- 134
Renegade 5.11 106
Repo Man 5.11- 131
Repose 5.10R/X 207
Reservoir Wall 89
Revenge of the Rock Gods 5.10+ 201
Rhythm Method 5.12 120
Ride the Pink Pony 5.11 46
Right Arm 5.10+ 150
Right Crack 5.12 94
Rimshot 5.11- 176
Rip Tide 5.11- 219
Rite to Life 5.10+ 197
Rites of Passage 5.11+ 174
Rochambeau 5.9 210
Rochambeau, Part II 5.11 212
Rock Lobster 5.11 120
Roofus 5.10+ 217
Root Canal 5.11+ 120
Rosholt's Disease 96
Round-up Route, The ? 176
Route of all Evil ? 84
Rowdy 5.10 195
Rte. 666 ? 84
Rubbin' the Nub 5.12- 130
Ruby Flame 5.11 196
Ruby's Cafe 5.13- 62
Rude Dudes 5.12 143
Ruins Crack 5.11 62
Rump Roast 5.11+ 148
Rump Roast II 5.11 200
Run Like Hell 5.10 161

S

Sabbath, Bloody Sabbath 5.12- 185
Sabbatical 36 5.10 204
Sabbatical Wall 204
Sacred Cow 151
Sacred Cow 5.12 151
Sacred Space 5.11 172
Salt Lake Special 5.12+ 186
Sample the Sausage 5.11- 152
Samurai Loving 5.10 143
Sardikar 5.10+ 180
Scarab 5.11 132
Scarface 5.11- 80
Scarface Wall 79
Scenic Line 5.10 195
Scorpion Corner 5.12 74
Scrunch 5.12 207
Second Choice 5.11 197
Second Meat Wall 141
Serrator, The 5.11- 210
Sesh One Cooking 5.11- 143
Shadows Route 5.10+ 167
Sharka Zulu 5.10+ 90
Shattered Faith 5.11- 98
Sheila Longstar 5.11- 60
Shivering Sheep 5.10+ 124
Short and Stupid 5.8+ 202

Short Loin 5.10 139
Shucka-bro 5.11 221
Sicilian, The 5.11 82
Sig Saur 5.12- 202
Signe Du Taureau 5.12+ 152
Silly Rabbit 5.12+ 214
Sinestra 5.11 150
Sipaku 5.12- 62
Six Star Crack 5.12 /5.13- 132
Six Star Left 132
Six Star Wall 132
Skid Row 5.11+ 126
Skidmarks 5.10 202
Slaughter House, The 5.10+ 148
Slice and Dice 5.12 210
Slim Chance ? 160' 65
Slot Machine 5.12- 90
Slug Wall, The 102
Snakeskin 5.10 96
Soul Fire 5.11- 180
South Face 5.7 168
South Six Shooter Peak 168
Soylent Green ? 143
Spaghetti Western 5.11 201
Spam ? 80
Spark it up Sparky 5.11- 194
Sparking Spurs 5.12 194
Sparkling Gefilte Fish 5.10 194
Sparkling Schnitzel 5.11- 194
Sparkling Touch 170
Sparkling Touch 5.11- 170
Sparks of the Tempest 5.11+ 194
Sparks Wall 194
Speedy Gonzalez 5.10/5.11 92
Split Pinnacle 5.9 34
Steel Pulse 5.11+ 83
Steer it Up 5.10 148
Steve Carruthers Memorial 5.11 152
Steve's Wimpout 5.10 201
Stiff Line 5.10 195
Sting, The 5.11 71
Streets of Delhi, The 5.11+ 149
Strike and Dip 5.12- 128
Strumpet 5.11- 88
Stupid Crack of the Desert 5.11+ 71
Suburbia 162
Sucker Crack 5.10+ 118
Sudden Impact 5.11 83
Sundance 5.7 34
Sunflower Tower 5.10+ 172
Super Cat of the Desert 5.12 106
Super Corner 5.11+ 44
Super Crack of the Desert 5.10 46
Super Dooper 5.11+ 44
Supercorner ? 47
Supercrack 5.10 46
Supercrack Buttress 40
Supervisor, The 5.12 97
SUV Crack 5.11 187
Swedin-Ringle 5.12- 65
Swedish Meatballs 5.11 141
Switching ? 192
Sylvester 5.11 114

T

T-Bones Tonight 5.12- 143
Tasmania 5.12+ 112
Technicolor 5.11+ 190
Technicolor Wall 189
Tender Vittles 5.12 108
Tenderloins 5.12 148
Tenderloins Wall 147

Index

Teri's Lieback 5.11 134
Texas Cake ? 219
Thank God For Pods 5.11+ 98
Thing, The 5.10 55
Think Pink 5.11- 56
Thinner 5.12+ 148
Third World Lover 5.10 124
Three Fools 5.10 92
Three Strikes You're Out 5.11 65
Thumbelina 170
Thunderbolts 5.10 171
Tip Layback 5.11+ 75
Tofu 5.10- 150
Tofu Crack 5.10 142
Tom Cat 5.10+ 105
Too Much Cake 5.11+ 47
Tooth Fairy 5.11- 122
Top Sirloin 5.11 142
Toprope Flake 217
Torque Wrench 5.11 83
Torte, The ? 88
Toss, The 5.10 204
Trial, The 5.10 161
Trick or Treat 5.11 220
Trick or Treat Wall 220
Tricks are for Kids 5.13 214
Tricks Wall 214
Trickster Coyote 5.11 72
Trip to the Vet 5.10+ 106
Trundle Alley 5.12 132
Tube Steaks Tomorrow 5.10+ 143
Tweety 5.11- 112
Twin Cam 5.12 151
Twitch! 5.11 84
Two Scoops 5.12 181
Two Timer 5.10+ 142

U

Ukranian Root Canal 5.10+ 118
Ultimate Crack 5.12+ 78
Unbelievable 5.12 122
Under the Big Top 5.11 73

V

Variety Pack 5.11+ 187
Vegetarian Corner 5.10+ 152
Virgin Voyage 5.10+ 129
Vision Quest 5.10+ 172
Vulcan Death Pinch 5.10 221

W

Wahinis 5.12+ 102
Walkin' Talkin' Bob 5.10- 126
Wall, The 161
Warm-up Handcrack 5.10+ 96
Warm-Up, The 5.9 62
Warren's Left-leaning Crack 5.11+ 72
Warren's Roof Crack 5.12 72
Wavy Gray 5.10- 84
Way Nutter 5.9 210
Way of Friends, The 5.11 172
Way Rambo 5.12- 210
We Love ? 219
Wee Doggie 5.10- 150
Whale's Back 5.11- 190
Where's Carruthers? 5.10+ 80
Where's the Bong? 98
White Patti 5.10 71
White Salamander 5.12 129
White Waltz 5.10 34
Wiggin' Out 5.10 158

Wiggins Chimney 5.9X 62
Wiggins I 5.11- 158
Wiggins II 5.12- 158
Wigglin' Worm 5.11 90
Wild Cat 5.11+ 104
Wild Flower 5.10 174
Wild West Show 5.10, A1 172
Winner Takes All 5.13- 134
Wishbone Suspension 5.11- 209
Wolf's Ear 5.11+ 200
Workin' Man 5.11- 204
Worm Hole 5.10+ 71
Wounded Knee 5.10+ 201
Wrath of Khan, The 5.10 218

X

X-tra Lean 5.11+ 142

Y

Y-Crack 5.10 73
Y-Crack Simulator 5.9 34
You Found It 5.12 132

Z

Ziji 5.12 173
Zitz 5.10 221
Zow 5.11 48

A Special Thanks to our Essay Contributors

Jeff Achey	178-179
Karin Budding	38
Marco Cornacchione	206
Micha Dash	154
Steph Davis	66
Stewart Green	100
Lisa Hensel	84
Jason Kieth	30-31
Karl Kelley	140
Alan Lester's ruler	25
Timmy O'Neill	164-165
Rebecca Roseberry	110
Bret Ruckman	198
Ed Webster	18-21

Our Photographers Rock

Jeff Achey	Nils Davis	Lisa Hensel
Joe Auer	John Dickey	Ben Moon
Steve Bartlett	Topher Donahue	Eric Pearlman
David Bloom	Eric Draper	Kris Passie
Andrew Burr	Richard Durnan	Mark Soot
Tommy Chandler	Laurence Gouault	David Vaughan
Michael Clark	Stewart Green	Leslie Warren
Josh Cross	Dan Hare	Ed Webster
	Glen Hartman	

Sharp End Advetisors made this book happen!

Axolotl Productions	67
Black Diamond	45
Climbing Magazine	68
Gearheads Outdoor Store	53
Desert Bistro	205
La Sportiva	115
Metolius	7
Neptune Mountaineering	39
Pagan Mountaineering	27
Petzl	back cover
Sterling Rope	116
Trango	85
Wilderness Exchange Unlimited	32

Sure Bets

Recommended Routes - All of the routes in this guide are worth doing, but these are the 4- and 5-star classics.

5.10- and Under

Batteries Not Included 5.9+, hands, 76
Binou's Crack 5.9, varied, 52
Bunny Slope 5.9+, hands, 196
Chocolate Corner 5.9, thin hands, 54
Generic Crack 5.10-, hands, 50
Incredible Spam Crack 5.9, hands, 148
Rochambeau 5.9, varied corner, 210
Short and Stupid 5.8+, thin hands, 202
#5 on Blue Gramma 5.9+, big hands, 36
#6 on Power Wall 5.8, twin thin-hands cracks, 76
The Warm-up 5.9, thin hands, 62
Wavy Gravy 5.10-, 84

5.10

Bad-Rad Duality Crack 5.10+, varied corner, 42
Black Uhuru 5.10+, thin-hands corner, 79
Blue Sun 5.10, splitter hands, 210
Cactus Flower 5.10+, fists and OW, 71
Cat Man Do 5.10, varied splitter, 113
Dirt Cheap 5.10+, stemming, 83
Drainpipe 5.10, thin hands, 55
Finger Fun 5.10, fingers, multi-pitch, 204
Incredible Hand Crack 5.10, hands, 43
Karin's Corner 5.10+, thin-hands corner, 152
Meow Mix 5.10+, varied corner, 114
Nagasaki 5.10+, varied corner, 126
Petrified Hornet 5.10+ 185
Pussy Wuss Crack 5.10+, OW, 118
Right Arm 5.10+, varied splitter, 150
Slaughterhouse, The 5.10+, enduro corner, 148
Sunflower Tower 5.10+, fingers, hands, 172
Supercrack 5.10, wide hands, 46
Three A.M. Crack 5.10, wide-hands corner, 42
Thunderbolts 5.10, face, 171
Tomcat 5.10+, hands, 105
Vision Quest 5.10+, wide hands to OW, 172
Warm-up Handcrack 5.10+, hand, 96
Wave, The 5.10+, varied corner, 43

5.11

Alley Cat 5.11+, thin hands, 108
Amaretto Corner 5.11+, thin hands corner, 46
Anasazi 5.11-, fingers in a corner, 47
At Your Cervix 5.11-, fingers in a corner, 143
Bachelor Party 5.11+, fingers to off fingers, 113
Battle of the Bulge 5.11, thin hands or LB, 56
Big Baby 5.11, OW, 60
Big Guy 5.11-, OW, 84
Black Corner 5.11, thin hands or LB, 64
Blue Gramma 5.11, fingers, 36
Cow Crack 5.11+, thin hands, 220
Coyne Crack 5.11+, thin hands, 44
Crack Attack 5.11-, thin hands, 58
Curiosity 5.11, flare, 111
Deseret Moon 5.11+, stemming to hands, 105
Dos Hermanos 5.11+, fingers to roof, 54
Double Trouble 5.11-, varied corner, 128
Excuse Station 5.11, tight hands, 89
Fat Cat 5.11-, big hands, 113
Fatted Calf 5.11-, thin hands
Fingers in a Light Socket 5.11+, fingers, 44
4x4 5.11-, fists, 186
Heat Searcher 5.11+, thin hands, 118
Jane Fonda Workout 5.11, thin hands to hands, 60
Johnny Cat 5.11+, big fingers, 112
King Cat 5.11+, LB to roof, 111
Kool Cat 5.11, fingers, 108
Learning to Crawl 5.11, bolted face, 170
Lightning Bolt Cracks 5.11-, multi-pitch, 167
Mad Dog 5.11+, thin hands, 111
Nine Lives 5.11+, hands to thin-hands splitter, 103
Our Piece of the Real Estate 5.11-, hands, 60
Overlook 5.11, thin hands, 92
Overthruster 5.11, tight hands, 220
Pente 5.11-, tight hands, 90
Pit Bull Terror 5.11, LB corner, 113
Polygrip 5.11+, fingers LB, 120
Puma 5.11+, fingers, 106
Quarter of a Man 5.11+, thin-hands corner, 62
Rock Lobster 5.11, hands to thin hands, 120
Scarface 5.11-, tight hands, 79
Sudden Impact 5.11, thin-hands corner, 83
S.C. Memorial 5.11, big hands, 152
Spaghetti Western 5.11, hands, 201
Technicolor 5.11+, LB, 190
Thank God For Pods 5.11+, thin hands, 98
Think Pink 5.11-, big-hands corner, 56
Three Strikes You're Out 5.11, LB, 65
Top Sirloin 5.11, thin-hands corner, 142
Torque Wrench 5.11, hands to flare, 83

Twitch 5.11, roof, 84
Variety Pack 5.11+, fingers and LB, 187
Wiggins I 5.11-, wide, 158
Wild Cat 5.12-, finger stacks/thin hands, 104
Whale's Back 5.11-, big hands, 190
X-tra Lean 5.11+, fingers, 142

5.12

Anunnaki 5.12-, varied splitter, 181
Bad Cat 5.12, fingers to thin hands, 112
Beauty and the Beast 5.12-, fingers, 128
Broken Brain 5.12, hands to thin hands, 158
Broken Tooth 5.12-, varied, 122
Camping Under the Influence 5.12-, big fingers, 144
Cat Burglar 5.12, tips, 112
Crankcase 5.12+, fingers, 187
Critic's Choice 5.12, fingers to hands, 197
Cyborg 5.12, big fingers, 94
Desert Shield 5.12, LB, 82
Digital Readout 5.12, tips, 62
Disco Machine Gun 5.12, thin corner, 59
Double Bock 5.12+, off-fingers, 182
F.F. 5.12, fists, 129
Family Home Night 5.12, finger stacks, 146
Frosted Flakes 5.12, fists, 96
Force It In 5.12, tips, 129
Fuel Injected Hard Body 5.12-, fingers, 50
Hydraulic Pump 5.12+, off-fingers LB, 186
Inflictor 5.12-, fingers, 120
Jonesin' 5.12-, enduro corner, 148
Let 'er Buck 5.12, bolted arete, 52
Middle Crack 5.12-, fingers, 94
Mondo 5.12-, fists, 117
Not That Funny 5.12-, switching corner, 82
Ocean Negro 5.12, 5.12+, multi-pitch, 54
Pistol Whipped 5.12, multi-pitch, 202
Power Line 5.12, fingers, 75
Sacred Cow 5.12, finger stacks, 151
Slice and Dice 5.12, finger stacks, 210
Slot Machine 5.12-, thin hands corner, 90
Supercat of the Desert 5.12, thin hands, 106
Swedin-Ringle 5.12-, varied splitter, 65
T-Bones Tonight 5.12-, thin, corner to roof, 143
Tenderloins 5.12, off-fingers, 148
Twin Cam 5.12, finger stacks, 151
Unbelievable 5.12, LB corner, 122
Way Rambo 5.12-, thin hands, 210
Wiggins II 5.12-, thin hands, 158
Ziji 5.12, fingers, 173

5.13

Air Swedin 5.13R, technical arete, 65
Belly Full of Bad Berries 5.13-, OW, 196
Death of a Cowboy 5.13-, tips roof, 83
Optimator 5.13-, finger stacks, 182
Pink Flamingo 5.13-, off fingers, 48
Ruby's Cafe 5.13-, fingers, 62
Six Star Crack 5.13-, thin hands, 132
Tricks are for Kids 5.13, finger stacks, 214
Winner Takes All 5.13-, fingers, 134

Other Resources

Climbing #128 by Steve Petro, 1991

Desert Rock by Eric Bjornstad, Chockstone Press, 1988

Indian Creek Climbs by Marco Cornaccione, Sharp End Publishing, 1999 edition

Rock Climbing Utah by Stewart Green, Falcon Press, 1998

Rock and Ice #23 by Ken Trout, 1988

Photograph by Chris Passie

Guidebooks   Videos   Women of Climbing Calendar

Sharp End Publishing
PO Box 1613 Boulder, CO 80306
p: 303. 444. 2698   f: 303. 413. 9757
toll free: 888. 594. 6398   www.sharpendbooks.com

Perennial Best Sellers

www.sharpendbooks.com

Colorado Bouldering   Phillip Benningfield
This is it — the ultimate guide to the vast bouldering of the mountain state. Countless problems, from high alpine areas to winter solar collectors, are included in this meticulously researched masterpiece. Praised for its accuracy, *Colorado Bouldering* includes hundreds of photo overlays and detailed maps.

Colorado

Black Canyon Rock Climbs   Robbie Williams
Black Canyon Rock Climbs does more than describe this premier adventure area's many routes; it also brings alive the flavor, history, and character of this primordial canyon. Over 20 essays and numerous photos from pioneering climbers pepper the book with insights and passionate reflections.

Classic Desert Climbs   Fred Knapp
No desert climber should be without this invaluable resource. An accurate and detailed guide to hundreds of the best sandstone climbs of Utah's Canyon Country, including Wall Street (Potash Road) and the bouldering around Moab. Other areas covered include: Arches Nat'l Park, Canyonlands Nat'l Park, San Rafael Swell, Colorado Nat'l Monument, Fisher Towers, River Road, and more. Humorous, insightful, and well researched.

Utah

Rock Climbs of Southwest Utah & the Arizona Strip   Todd Goss
The area around St. George, Utah is THE cold weather destination. Todd Goss's full-color guide covers 45 crags on seven rock types, featuring such renowned areas as the Virgin River Gorge, Utah Hills, Crawdad Canyon, Snow Canyon State Park, and many more.

Double Down: A guide to the best of Vegas Limestone & Sandstone   Rob Floyd
The sandstone of Red Rocks has long drawn the Spring Break crowd to the rock of Las Vegas. Now, with the popularity of its limestone crags, climbers visit during all seasons. *Double Down* distills the best of Vegas climbing into a single reference for the visitor wishing to make the most of their climbing vacation.

Nevada

What's New

Enchanted Rock Sean O'Grady
Located in the West Texas Hill Country near Austin, Enchanted Rock receives over 350,000 visitors a year and offers more than 300 roped routes and a virtually untapped bouldering scene. *Enchanted Rock: A Climber's Guide* is the most comprehensive guide in over 13 years. Full route descriptions include gear suggestions, bolt counts, and route recommenda-

Texas

Sandia Rock Mick Shein
Towering over the high desert city of Albuquerque, the Sandia Mountains are arguably New Mexico's finest backcountry climbing area. Adventure awaits for the beginner as well as the seasoned veteran in this varied area.

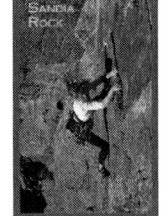

New Mexico

The Ripper Ben Bruestle
The Wet Mountains, a hidden gem of Southern Colorado climbing, boasts steep sport granite, multi-pitch adventure climbs, ice and historic sandstone bouldering. Front Range climbers are flocking to check out the quality granite of Tanner Dome.

Colorado

Coming Soon: Colorado Bouldering 2008 Editions
Phillip Benningfield

The ever-popular Colorado Bouldering guidebooks are being remastered as full-color guides, divided into regions: Front Range and Mountains. The expected release should be the summer of 2008.

Colorado

A Bouldering Guide to Utah
Jeff Baldwin, Mike Beck, and Marc Russo

The definitive guide to Utah bouldering includes Little Cottonwood, Joe's Valley, Ibex, Triassic, Moab, Huntington, Price, Wasatch Front, Maple, Cedar City, Big Rocks, St. George, and the High Uintas. Photo overlays, overview maps, and inspirational action pics make this the bouldering guide of choice.

Utah

Betty and the Silver Spider
Welcome to Gym Climbing
Craig Luebben/Jeremy Collins

Join Betty and Moe as they venture into the world of gym climbing, gaining the know-how required to send the plastic testpiece of the Silver Spider route. Along the way the reader is taught knots, belaying, toproping, leading, bouldering, gym etiquette, safety measures, techniques, and much more. Collins' insightful eye captures the nuances of gym climbing that will entertain the novice climber as well as the veteran.

Instructional

www.sharpendbooks.com   888.594.6398

Visual Media Available from Sharp End

Fit Life Pilates
VHS
For peak athletic performance

Inertia 1 & 2
DVD
Pure Inspiration

A Day in the Life
VHS
Five women who climb

Scary Faces
VHS
Strung out and run out in Boulder, Colorado

Front Range Freaks
DVD/VHS
Vignettes that really amuse

Friction Addiction
DVD/VHS
Classic South Dakota Bouldering

Upcoming Titles

Taos Rock
by Jay Foley
Spring 2004

Gunnison Rock
by Leo Malloy
Fall 2004

Women of Climbing Calendar
Available Annually

Oklahoma Select
by Tony Mayse
Spring 2004

Sharp End Publishing is continually looking for core rock climbers interested in authoring new regional and destination titles.
Please query us with your ideas.
sharpend@comcast.net
p: 303. 444. 2698

Prospective Authors

231

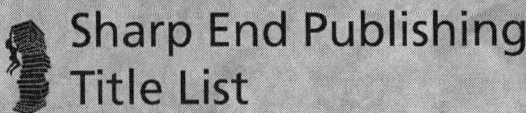

Sharp End Publishing Title List

Title	Price	Author
Betty and the Silver Spider	$12.95	Luebben/Collins
Black Canyon Rock Climbs	$28.00	Williams
A Bouldering Guide to Utah	$34.95	Baldwin/Beck/Russo
Castles in the Sand: A Climber's Guide to Sedona and Oak Creek Canyon	$24.95	Bloom
Classic Boulder Climbs	$9.95	Knapp
Classic Desert Climbs 2nd Edition	$14.00	Knapp
Colorado Bouldering	$28.00	Benningfield
Colorado Bouldering 2	Sold Out	Benningfield/Samet
A Day in the Life: 5 Women Who Climb (VHS)	$19.95	Integrity 7
Double Down: A Select Guide to Vegas Limestone and Sandstone	$14.00	Floyd
Enchanted Rock: A Climber's Guide	$16.95	O'Grady
Fit Life Pilates (VHS)	$15.00	Melissa Griffith
Friction Addiction (VHS and DVD)	$30.00	Smith
Front Range Freaks (VHS and DVD)	$30.00	Mortimer
Front Range Topropes	$16.95	Knapp
Indian Creek: A Climbing Guide	$32.95	Bloom
Inertia 1 & 2 (DVD)	$24.95	Integrity 7
The Legendary Wild Iris	$10.00	Piana
Life by the Drop: Ice and Mixed Climbs Surrounding CO's San Luis Valley	$14.00	Hunt
Mountain Biking Colorado's Western Slope	$9.95	Benningfield
The Park: Climbs of Rocky Mountain National Park	$9.95	Knapp
Rifle: Climbers' Guide to Rifle Mountain Park	Sold Out	Saab
The Ripper: Rock, Ice and Bouldering in the Wet Mountains near Pueblo, CO	$14.00	Bruestle
Rock Climbs of Southwest Utah and the Arizona Strip	$32.95	Goss
Sandia Rock	$14.95	Schein
Serious Play: An Annotated Guide to Front Range Classics 5.2-5.9	$18.00	Dieckhoff
Scary Faces Video	$30.00	Mortimer
Shelf Road Rock	$12.95	Knapp
Shelf Road's Cactus Cliff & Spiney Ridge	$8.95	Thompson
Spearfish Canyon Limestone	$14.95	Junek
Sport Climbs of Sinks Canyon	$11.95	Piana
South Platte Rock	$12.95	Trout
Tuolumne Topropes	$10.95	Floyd
Winter Trails of the Front Range	$7.95	Oliver
Yosemite Topropes	$8.95	Floyd
Zion Rock	$14.00	McAfee
Women of Climbing Calendar	$15.95	NA
Women of Climbing Thailand Poster	$7.95	NA